Palgrave Shakespeare Studies

General Editors: **Michael Dobson** and **Gail Kern Paster**

Palgrave Shakespeare Studies takes Shakespeare as its focus but strives to understand the significance of his oeuvre in relation to his contemporaries, subsequent writers and historical and political contexts. By extending the scope of Shakespeare and English Renaissance Studies the series will open up the field to examinations of previously neglected aspects or sources in the period's art and thought. Titles in the *Palgrave Shakespeare Studies* series seek to understand anew both where the literary achievements of the English Renaissance came from and where they have brought us.

Titles include:

Pascale Aebischer, Edward J. Esche and Nigel Wheale (*editors*)
REMAKING SHAKESPEARE
Performance across Media, Genres and Cultures

Jane Kingsley-Smith
SHAKESPEARE'S DRAMA OF EXILE

Palgrave Shakespeare Studies
Series Standing Order ISBN 1–4039–1164–9 (hardback) 1–4039–1165–7 (paperback)
(*outside North America only*)

You can receive future titles in this series as they are published by placing a standing order. Please contact your bookseller or, in case of difficulty, write to us at the address below with your name and address, the title of the series and the ISBN quoted above.

Customer Services Department, Macmillan Distribution Ltd, Houndmills, Basingstoke, Hampshire RG21 6XS, England

Remaking Shakespeare

Performance across Media, Genres and Cultures

Edited by

Pascale Aebischer

Edward J. Esche

and

Nigel Wheale

First published 2003 by
PALGRAVE MACMILLAN
Houndmills, Basingstoke, Hampshire RG21 6XS and
175 Fifth Avenue, New York, N.Y. 10010
Companies and representatives throughout the world

PALGRAVE MACMILLAN is the global academic imprint of the Palgrave Macmillan division of St. Martin's Press, LLC and of Palgrave Macmillan Ltd. Macmillan® is a registered trademark in the United States, United Kingdom and other countries. Palgrave is a registered trademark in the European Union and other countries.

ISBN 1–4039–1266–1 hardback

This book is printed on paper suitable for recycling and made from fully managed and sustained forest sources.

A catalogue record for this book is available from the British Library.

Library of Congress Cataloging-in-Publication Data
Remaking Shakespeare: performance across media, genres, and cultures/edited by
Pascale Aebischer, Edward J. Esche, and Nigel Wheale.
        p.cm. – (Palgrave Shakespeare studies)
      Includes bibliographical references and index.
      ISBN 1-4039-1266-1
        1. Shakespeare, William, 1564–1616–Adaptations–History and criticism. 2. Shakespeare, William, 1564–1616–Film and video adaptations. 3. Shakespeare, William, 1564–1616–Dramatic production. I. Aebischer, Pascale, 1970–II. Esche, Edward J., 1953–III. Wheale, Nigel. IV. Series.

PR2880.A1R46 2003
822.3′3–dc21   2003045684

10 9 8 7 6 5 4 3 2 1
12 11 10 09 08 07 06 05 04 03

Printed and bound in Great Britain by
Antony Rowe Ltd, Chippenham and Eastbourne

Contents

SPECIAL CREDITS:

List of Figures

Acknowledgements

My principal debt in compiling and editing this volume is to Nigel Wheale and Ed Esche, who generously invited me to join their conference organisation committee for Scaena: Shakespeare and His Contemporaries in Performance (Cambridge, August 2001). All the chapters in this volume are drawn from this conference and I am very glad indeed of the opportunity it gave me to facilitate and participate in the heated and stimulating debates which ultimately resulted in this book. I am particularly grateful to Nigel Wheale for taking the time to discuss the project and collaborate on the Introduction.

I would not have been able to help organise the conference or edit this book without the financial support of the Swiss National Science Foundation and the Research Fellowship granted by Darwin College, Cambridge. Darwin not only provided an institutional 'home'; its members also provided personal and technical support with the editorial work. For the final months of this project I received the support of the Department of English at the University of Leicester. I am deeply grateful to Angie Kendall (Leicester) for her unstintingly generous and meticulous help with the arduous task of copy-editing.

Among the personal debts of gratitude, I owe most of all to Barbara Hodgdon, a source of inspiration, a guiding hand and a true friend whose gentle advice has left a subtle trace throughout this volume. I would like to thank Sharon O'Dair for the remarkable zest with which she responded to a number of essays included here and to express my obligation to all the contributors who read one another's essays and were willing to engage in a dialogue with each other, making my task as an editor not only easier but also immensely engrossing. I feel privileged to have been allowed to exchange ideas with so many fine and enthusiastic scholars. Further thanks are due to Elsie Walker and Anne Zimmermann for their timely, comprehensive and well-informed thoughts on postcolonial criticism, and to Ian Gadd for many fascinating and instructive exchanges about recent trends in bibliography. Drew Milne, Gordon MacMullan and Robert Shaughnessy were all instrumental in encouraging me to invest myself fully in the preparation of this book. As a first-time editor, I am especially beholden to David Hillman and Lukas Erne, who pointed me in the right direction and helped with canny advice about editorial methodology and warnings of potential pitfalls. David Jones, meanwhile, made sure that I did not lose my way.

Finally, I would like to thank the following individuals and institutions for granting permission to reproduce materials in this book: the Beinecke Rare Book and Manuscript Library (Yale University), Peter Novak, Carlin Music Corporation, South Pacific Pictures ©, The Playmarket (Wellington), David Geary, Margaret Healy, Mark Houlahan, Michael Hurst, Penny Woolcock, Seb Grant, Mrs Burgess, the Estate of Anthony Burgess, Artellus Ltd and the Harry H. Ransom Research Center (University of Texas). Special thanks to the Amaryllis Theatre Company in Philadelphia and to Harvey Finkle: Impact Visuals for permission to reproduce the images in Chapter 2.

PASCALE AEBISCHER
University of Leicester

Notes on the Contributors

Pascale Aebischer is a Lecturer in Shakespeare and Renaissance Literature at the University of Leicester. She is the author of *Shakespeare's Violated Bodies: Stage and Screen Performance* (forthcoming 2004) and co-editor of *Personation and Performance: Staging Early Modern Subjectivity* (2003). She has also published articles on drama theory, Restoration comedy, George Vandenhoff's theatrical memoirs and Henry Green's *Blindness*.

Paromita Chakravarti is currently finishing her D.Phil. on Renaissance folly at Oxford. She teaches English at the University of Jadavpur, Calcutta, India. She has written on medical constructions of early modern folly, on post-colonial Shakespearean pedagogy and on Shakespeare in the popular media. She has translated Tagore's short stories from Bengali to English. She is interested in the history of psychiatry, translation theory and women's writing.

Jean Chothia is a Fellow of Selwyn College, Cambridge and a Senior Lecturer in the Cambridge University Faculty of English. Her publications include *Forging a Language: a Study of the Plays of Eugene O'Neill* (1979); *Directors in Perspective: André Antoine* (1991); *English Drama, 1890–1940* (1996), and an edition, *'The New Woman' and Other Emancipated Woman Plays* (1998). Research interests include dramatic language and Shakespeare in the theatre and on film. She is currently working on the staging of crowds and insurgency.

Edward J. Esche is Principal Lecturer in English at Anglia Polytechnic University. He was the general editor for the *Ideas and Production* Open University book series between 1990 and 1993 and has since edited Thomas Middleton's *The Witch* (1993); Marlowe's *Massacre at Paris* (1998), and the collection of papers *Scaena: Shakespeare and His Contemporaries in Performance*. His research focuses on Shakespeare, Renaissance drama and modern drama.

Susanne Greenhalgh is Senior Lecturer in Drama at the University of Surrey, Roehampton, where she also teaches Film and Television Studies. She has published essays on a wide range of subjects, including television adaptations of medieval drama and children's literature, and is currently preparing an edited essay collection, *Shakespeare's Children/ Children's Shakespeare*.

Barbara Hodgdon, Adjunct Professor of English and Drama at the University of Michigan, is the author of *The End Crowns All: Closure and Contradiction in Shakespeare's History* (1991); *The First Part of King Henry the Fourth: Texts and Contexts* (1997), and *The Shakespeare Trade: Performances and Appropriations* (1998). She served as guest editor for a special issue of *Shakespeare Quarterly* (Summer 2002) on Shakespeare films, and is currently editing *The Taming of the Shrew* for the Arden 3 Shakespeare, and co-editing, with William B. Worthen, the *Blackwell Companion to Shakespeare and Performance*.

Peter Novak is an Assistant Professor in the Department of Visual and Performing Arts at the University of San Francisco where he also co-directs the Performing Arts and Social Justice Program. His most recent research focuses on the relationship between American Sign Language and film theory. He is an associate editor for *Peace Review* and is currently editing a special section on art and social justice.

Robert Shaughnessy is Reader in Drama, Theatre and Performance at the University of Surrey, Roehampton. He is the author of *Representing Shakespeare: England, History and the RSC* (1994) and *The Shakespeare Effect: a History of Twentieth-Century Performance* (2002); and has edited *Shakespeare on Film* (1998) and *Shakespeare in Performance* (2000). He is currently writing *The Complete Critical Guide to William Shakespeare* and is researching Shakespeare's impact upon the national cultures of the British Isles.

Catherine Silverstone has recently completed a D.Phil. thesis on Shakespeare and performance at the University of Sussex. She has published on the subject of Shakespeare and teaching practice and has taught courses on literary theory and early modern drama.

Kay H. Smith is a Professor in the Department of Interdisciplinary Studies at Appalachian State University in Boone, North Carolina. Her essay in this volume is based on her presentation of the 2001 Burgess Lecture at the Anthony Burgess Center, University of Angers, France. Smith's interests include Shakespeare and film: her essay ' "Hamlet, The Revenge, Part Eight": Sampling Shakespeare in a Postmodern World' is forthcoming in *College Literature*.

Poonam Trivedi, Reader in English, Indraprastha College, University of Delhi, India, received her doctorate from the Shakespeare Institute, UK on the Problem Plays. She has published articles on Shakespeare and feminism, Shakespeare and performance and is currently working towards a book on the performance of Shakespeare in India.

Nigel Wheale's books include *The Postmodern Arts* (1995) and *Writing and Society. Literacy, Print and Politics. Britain 1590–1660* (1999).

Ramona Wray is a Lecturer in English at Queen's University, Belfast. She is the author of *Women Writers of the Seventeenth Century* (2003) and the co-editor of *Shakespeare and Ireland: History, Politics, Culture* (1997) and *Shakespeare, Film, Fin de Siècle* (2000). She is currently co-editing *Reconceiving the Renaissance: a Critical Reader*.

1
Introduction

Pascale Aebischer and Nigel Wheale

The Deaf have always had their own language, impenetrable to most of us who are equipped with hearing. The speech of the Deaf is a gestural discourse which can easily be turned against the uncomprehending world around it. But the performance of signers may move those who hear too, even though they cannot understand. There is the intense pleasure in watching a skilled signer working to the side of a stage as they articulate the dialogue of a play or opera for the benefit of their unhearing audience; sign-communicators practise a kind of sur-titling which graces the work of the actors or singers. Signing is an acutely expressive medium, a wordlessly eloquent performance, as Leonardo da Vinci knew when he suggested that painters could make their figures more articulate if they copied 'the motions of the dumb, who speak with movements of their hands and eyes and eyebrows and their whole person, in their desire to express that which is in their minds'.[1] Within every community of language speakers there must always have been idiolects practised by those who could only sign, a system of communication in every way as articulate as the speech or writing which surrounded them. Socrates invoked this gestural language as he discussed the relation between words and meanings; Montaigne was convinced that signing language was 'nothing short of perfect' as a means of communication.[2] Yet deafness as represented in Shakespeare is a terrible privation, 'mulled, deaf, sleepy, insensible', 'ruthless, dreadful, deaf, and dull';[3] one human quality which seemingly failed to engage the author's imaginative sympathies. There may well have been Deaf auditors among the playgoers on Bankside, in the period when you went 'to hear' rather than 'see' a play, since following the rhetoric of a drama or sermon was such a developed form of attention. What might Shakespeare's Deaf audience have been signing to each other in the Globe, as they lip-read the soliloquies which have entered so many ears?

1

Peter Novak's essay 'Shakespeare in the Fourth Dimension: *Twelfth Night* and American Sign Language', creates a vivid agenda for each of the contributions which follow it in this collection: to what extent is any performance of Shakespeare a radical transposition of the given text? What becomes of that originating text as it is placed into contexts and translated into actions far removed from the culture of early modern London? And most directly: 'It is no longer possible to think of texts as disembodied objects, or of reading without the physical presence of an actor and character. American Sign Language forces a reconsideration of every standard definition of literature, author, writing, and reading.' Any performance or appropriation of an old text must bring that play into the present: an exact replica of an afternoon's entertainment in the Elizabethan theatre is frankly unattainable – and how shocking that might be, if it were possible. The earliest sketch that has survived of a scene from Shakespeare-in-performance seems to show a disturbingly eclectic taste in costume and design. Henry Peacham's tableau-illustration of *Titus Andronicus* mingles classical togas and Elizabethan armour together with designer-medieval dresses, forming a perfect 'precedent for modern productions which are determinedly eclectic in their dress, combining ancient and modern'.[4] The point is this: these plays were in all kinds of interesting flux from their moment of inception – in terms of textual status, gender and race representation, audience address, political nuance. The text called 'Shakespeare' was ripe for re-accentuation, recontextualisation, 'tradaptation' from the moment it hit the boards,[5] and not long after, the bookstalls.

The prefix 're-' in our title stands for the repetition and reproduction that is intrinsic to every engagement with Shakespeare, whether via editions, performances or rewritings and transformations into different artistic and cultural forms – television, cinema, music, visual art or souvenirs from Stratford-upon-Avon.[6] Such reproduction is inevitably conservative in so far as its totem is a Shakespearean 'essence' that is valued enough to be reproduced – no matter whether the ultimate aim be to bury or praise the 'Shakespeare' in question. The traditional bibliographers' attempt to recover 'some singular, original authorising text',[7] no less than the new Globe theatre's project to create 'performance conditions reproducing those of Shakespeare's time',[8] is flawed by the unavoidable imposition of turn-of-the-millennium frameworks on their supposedly authentic reconstructions and discoveries. Whenever Shakespeare is put into new textual forms and novel historical, geographical, or cultural contexts, dual if not multiple authorship is involved. Re-production of Shakespeare, biographical, theatrical, novelistic, cinematic or musical, in new translations or editions, is predicated on a negotiation with the textual traces left in Quartos, Folios and historical records. It is subject to a process of what we may call, extending the meaning of a term proposed by Jeffrey Masten, a 'diachronic collaboration' between today's reproducers of Shakespeare in whatever form (including rewritings that irreverently talk back to Shakespeare) and the playtexts and other documents relating to the playwright's life and work.[9] As Michael Bristol argues,

> Every staging of a Shakespeare play results from a dialogue between the historical moment of its creation and the contemporaneity of the *mise-en-scène*. At the same time, the thought of the author and of his community continues to resonate even in the most self-consciously modernizing interpretation.[10]

Accepting that today's Shakespeares always implicitly assert both their relation to and difference from their early modern pretexts means rejecting the value judgements that have haunted the form of performance criticism which seeks to establish degrees of 'faithfulness' to the Shakespearean originals.[11] It means accepting remade 'Shakespeare' as a modern performance or cultural text in its own right, looking not solely at the diachronic collaboration with the originating text, but, more importantly, at the context informing the modern version together with the cultural work in which it involves its audiences.

This dual focus on the new textual forms of 'Shakespeare' in the widest sense – the playtexts, their perceived 'essence', the historical individual – and on their specific contexts, is shared by all the essays in our collection. Located at the intersection of Shakespeare studies, performance studies and cultural studies, the essays address the question of how Shakespeare's plays affect and are affected by their environments as they are transposed into a variety of media, cultures and historical moments. Shakespeare is increasingly decentred as the essays explore productions that use his plays and name as pretexts for cultural and ideological negotiations that are often more relevant to their immediate context than to Shakespeare's plays themselves. This decentring of Shakespeare is evident not only in the comparative neglect of the actual playtexts as 'Shakespeare' becomes a faint cultural memory, an association we may have when we listen to a tune that we vaguely recognise as belonging to the soundtrack of a Shakespeare film, or a few literary anecdotes about Shakespeare's dark lady and marital discord (see Shaughnessy and Smith). It is also apparent in the geographical distribution of the productions: only Susanne Greenhalgh's contribution is concerned with an RSC production premièred in Stratford-upon-Avon. But even this essay is ultimately centrifugal, concerned as it is with Bogdanov's multiculturalism and the RSC's outreach work from Stratford-upon-Avon in the company's touring destinations, from the theatre to the television and computer screen. Rather than offering a textual and geographical centre, this volume develops insights into the vitality of Shakespeare in different media and geographical locations, for example a digitised American Sign Language translation of *Twelfth Night* (Novak), a number of productions at Indian Shakespeare festivals (Trivedi), Shakespeare in British housing estates or on the pre-war American stage (Greenhalgh and Chothia), and the strangely 'homeless' productions of *Love's Labour's Lost* and *The Tragedy of Hamlet* directed by Kenneth Branagh and Peter Brook respectively (Wray and Hodgdon).

The essays therefore raise issues that transcend the individual performances and texts they discuss, providing significant contributions to the fields of performance studies and postcolonial studies and tackling theoretical issues of adaptation and genre in practical terms. The cultural, ideological and institutional diversity of the authors, whose contributions arise out of work presented at Scaena: Shakespeare and His Contemporaries in Performance (Cambridge, August 2001), gives each essay a unique approach to the contentious issue of remaking Shakespeare.

Shakespeare retextualised and recontextualised

Since their first reproduction in print, Shakespeare's plays have been recast in numbers of new forms that complicate the relationship between the original playtexts and their subsequent incarnations. Granted, Shakespeare today is still reproduced in numerous performances that aspire to maintain fidelity to the author's intentions, and in editions which strive to recover some original form of the text. But even scholarly editions aiming for editorial objectivity, as Robert Shaughnessy shows here, are ideologically inflected in their introductions, mirroring the cultural contexts in which they were composed.[12] Yet increasingly many of today's Shakespeares appear not in editions and conservative theatrical productions but in a plethora of contemporary formats – novel, horror, screenplay, musical – in foreign performance traditions – *kathakali, theerukootu* and *kudiattam*, for example – and in a bewildering range of media-forms, from film via video to DVD, CD-ROM, and the internet. Stage productions themselves often retextualise Shakespeare in radical ways: when in *The Tragedy of Hamlet* Peter Brook reshuffles Shakespeare's lines, this is, Barbara Hodgdon suggests, an ideologically-inflected 'act of resistance' through which the retextualisation 'enables spectators to see or to *re*-see what has been covered by cultural-ontological habits of mind'. While each of these new forms can be read as an independent cultural 'text', their textualities are distinct and allow for types of interaction that are specific to each.

Several essays address the ephemeral nature of theatrical performance and the difficulties involved in reconstructing the occasion, whether from archival materials such as prompt-books, photographs and reviews, or from the author's own memory. While Peter Novak's description of the translation of Shakespeare into the 'literature of the body' of American Sign Language leaves no doubt about the textual nature of performance, evoking William B. Worthen's assertion that performance 'is a means of textualising the body',[13] he also provokes troubling questions about our ability to 'fix' such a performance text. Even if, as here, the translation is 'textualised' in the sense of being given a stable, reviewable, material form through a digitised recording of the performed translation that functions as a script from which the actors can learn their 'lines', this new version remains disturbingly unstable. In fact, due to the double nature of sign language in which Shakespeare is both literature *and* performance, a more fluent performance necessarily 'makes for a better translation', disrupting the fixity of the text together with its authorship. The sign-language actors are, quite literally, co-authors of this remaking of the Shakespeare which they embody in their fleeting performance. This could be said to be an extreme example of what holds true of any theatrical staging, where in strict terms every performance is a different retextualisation of Shakespeare.[14] The textual multiplicity and instability current trends in textual criticism identify as intrinsic to plays in general and Shakespeare in particular is therefore also characteristic of Shakespeare's more recent transpositions in the theatre.[15]

Even formats such as film and video that promise to provide 'a new monolithic and stable "text" – the ideal performance, recorded on tape, edited and reshaped in post-production, available for re-viewing' – eventually prove to be contingent.[16] Films such Branagh's *Love's Labour's Lost*, as discussed here by Ramona Wray, exist in multiple versions to allow for post-screen-test alterations, showing the influence of context and reception on textual forms that are normally identified with a single dominant *auteur*. A different type of instability can be found in films that exist in a single version, for, as Jean Chothia points out, what changes subsequent to a film's first run is 'the viewing situation, as the film is transposed to the small screen, in study or living room, or seen in the cinema in an ageing print'. The context of reception alters the meaning of the text, explaining why productions may fail to translocate effectively, either in time or space.

An understanding of context is therefore essential in establishing the meaning of retextualised Shakespeares, both in their production and their reception. In Peter Novak's American Sign Language translation and production of *Twelfth Night*, written for and watched by a particular Deaf community, the translation or 'tradaptation' incorporated, most literally, insights from the critical work of Stephen Greenblatt and Dympna Callaghan. Since in American Sign Language 'discourse is intimately connected to the presence of a signer – an individual body within a specific cultural, ideological and linguistic community', in Novak's production the signing actors and the space surrounding them became both text and context. Their performance bodied forth their own environment, Shakespeare's playtext, *as well as* twentieth-century literary criticism and its interpretation of the early modern social and cultural contexts that informed Shakespeare's writing. Recontextualisation, Novak suggests in his essay, 'highlights different issues that cannot be foregrounded in the same way through the written text alone'. Such a performance can hardly be described as a reduction of the meaning of the Shakespearean text, since what it achieves is a simultaneous presentation of both the playtext *and* the interpretative frameworks that make it intelligible to a specific community.

While Novak's American Sign Language *Twelfth Night* would, no doubt, be seen by some as an appropriation of Shakespeare, together with all the connotations of usurpation and theft which this term carries,[17] it might be preferable to revert to the less judgemental word 'remaking' that may embrace any reproduction of Shakespeare in any context other than that of early modern English theatre and the specific company for which the plays were first written. Thomas Cartelli carefully distinguishes between adaptation, which 'seek[s] to reproduce in [a] faithful or sustained way what it "abducts" from its objective', and five different types of appropriation: satiric, confrontational, transpositional, proprietary and dialogic. While these can be useful in suggesting differences in the reproducers' attitudes towards their Shakespearean pre-texts, the term 'appropriation' is ultimately no more precise than our deliberately more inclusive term 'remaking'. As Cartelli himself admits, the association of 'appropriation' with 'some form of subversive or oppositional intervention in an established discourse' is contradicted by the fact that 'appropriation, particularly in its proprietary mode, has been the favored practice of parties devoted to the nationalization, domestication, naturalization, and institutionalization of Shakespeare'.[18] Remaking is a neutral term which can include everything from Michael Bristol's 'big-time Shakespeare' (the 'institutionalization of the Bard') to the 'small-time Shakespeare' Christy Desmet describes as 'individual acts of "re-vision" that arise from love or rage, or simply a desire to play with Shakespeare'.[19] 'Remaking' allows us to perceive links between recontextualised Shakespeares that would otherwise be obscured by the ideological divisions of the terminology. For example, rather than focusing on the conservatism of Kenneth Branagh's film of *Love's Labour's Lost*, Ramona Wray's emphasis on awareness of contexts of production and reception reveals links between this film, the problems associated with the differential reception of Annette Leday's *kathakali* production of *The Tempest* in the west and the east (Trivedi), and the stylistic and generic choices of the two British TV *Macbeth*s discussed by Susanne Greenhalgh.

Similarly, Peter Novak's and Barbara Hodgdon's concentration on the actor's body as both text and context highlights the relationship between the quintessentially western productions they analyse and the postcolonial productions discussed by Chakravarti, Silverstone and Trivedi. If we accept the premise that each performing body partakes in remaking Shakespeare and that bodies can indeed be 'read' as 'texts', then the gender, race and cultural encoding of the performers' bodies become part of the meaning of remade Shakespeare. This is particularly true of the adaptations of *Othello* in colonial and postcolonial spaces. Paromita Chakravarti explains that while 'a white actor can be thought able to represent Othello's blackness, a black or Asiatic actor is considered capable only of demonstrating his own negritude'. When the Bengali performer of Othello in *Saptapadi*, a postcolonial cinematic negotiation of the play set in the context of British India, blackens his face in an implicit refusal of any association of his own skin colour with 'blackness', the actor's body is obviously charged with a political significance that exceeds the Shakespearean pre-text.

If the blacking-up of a Bengali Othello is understandable as a political statement about the common Aryan ancestry of colonisers and colonised within the context of 1960s Bengal, Catherine Silverstone demonstrates how the blacking-up of an actor of mixed-race (though predominantly European) descent has a distinctly different significance in late twentieth-century New Zealand. Obviously, as Ania Loomba and Martin Orkin caution, 'post-colonial studies... [do not constitute]... a homogeneous body of writing, or a single way of approaching the question of colonial power relations'.[20] The authors of the essays motivated by postcolonial concerns are highly sensitive to the ways in which the recontextualisations of Shakespeare they consider are shaped by their individual contexts of creation and reception. They are alert to Loomba's warning that 'if it is uprooted from specific locations, "postcoloniality" cannot be meaningfully investigated, and instead, the term begins to obscure the very relations of domination that it seeks to uncover'. What emerges from these essays is a sense of the diversity and richness of the various postcolonial contexts, distinguishing clearly between Shakespeare's influence in the 'settler culture' of New Zealand,[21] the postcolonial situation of India and, more specifically still, that of contrasting Indian states at different historical moments.

This perception holds true for all our contributors. Whether the focus is on the racialised geographical space of New York in the 1950s that provides the backdrop to *West Side Story* (Shaughnessy) or on the idiosyncratic 'Britishness' of the films directed by Penny Woolcock and Kenneth Branagh (Greenhalgh, Wray), the authors are acutely aware of the significance of the specific contexts of the Shakespeares which they consider. One crucial effect of the essays' emphasis on the importance of context is to dislodge Britain and the United States as the dominant cultures whose contexts need no explication; Europe and North America are dethroned as the sovereign subjects of history and literary criticism. These productions from around the globe provide localities in all of which Shakespeare is, as Dennis Kennedy reminds us, essentially foreign: because of his 'distan[ce] in time, language, and thought,... Shakespeare doesn't belong to any nation or anybody: Shakespeare is foreign to all of us'.[22]

Nevertheless, the Britishness of Shakespeare remains an essential component of remade Shakespeare. An important strand in the essays is the value of Shakespeare as a British cultural commodity, promoted by the Labour government and endorsed by the Royal National Theatre and Royal Shakespeare Company. In a neo-colonial gesture, Shakespeare is exported to former colonies at the same time as he is re-imported to the British heartlands, an ethnically-mixed housing estate of Ladywood where he assumes the same 'civilising' educational role he played in the establishment of the Empire (Greenhalgh). It becomes apparent that Shakespeare's Britishness is an important means of self-definition in a postcolonial Britain that, 'by an ironic act of symmetry, is undergoing the same uncertain groping towards defining itself as are the countries that were once colonised by Britain'.[23] Shakespeare's Britishness is asserted in the most surprising contexts, as Chakravarti's Bengali actors receive incongruous RP voice-overs for their performance of *Othello*, or as a musical version of Shakespeare's life, to be filmed by a Hollywood studio, is partly legitimised through a spate of successful British musicals and the employment of a British writer for the screenplay (Smith).

However, as Neil Taylor remarks, 'Just as the non-British English-speaking film industry has always had to cope with Shakespeare's Englishness, the British film industry has always had to cope with the dominance of Hollywood in the industry as a whole'.[24] Hollywood looms large in many of the essays included in this volume, for even when the films under discussion specifically define themselves in opposition to it, Hollywood remains an ideological context within or against which all encounters with Shakespeare-on-film are always already inscribed. 'Hollywood' is perceived as a mode of production that imposes simplifying and popularising structures via narrative, often in conflict with the Shakespearean texts it attempts to remake. Anthony Burgess's resistance to the 'ghastly' idea of making a musical hero out of Shakespeare is an instance of the widespread feeling about the incompatibility of Shakespeare and Hollywood, whose influence manages to turn the sombre conclusion of Shakespeare's *Love's Labour's Lost* into a more hopeful, if not downright happy ending. Kenneth Branagh, the most prolific Shakespearean film-maker of the 1990s, has had a predictably complex relationship with the American film-metropolis and remains vulnerable to the criticism of being uncritical in respect of both Hollywood and Shakespeare. If his films do indeed 'represent an unconventional marriage, something like that we might imagine for Beatrice and Benedick, between Shakespeare and Hollywood',[25] the box-office flop of his musical *Love's Labour's Lost* is the result of bitter marital strife. Ramona Wray argues that the film's commercial failure is the result of a fundamental generic mismatch in which Shakespeare's Britishness and Branagh's nostalgic patriotism are incompatible with the film's generic aspiration to be a Hollywood musical. It is only by considering the genres and defining contexts which frame Branagh's film that the complex nature of his failure becomes clear.

Remaking Shakespeare

This volume opens and closes with discussions of 'embodied' Shakespeares in two essays that are acutely aware of the textuality, semiotics and mnemonics of the actor's body. Beginning with Peter Novak's account of the incorporation of text and context through sign language, various postcolonial and theoretically-informed essays precede Susanne

Greenhalgh's examination of contemporary British Shakespeares at the centre of the collection. In Penny Woolcock and Michael Bogdanov's highly situated, neo-colonial enterprise Shakespeare is imported into the multicultural housing estate of Ladywood, a project taken to be emblematic of the social and political forces at work in Britain at the turn of the millennium. Greenhalgh contrasts this project with Gregory Doran's decontextualised TV adaptation of his RSC *Macbeth*, representative of the commodification of Shakespeare as a cultural export that is increasingly the only global impact that 'British Shakespeare' can still claim to have. The essays that follow explore Shakespearean remakings in increasingly 'mainstream' forms, including musicals, but which are no less culturally and geographically situated than their postcolonial counterparts. Our collection concludes with Barbara Hodgdon's 'Hamletic' reading of bodies and performances that allusively touches on many of the issues raised throughout.

In the opening essay, Peter Novak effectively initiates a new critical field with his exploration of the implications of translating Shakespeare into American Sign Language, and he raises crucial theoretical questions about the ability of performance studies to translate performance back into written words. 'Writing about sign language', he suggests, 'is like dancing about architecture.' His analysis of an American Sign Language production of *Twelfth Night* (Philadelphia, September 2000) sets the agenda for the whole collection, destabilising the opposition between text and performance common in conventional performance criticism and proposing that, at least in the context of sign language, performance and text are indistinguishable. Performance is here shown to retextualise Shakespeare's words in American Sign Language, theatrical performance, and digital recording of translation and performance. To analyse such a 'somatic form of literature', Novak insists, 'there must be an epistemological shift away from considering the performance text from an oral/aural perspective to one that reads the performance through the lens of a visual poetics and as a visual artefact within a specific linguistic and cultural community'. This involves recognising how rhyme and verse can be expressed spatially, making over Shakespeare's poetry without the dimension of sound. Novak's essay is provocative in suggesting that the medium of American Sign Language allows the translator/signer to inscribe 'historical and social notions of gender and power onto the body in ways that English [and, by implication, Shakespeare] cannot'. Transposition into another medium is thus implicitly described as a critical intervention in which the new medium's difference from the Shakespearean playtext and original performance conditions is seen as a factor that enables the interpreter to highlight issues that, while inherent in the source-text, may be particularly salient when set into a different, postmodern, context.

Paromita Chakravarti's discussion of the film *Saptapadi*, a response to *Othello* set in the postcolonial environment of 1960s Bengal, focuses less on the medium than on the interactions between Shakespeare's play and the cultural and historical context within which it is mobilised. In an essay attuned to the precise cultural capital which Shakespeare represents in postcolonial India even today and that traces the power of Shakespeare's plays back to colonial educational strategies, Chakravarti provides a reading of a film that, although little known in the west, remains popular in Bengal. *Othello* is clearly a play whose meaning is conditioned by the political climate in which it is performed. In objecting to the conflation and homogenising of different postcolonial contexts and postcolonial subjects, Chakravarti explores the particular implications of the performance of 'race' for Indians. *Saptapadi*'s romantic melodrama recasts Shakespeare's play in order to question racial stereotyping and create new possibilities for sexual freedom. 'At the cost of glossing over the misogyny and racial prejudices embedded in the text', Chakravarti concludes, *Saptapadi*, with its escapist happy ending for the lovers 'wrests from it a sense of freedom and modernity' which, though severely circumscribed, is nevertheless meaningful in its provision of a space for intercultural dialogue.

Poonam Trivedi's exploration of a number of Indian productions of Shakespeare's plays, including Annette Leday's *kathakali* production *Der Sturm* (*The Tempest*), provides an informative context for understanding Chakravarti's contribution. Trivedi gives a critical account of recent publications, productions, conferences and informal exchanges through which she questions the tendency of western postcolonial criticism to see the otherness of 'diasporic Shakespeares' as 'a kind of pollution of Shakespeare'.[26] The main difficulty of current postcolonial criticism, Trivedi suggests, is the absence of a theory of 'other' Shakespeares, an absence which makes it difficult even for Asian critics and audiences to set aside lingering colonialist attitudes and accept Asian productions and rescriptings as no less valid than conventional western performances of the classic. Rather than seek for the basis of such a theory in western models, Trivedi proposes that 'Indians especially could advantageously take a leaf out of their own indigenous literary tradition where translation, adaptation, rewriting and transformation are sanctioned practices of literary creation. Unlike the western tradition in which even translation is a "fall" from the origin and a condition of "exile"', she argues, 'the Indian literary tradition recognises these practices as legitimate modes of alterity'. When performed and read within Asian culture, both Shakespeare and the theoretical and critical frameworks that enable an understanding of his works may be constructively reshaped.

Trivedi's concern with the theoretical crisis of postcolonial criticism and Chakravarti's engagement with *Othello* in the specific postcolonial context of Bengal are complemented by Catherine Silverstone's analysis of contrasting remakings of *Othello* in New Zealand. Like Chakravarti, Silverstone seeks to 'extend discussions on *Othello* and blackness which have read the play predominantly in terms of a black Africanist presence'. In her analysis of the play's cultural impact, Silverstone discusses the disturbingly conservative negotiations with *Othello* in New Zealand soap operas and high school exam questions. Her essay culminates in a discussion of *Manawa Taua*, a controversial dramatic rewriting of the play set in colonial times. In its distinction between the postcolonial appropriations of Shakespeare in Africa, the Caribbean and India, so modish in current postcolonial critical discourse, and the different ways in which Shakespeare is used to articulate issues of race and cultural domination in the settler culture of New Zealand, Silverstone's essay represents an important act of resistance to the globalising tendency of much postcolonial criticism.

In a final twist to the discussion of postcolonial Shakespeares that animates the three preceding essays, Greenhalgh's assessment of two British televised productions of *Macbeth* shows neo-colonial attitudes at work in Britain itself. As Greenhalgh is quick to point out, Penny Woolcock's *Macbeth in The Estate* (BBC2 1997), a documentary that shows director Michael Bogdanov at work on Shakespeare with inhabitants of a Birmingham inner-city estate, reveals attitudes towards culture, ethnicity and education that are disturbingly close to those critiqued and analysed by Chakravarti, Trivedi and Silverstone. More important to Greenhalgh's argument, however, is the two productions' recasting of Shakespeare into subtly different televisual genres, contrasting Woolcock's 'performative documentary' with the 'documentary style' of Gregory Doran's RSC/Channel 4 production (1999–2001). Although both productions can be broadly associated with 'the documentary' and both recontextualise *Macbeth* as a modern-day, modern-dress tragedy informed by media coverage of crime and warfare, Greenhalgh's analysis illuminates the crucial interdependence of genre and ideology that accounts for the videos' differing reception and future marketing potential.

The emphasis in Greenhalgh, Chakravarti and Silverstone's contributions on 'Shakespeare' as a British cultural export that may be appropriated in other cultural contexts, and through which new political meanings may be negotiated and articulated, also informs the next essay. In her comparison of Orson Welles's 1937 American stage adaptation *Caesar* with Joseph L. Mankiewicz's 1953 film of *Julius Caesar*, Jean Chothia insists on the historical specificity of each production's political implications and reads their treatment of the killing of Cinna the poet as an indicator of their respective political climates. She suggests that whereas the criticism of Fascism was blatantly obvious to contemporary viewers of Welles's adaptation, the later film's deliberate 'avoidance of issues that might challenge the present moment' constitutes in itself a statement on the McCarthy era. No recontextualisation of Shakespeare, however depoliticised, Chothia contends, is ever devoid of ideological implications.

A second strand of Chothia's argument, which itself picks up on undercurrents in Silverstone's essay and harks back to Novak's engagement with the radical remakings of performance, is concerned with the difficulties inherent in the recovery of past performances and lost documents. Where Chothia speculates about Orson Welles's lost screenplay of *Julius Caesar*, Kay H. Smith celebrates the survival of Anthony Burgess's 1968 manuscript screenplay for a fictional musical biography of Shakespeare and investigates its potential for performance. In an article that is attentive to the cultural climate of the late 1960s and that firmly embeds the screenplay in the context of Burgess' work, Smith discusses Burgess's return to the territory of his fictional biography of Shakespeare, *Nothing Like the Sun*, and his attempt to stay true to some mythical essence of 'Shakespeare' without reusing the same historical documents. She details the sometimes hilarious difficulties Burgess encountered in setting 'Will' into the context of a musical comedy so as to satisfy Warner Brothers' desire to capitalise on both the cultural signifier of Shakespeare and the newly popular genre of the British musical. While the essay introduces us to an unduly neglected screenplay, it also widens the previous contributions' interest in 'Shakespeare' as a British cultural export. Smith furthermore raises new questions about the popular fascination with Shakespeare's biography. In assessing the generic appropriateness of the musical for a treatment of Shakespeare she considers the negotiations between the author/*auteur*'s vision and the economic and ideological pressures of the production company.

If Burgess's screenplay was doomed to be scrapped because of studio pressures and a fundamental shift in tastes that coincided with its composition, Ramona Wray's essay on Kenneth Branagh's attempt to generically reshape *Love's Labour's Lost* as a Hollywood musical and to recontextualise it within the pre-war period traces its commercial failure to similar pressures. Wray suggests that because of the current uncertain cultural status of the musical, the film creates a discrepancy between the *auteur*'s original conception and the target audience's expectations. Branagh's film, she claims, 'is caught in a limbo between venerating the bard and the rejuvenation and manipulation of Shakespeare on the popular screen and in mass media more generally'. Wray's attention to the way the film's implicit patriotic and nostalgically British sensibility runs against the grain of its generic aspirations, setting up a disjunction between genre and nation, gives a new spin to the previous essays' consideration of Shakespeare's value as a British cultural icon.

Wray's stress on the importance of cultural contexts and the negotiations between Shakespearean production and reception is shared by Robert Shaughnessy. In an essay that takes in Peggy Lee, John Dover Wilson and other Shakespearean editors, *West Side Story*, Zeffirelli's stage and screen versions of *Romeo and Juliet*, the Rolling Stones and Nino Rota's perennial Love Theme with its subsequent appropriations, Shaughnessy explores the intricate and often surprising forms of dialogue that developed between the text, films and performances of *Romeo and Juliet* in the second half of the twentieth century. As Shaughnessy moves between productions of the play on stage, screen and in scholarly editions, he traces the increasing impact of distinctly contemporary conceptions of youth as a metaphor of social change on the recasting of the play in 'high' and 'popular' culture alike. In tune with the other essays in the volume, Shaughnessy stresses the enabling potential of Shakespearean remakings, showing how the recontextualisation of *Romeo and Juliet* in New York's West Side allowed Bernstein to negotiate the possibility of interracial pairing at a discreet distance and how the use of Rota's Love Theme in a BBC programme enabled listeners to trope their own tragic loves and lives through Shakespeare.

The volume concludes with Barbara Hodgdon's meditation on 'reincarnation', her metaphor for the 'Shakespearean repetition compulsions at work in late twentieth- and early twenty-first century performative culture'. The new contexts into which Shakespeare is put, in Hodgdon's essay, are the bodies of the actors no less than the political and cultural climates within which they perform. In a return to Novak's insistence that text is inscribed on and through the body, Hodgdon considers three turn-of-the-millennium performances of *Hamlet*, proposing that 'giving *Hamlet* theatrical life is always already an exercise in reincarnation, a surrogate performance taking place in a memory space on which modernity presents "period revivals" from the Shakespearean canon.' In considering the embodied acting of Simon Russell Beale, Adrian Lester and Ethan Hawke, Hodgdon reflects on *Hamlet*'s compulsive evocation of cultural memory and the predication on its own disappearance that is a crucial feature of all performance. As with the 'Shakespearean' tunes discussed by Shaughnessy, Hodgdon sees *Hamlet* as a stimulus for intensely personal memories 'that [enter] each spectator's associative field'. Hamlet and his performers become the pretext for the critic's own engagement with the remembrance, loss and grief that are the subject of the play no less than of the experience of theatre going.

Notes and references

1. Jonathan Rée, *I See A Voice. A Philosophical History of Language, Deafness and the Senses* (London: HarperCollins Publishers, 1999) 120.
2. Rée 119, 121.
3. First Servingman denouncing the lethargy of Peace, *Coriolanus*, 4.5.229; and Aaron describing the woods to Chiron and Demetrius, *Titus Andronicus*, 2.1.128. All quotations from Shakespeare's plays in this Introduction are taken from *The Complete Works*, ed. Stanley Wells and Gary Taylor (Oxford: Clarendon Press, 1988).
4. Jonathan Bate, ed. *Titus Andronicus* (London and New York: Routledge, 1995) 43.
5. The term, which is gaining popular currency, was possibly first coined by Robert Lepage, who in an interview in the *Guardian* on 5 October 1994 used it 'to convey the sense of annexing old texts to new cultural contexts' (Jatinder Verma, 'The Challenge of Binglish: Analysing Multi-Cultural Productions,' *Analysing Performance*, ed. Patrick Campbell (Manchester: Manchester University Press, 1996) 196).
6. For a reading of the Shakespeare souvenir trade, see Barbara Hodgdon, 'Stratford's Empire of Shakespeare; Or, Fantasies of Origin, Authorship, and Authenticity: The Museum and the Souvenir,' *The Shakespeare Trade: Performances and Appropriations* (Philadelphia: Univ. of Pennsylvania Press, 1998) 191–240.
7. Laurie E. Osborne, 'Rethinking the Performance Editions: Theatrical and Textual Productions of Shakespeare,' *Shakespeare, Theory, and Performance*, ed. James C. Bulman (London: Routledge, 1996) 169.
8. Item 2 of the online mission statement of the Globe theatre (*http://www.shakespeares-globe.org/mission-statement.htm*) as seen on 17 July 2000.
9. Jeffrey Masten, 'Playwrighting: Authorship and Collaboration,' *A New History of Early English Drama*, ed. John D. Cox and David Scott Kastan (New York: Columbia University Press, 1997) 378. Masten defines the term as 'the writing of several playwrights on a playtext at different times (revision) and the manifold absorption and reconstitution of plays and bits of plays by playwrights writing later.'

10. Michael D. Bristol, *Big-time Shakespeare* (London: Routledge, 1996) 13.
11. The discourse of faithfulness, Robert Shaughnessy convincingly argues, is in fact ideologically charged: 'being "true to Shakespeare" is as much about endorsing the conservative values with which his work has been traditionally associated – order, hierarchy, Christianity, nationalism, militarism, compulsory heterosexuality, and so on – as it is about preserving the letter of the text' ('Introduction' *Shakespeare on Film*, ed. Robert Shaughnessy (Basingstoke: Macmillan – now Palgrave Macmillan, 1998) 4).
12. See, for instance, Laurie E. Maguire, 'Feminist Editing and the Body of the Text,' *A Feminist Companion to Shakespeare*, ed. Dympna Callaghan (Oxford: Blackwell, 2000) 59–79, for a discussion of how the playtexts themselves, thanks to gendered editorial choices, are ideologically inflected in supposedly 'neutral' scholarly editions.
13. William B. Worthen, *Shakespeare and the Authority of Performance* (Cambridge: CUP, 1997) 148.
14. The extreme view that any amount of variation constitutes a new text is held by Zeller, Danto and Jacobs (see Eric Rasmussen, 'The Revision of Scripts,' *A New History of Early English Drama*, ed. John D. Cox and David Scott Kastan (New York: Columbia University Press, 1997) 458; and Sarah Rubidge, 'Does Authenticity Matter? The Case For and Against Authenticity in the Performing Arts,' *Analysing Performance: A Critical Reader*, ed. Patrick Campbell (Manchester: Manchester University Press, 1996) 220–1.
15. See, for instance, MacDonald P. Jackson, 'The Transmission of Shakespeare's Text,' *The Cambridge Companion to Shakespeare Studies*, ed. Stanley Wells (Cambridge: CUP, 1986) 166, who also notes that 'Plays are textually the least stable of all literary forms.' For a wider view, see David C. Greetham, *Textual Scholarship: an Introduction* (New York: Garland, 1994) 335–46.
16. Douglas Lanier, 'Drowning the Book: *Prospero's Books* and the Textual Shakespeare,' *Shakespeare, Theory, and Performance*, ed. James C. Bulman (London: Routledge, 1996) 203–4.
17. Christy Desmet, in her introduction to *Shakespeare and Appropriation*, ed. Christy Desmet and Robert Sawyer (London: Routledge, 1999) 4, comments: 'The word "appropriation" implies an exchange, either the theft of something valuable (such as property or ideas) or a gift, the allocation of resources for a worthy cause (such as the legislative appropriation of funds for a new school).'
18. Thomas Cartelli, *Repositioning Shakespeare: National Formations, Postcolonial Appropriations* (London: Routledge, 1999) 17–18.
19. Christy Desmet 2.
20. Ania Loomba and Martin Orkin, 'Introduction: Shakespeare and the Postcolonial Question,' *Post-Colonial Shakespeare*, ed. Ania Loomba and Martin Orkin (London: Routledge, 1998) 7.
21. Thomas Cartelli describes 'settler colonies' – as opposed to the ' "invaded colonies" like India and Nigeria or the "slave colonies" of the West Indies' – as having 'developed as "filial" and "affiliated" extensions of the "mother" country' that 'have "grown up" in a responsive relationship with the mother country...and "separated" upon their maturation without the violence and loss of life that attended, say, the "separation" of Kenya or India from England' (7). Ania Loomba is more suspicious of the settler cultures' appropriation of

postcolonial status: 'White settlers were historically the agents of colonial rule, and their own subsequent development – cultural as well as economic – does not simply align them with other colonised peoples.' However, she admits that 'at the same time, we cannot simply construct a global "white" culture either' (9, 10), opening a space for Catherine Silverstone's nuanced consideration of the distinctive settler context of New Zealand in this volume.

22. Dennis Kennedy, 'Introduction: Shakespeare Without His Language,' *Foreign Shakespeare: Contemporary Performance*, ed. Dennis Kennedy (Cambridge: CUP, 1993) 16, 13.
23. Jatinder Verma 196.
24. Neil Taylor, 'National and Racial Stereotypes in Shakespeare Films,' *The Cambridge Companion to Shakespeare on Film*, ed. Russell Jackson (Cambridge: CUP, 2000) 264.
25. Samuel Crowl, 'Flamboyant Realist: Kenneth Branagh,' *The Cambridge Companion to Shakespeare on Film*, ed. Russell Jackson (Cambridge: CUP, 2000) 237.
26. Trivedi quoting Inga-Stina Ewbank's description of British attitudes in 'Shakespeare Translation as Cultural Exchange,' *Shakespeare Survey* 48 (1995): 2.

2
Shakespeare in the Fourth Dimension: *Twelfth Night* and American Sign Language

Peter Novak

'As the tongue speaketh to the ear, so the gesture speaketh to the eye.'

Francis Bacon

This chapter is a written and visual presentation of the practical and theoretical implications confronted in translating Shakespeare's *Twelfth Night* into American Sign Language (ASL). It is divided into two sections: the first provides some linguistic background information on the nature of ASL, and the second details specific issues of dramatic literature and the resulting translation of *Twelfth Night* into a somatic form of literature. With artists and scholars increasingly turning their attention to the representation and translation of gestures, this translation stands at the centre of two distinctly different cultures: the hearing world with Shakespeare as one of its greatest poets, and the visual/gestural language of the American Deaf.[1] An ASL translation of *Twelfth Night*, I want to suggest in this essay, does not remove from Shakespeare the sound of the language. Neither does it eliminate the intricate rhymes and puns based on homonyms, or the articulations of speech that help the listener move through a dependent clause to the end of a thought. Rather, an ASL translation searches for a new paradigm of communication that decodes Shakespeare's spoken text and reproduces it visually. At the centre of this new 'text' lies a literature of the body, a corporeal artefact that will expand conventional notions of language, gesture and culture.

No published works have detailed the process of translating Shakespeare into ASL or adequately investigated the theoretical questions raised by ASL in theatrical performance. Deaf theatres and universities in the United States do produce Shakespeare, but rarely. The National Theater of the Deaf (by far the best-known American theatre of the Deaf) has produced only one Shakespearean play in its thirty-five-year history, an adaptation titled *Ophelia*, and has only recently completed two hour-long adaptations of *Othello* and *Macbeth*. This lack has in part arisen because Shakespeare's language poses special problems: the verse structure, the imagery and the archaisms all present linguistic and cultural challenges in a visual and gestural language. Translations are also few because they are so time- and research-intensive. When translations are produced in ASL, the time requirements of a staged production force the focus on rehearsal and give the translation short shrift. In most ASL translations of Shakespeare, each actor is responsible for interpreting his or her own lines; this practice lacks a coherent methodology grounded in critical, historical and theoretical investigations of the play.

To address these problems, and to create a scholarly translation of the play, Yale University's Digital Media Center for the Arts provided me with a grant to create and archive the translation onto CD-ROM. In tandem with the translation process were plans for a fully-staged Equity production of the translation in Philadelphia in September of 2000.[2] During the preceding eighteen months, a core team of four translators (two Deaf and two hearing) worked on a collaborative translation of *Twelfth Night* with the resulting text recorded onto four CD-ROM discs. When rehearsals began, a bank of computers outside the rehearsal hall provided the Deaf actors with their 'script', a digitised version of the translation created and signed by the translation team. The performance incorporated hearing actors (who knew sign language) to create the 'voices' for the characters so that the play would be accessible to both Deaf and hearing audiences simultaneously.

This bifurcation of voice and body during the production of the play allows a critic to analyse one function, or the other, or both at the same time. What emerges, then, in the performance of the translation is a series of different but simultaneous texts in simultaneous juxtaposition. The result for the hearing audience was a visual and aural dissonance. They are, in essence, hearing one language (Shakespeare's text) while simultaneously seeing an altogether different one (ASL). The advantage for the hearing audience is that they do, in fact, watch a translation, an augmentation of the ASL performance with temporal sounds of the spoken language – in essence, they *see* Shakespeare for the first time. The theoretical implications for this will be discussed later in this chapter.

The distance between Shakespeare and sign language is not so far as one might expect. The renderings of seventeenth-century Englishman John Bulwer have often been used to cite a physical manifestation of Elizabethan stage acting. Himself a teacher of the Deaf and a physician, Bulwer published both his *Chirologia: or the Natural Language of the Hand* and *Chironomia: or The Art of Manual Rhetoric* in a combined work in 1644. A third work, *Cephalelogia/Cephalenomia*, was never completed, but its premise was to be a catalogue of gestures belonging to the head, just as the *Chirologia* was for the hands. Bulwer's renderings are instrumental for translators whose work depends on historical documentations of the face and hands and for what 'it implies about the extraordinary visibility of hands in Elizabethan society, and on Shakespeare's stage in particular'.[3] While some of Bulwer's chirograms depict facial expressions and body movement that accompany a given gesture, most often the hands are separated from the body, presenting distinct units of meaning (See Figure 2.1).

Bulwer's understanding of gesture was intimately tied to his belief that the hands and their gestures are better able to communicate cross-culturally than are spoken languages. The hand, he wrote, 'speaks all languages, and as an universal character of reason, is generally understood and known by all nations among the formal differences of their tongue'.[4] He meticulously detailed handshapes without the requisite movements that lead to them, admitting that 'the necessary defect of the Chirograms in point of motion and percussion, which Art cannot express, must be supplied with imagination'.[5] The static nature of these representations usually depicts only one moment within a continuum of emotions and physical expressions. What must be 'imagined', according to Bulwer, are the interstitial moments of vast and varied magnitude – movements that require the capturing or simulation of movement through time. The difficulty for Bulwer, indeed for any ASL translator or

Figure 2.1   From Bulwer's *Chirologia* (1644)

performance theorist, is to describe in words or static images the movement and 'inflection' of the body.

Shakespeare's language was visceral, intended for the playhouse. J. L. Styan writes that Shakespeare wrote a 'gestic poetry',[6] where words and movement combined through the physical presence of an actor. Oftentimes the reliance on Shakespeare's written texts overshadows the performance of those texts in the three dimensions of theatrical space. Our understanding of language, literature and poetry is bound by spatial metaphors just as space is integral to any definition of art, sculpture, dance and theatre. There is an intertextuality between the metaphors in our language and the creation of our art, but, as W. J. T. Mitchell writes, 'Spatial form is no casual metaphor but an essential feature of the interpretation and experience of literature' in all ages and cultures.[7] Poetry then paints for us a spatial dynamic, a rendering of sound as it moves through space.

Most written languages have a significant body of literature, and translators can cull from that historical canon in the translation process. Marcel Schwob and Eugène Morand, for example, had difficulty translating the second part of Hamlet's line 'When the wind is southerly I know a hawk from a handsaw' (II, ii, 374–5) in their 1899 translation of the play into French.[8] Their solution was to translate the line as: 'Je connais bien un cygne d'un corbeau,' or 'I know a swan from a raven.' They borrowed the image directly from an earlier text, François Villon's 'Ballade du concours de Blois' and filled their translation with other references from fifteenth- through seventeenth-century French poets – effectively re-creating for French readers a culturally encoded *Hamlet* replete with archaisms and other culturally significant images and references.[9] Such translating for a specific context seems natural in French which has other 'texts' from which to draw. ASL, though, has no previous (con)texts.

While the histories of sign language in both France and the United States date back several hundred years, there is no recorded history of ASL – so that any intertextual relationship with that linguistic heritage is impossible. The Deaf population that inhabited Martha's Vineyard at the end of the seventeenth century, for example, used a sign language significantly different than the one used today. Study of ASL is limited to those moments that have been visually recorded, fixed in time and space like a written/printed text, only using videotape. Without such documentation, ASL shares a common bond with other oral languages and cultures: linguistic anthropologists must dig for historical re-creations among the bodies of today's practitioners of the language. Or we rely on other visual histories to inform our understanding of any given text.

Not until the late 1960s did linguists pioneer the study of ASL as a language separate from English, distinct in linguistic and stylistic complexity. Contrary to popular belief, ASL is not a derivative or 'simplified' version of English encoded on the hands. Because it is visual and gestural rather than oral and aural, it contains intrinsic structures and processes different from English and other spoken and written languages. Neither are signed languages, as many assume, 'universal'. Gestures are broadly conceived of as 'universal' inasmuch as any gesture, such as pointing or indexing, is universal, but there remains no universal sign language. While Great Britain and the United States share English as a common language, the two sign systems, ASL and British Sign Language (BSL), are completely separate languages – a BSL translation of *Twelfth Night* will be strikingly dissimilar to an ASL translation. Deaf people, however, in neurolinguistic studies, have been found to assimilate into foreign Deaf cultures and languages at a much more accelerated pace than the hearing population can learn spoken languages. The reason for this, quite simply, is that the body as a whole has a greater capacity for memory than the speech and hearing centres of the brain. For the Deaf, the body *re-members*: the body incarnates language and reincarnates both memory and texts through performance – something akin to what Barbara Hodgdon suggests in her essay, but with the authentically embodied language of ASL.

American Sign Language functions by situating the speaker or signer in relation to others and to geographical environments in order to express semantic content. Writing occurs in the two dimensions of text and speech through time, as sound waves move through space. ASL combines the three dimensions of the signer's body and the world around her with temporal movement through that space. As a result, ASL is a fully four-dimensional language, using space *and* time in a more intrinsically performance-oriented medium than in written or spoken languages. As Oliver Sacks explains, 'We see, then, in Sign, at every level – lexical, grammatical, syntactic – a linguistic use of space: a use that is amazingly complex, for much of what occurs linearly, sequentially, temporally in speech, becomes simultaneous, concurrent, multileveled in Sign.'[10] Paradoxically, ASL is an 'oral' language – communication is disseminated through individual contact with another signer. Therefore, there is no 'disembodied' text or 'voice' in ASL; rather, discourse is intimately connected to the presence of a signer – an individual body within a specific cultural, ideological and linguistic community.

In spoken language, the sounds of individual words as well as their pitch, inflection, tempo and rhythm convey meaning. American Sign

Language is a visually-based language, so it may seem obvious that the sense of sight is the most important means of communicating linguistic information. Underpinning this recognition, however, is an entirely new epistemological paradigm – a shift away from the privileging of both the oral/aural word that was predominant in Shakespeare's theatre, as well as from the written text and its hold on the primacy of a canon of transcribed literature. Rather than having a body of literature, ASL creates a literature of the body, replacing spoken/written words with a semiotic reliance on visual information. In ASL, even time is established not through conjugation of verbs, but through a relationship to the signer's own body. Everything signed forward in front of the body is in the future, anything behind the body is in the past. For example, the sign for 'tomorrow' moves forward across the cheek, while 'yesterday' moves backward, and the word 'recently' scratches the cheek just a little in front of the past. Practically, then, the signer is always in the present moment, always a corporal reminder of presence through the individual body.

As this example underscores, meaning is communicated not only through hand movements. The rest of the body and the space that surrounds it have linguistic significance. The shape, position and move-ment of the hands, as well as body movements, gestures and facial expressions all combine to create meaning in ASL. For example, signers often shift their body to indicate that they are speaking as another person or role-playing while they narrate a previous conversation between two or more people. Their facial expressions indicate questions, emphasise emotions and add inflection. All these factors contribute to the semantic structure of American Sign Language. Simultaneity of movement, signs, gestures and facial expressions gives ASL an extremely wide range of interpretation and makes it notoriously difficult, if not impossible, to transcribe.

To paraphrase Robyn Hitchcock, writing about sign language is like dancing about architecture. Signed languages resist not only ortho-graphic transcription but also any systematic method of description. Written descriptions need to become so elaborate in order to convey the semantic content of a sign that they belie the economy intrinsic to signs. This problem is not new to scholars and theatre practitioners who have attempted in vain to document the body in space and its effect in performance. Theories of acting, rhetoric and performance have always grappled with how the body fashions itself in space, especially within the context of public performance. ASL is a performed language. Analysis of any performance requires consideration of a dizzying number of variables, since description of even a simple, continuous, linear motion requires a means of plotting both movement through space and movement through time, movement that is grammatically dispersed throughout the body.

There is a natural comparison between what theatre semioticians like Keir Elam describe as the dramatic text (that written *for* the theatre) and the performance text (that produced *in* the theatre).[11] That distinction is built into in the structure of ASL. It becomes impossible to separate the performance-related dimensions of the translation from purely literary ones, since they share a dialectical relationship. Yet the linking of these two 'texts' has always been problematic for those critics who cite the primacy of the written text over and above the performance text as more 'faithful' to Shakespeare's original. By combining the performance and dramatic text, the ASL translation reveals a new definition of the textualised body.

Critics will argue that a performed text actually narrows the plurality of meanings in a written text – that 'the play-in-performance necessarily interprets the text' and as such reduces the possible number of meanings from infinite to limited.[12] Nonetheless, any suggestion that meaning in an ASL text is necessarily more restricted because it is 'performed', is based on the premise that performance cannot convey the linguistic complexity of a written text. Although any translation always involves an act of interpretation, few dispute that with translations into French, Italian and other spoken languages, the plurality of meanings dictated by a written text may well be as broad as that of the original. But the intrinsically performative and visual nature of ASL requires a new analysis of performance texts, one based on the understanding of the ASL performance *as* literature *and* performance simultaneously.[13] In other words, there must be an epistemological shift away from considering the performance text from an oral/aural perspective to one that reads the performance through the lens of a visual poetics and as a visual artefact within a specific linguistic and cultural community.[14] Only then can the ASL translation be just as broadly interpreted as a written text, albeit from a distinctly unique and visual 'perspective'.

Reincarnating Shakespeare's *Twelfth Night*

When André Gide first published his translation of *Hamlet* in 1945 he eschewed verse in favour of prose. Gide wanted to modernise *Hamlet* for contemporary French audiences and was roundly criticised by poet Yves Bonnefoy who 'argued that separating form from content makes one lose all sense of the original'.[15] Bonnefoy, whose own verse translations of the play saw at least four separate incarnations, believed that earlier prose translations of *Hamlet* were 'Shakespeare décorporé' or Shakespeare disembodied, because they lacked the power of verse to incarnate the words.[16] The central problem for an ASL translation of *Twelfth Night* is similar: how to convey the intricacies and nuances of Shakespeare's language – poetry, prose, songs and puns – without the sense of sound.

In most spoken languages, verse metre is essentially a convention of patterned stresses. Stress is a natural aspect of the sound of individual words. Metre, however, is an artificial construct imposed upon language. While sound is what establishes the natural stress of a word in English and other spoken languages, sound cannot be the basis for word stress and, therefore, metrical structure in ASL. Similarly, the concept of rhyme which is based upon a musicality of identical sounds made in the last syllables of words is equally foreign in ASL. Because of its visual/gestural modality and lexical and semantic use of space, a specific type of signs, namely classifiers, contribute to the overall basis for discussion of the poetic nature of ASL.

Classifiers are commonly defined as a set of signs which are made with a specific handshape and represent a noun's shape, size and location as well as other defining physical characteristics. Because they can replicate a formal structure through repetition of movements, handshapes or locations, they are understood as a form of verse in ASL. Classifiers do not have precise counterparts in English, and transcribing them is often difficult because of their specific movements. They can represent individuals, vehicles or animals, and inanimate objects; they 'represent some mimetic elaboration to convey, for instance a more precise description of an event or of a quality'.[17] They may also act as predicates. Classifiers can be used in an infinite number of ways – two people may describe a similar object or event by using completely different classifiers and in different ways, providing ASL users with enormous creative flexibility.

The classifiers in Figure 2.2 are commonly named the 1-Classifier, 2-Classifier and the 5-Classifier for obvious reasons. The 1-Classifier can be used to represent a person walking, or a flagpole, or, placed horizontally, a log or a pencil, etc. The second could be two people walking together, or a man standing on his head, among two possibilities. If turned so that the fingers point downward, it could represent a person standing, or the fingers could move to indicate a person walking, or rolling on the ground in laughter, or sleeping in a bed, etc. If the right

Figure 2.2   Examples of classifier handshapes

Figure 2.3   Using the 1-Classifier

hand makes a 2-Classifier and puts it on the 1-Classifier of the left hand, it could be a person sitting on a log. The seemingly infinite number of variations of these two classifiers alone illustrates the construction of a complicated mimetic narrative. In the images in Figure 2.3, the 1-Classifier is used on both hands to represent two people separated in space, one far stage right and the other far stage left. He names them as Orsino (right hand) and Olivia (left hand) to represent those characters. Feste is often seen at both households where he entertains. He shows this visually by moving himself between the two classifiers. When he says to Viola, 'I think I saw your wisdom there,' he simply moves the classifiers back and forth in front of Viola, manipulating the space around her, suggesting her complicity in playing both houses at once, too. Figure 2.5 explains why Olivia and Orsino are configured in space on opposite sides of the stage, establishing the two characters easily and elegantly through the use of the 1-Classifier.

Rhymed verse also appears in the translation through a variety of means. Often rhyme is created by beginning a line in one location

(for example to the right of the body) and ending it in the same location, or by a comparable opposite movement. Deaf poet Clayton Valli
has established ASL rhyming structures according to a visual and kinetic
model rather than an auditory and written one. Valli differentiates
among six separate manifestations of ASL rhyme based on visual perception, defining rhyme as a repetition of 'handshapes, movements,
nonmanual signals, locations, palm orientation, handedness, or a combination of these'.[18] His thorough and succinct definitions present a
huge array of verse possibilities for the ASL translator. My decision was
to translate into this 'visual rhyme' only the passages of text written in
rhymed couplets. The example from the translation below shows how
similar handshapes create visual verse when Olivia finds herself
enthralled by Viola during their first meeting:

> I do I know not what and fear to find
> Mine eye too great a flatterer for my mind.
> Fate, show thy force, ourselves we do not owe.
> What is decreed must be, and be this so!
>
> (1.5. 298–301)

There are at least six separate signs that use the same 5-Classifier in these
lines from the translation, glossed in English as: *afraid, overwhelmed,
whatever, plan, my* and *god*. They make up the majority of the signs
within the line. The images below in Figure 2.4 represent the last line
'What is decreed must be, and be this so.'

Because the sign for *plan* is made with two open-palmed 5-Classifier
handshapes, Olivia uses the handshape to resemble two pages of a book,
comparing the difference between God's plan and hers. You can see her

Figure 2.4   Illustrating visual rhyme in ASL

head move between the two as she reads one 'plan' against the other. Not knowing what God has in store, she 'closes the book on her future' and thus unites the two plans. She then folds her hands together, as if in prayer, which visually resembles the last image of the sign for 'marriage'. The translation depicts a sense of closure, completion and transition to the next scene while simultaneously foreshadowing the ultimate act of every Shakespearean comedy, marriage.

ASL performance tends to create a spatially constructed world within which the signer locates herself. This traditional 'signing space' envelops the body from mid-torso to approximately six inches above the head (see central character in Figure 2.5 below). The linguistic construction of space allows signers to draft, on a smaller scale, the space that surrounds them and their relationship to that space or to other objects, or between objects. For example, if an actor points into the wing space off stage left, and gives it a name 'the orchard', then that space off stage left will always be the orchard until the scene changes to another location – Orsino's house, for example. The space can change meaning when the signer changes subject or re-identifies that space. Each entrance and exit, whether up, down, left or right, as well as the entire dramatic world of the play had to maintain a spatial logic consistent with the ASL translation.[19]

From the beginning of the translation process then, the scenic elements of the play's production were necessarily dependent upon how

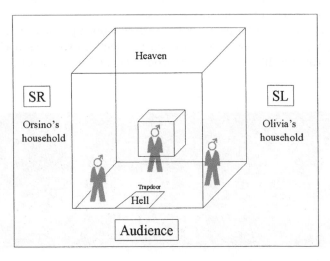

Figure 2.5   Spatial configuration for ASL translation

the translation constructed the physical world of the play. In the illustration above (Figure 2.5), the major characters inhabited two sides of the stage, each intended to represent either Olivia's domain, or Orsino's, automatically establishing a visual and spatial relationship between the two at opposite ends of the stage. Whenever characters referred to either Orsino or Olivia, they would index (point) to that location (whether or not Olivia or Orsino were actually present did not matter) usually followed by or accompanied with a glance in the same direction. Such movement located those characters as fixed 'realities' throughout the play, while the remainder of the dramatic world, such as specific rooms within each house, the town, the orchard, the sea, etc., was established in relation to these two poles. 'Hell' was always positioned down stage centre under the trapdoor, in the same location as Malvolio's darkhouse. This physical inter-relationship of signer to the surrounding dramatic world of the play establishes visual relationships between objects, spaces and characters that simple English narrative does not allow. Space becomes linguistic.

ASL can also render historical and social notions of gender and power onto the body in ways that English cannot. In ASL, status, class or power is visually relational; those with greater status are located in space over and above those with lesser status. The distance between the two objects or individuals indicates their relative relationship and power differential. These proxemic relations have an enormous capacity to reveal information about class, social standing and relationships of power and oppression. Originally meant to be an understanding of architectural space, proxemic theory lends itself well within an ASL discussion of signing space and how the signer manipulates herself spatially in relationship to objects, the audience, other actors/characters and even to herself.[20]

With the ability to render these relationships on the body, ASL transforms hidden or historical assumptions and meanings in English into visual constructs and images. Figure 2.6 provides an example of Olivia's own linguistic internalisation of paternalism and oppression through the visual syntax of ASL. In Figure 2.6 Orsino is represented by the raised 1-Classifier of the right hand, while Olivia represents herself by the lower 1-Classifier of the left hand. Olivia always locates Orsino in space at a level above herself, and maintains the less powerful position in the relationship throughout the play. Notice that Olivia locates Orsino and herself with the same spatial characteristics represented in Figures 2.3 and 2.5 above in order to maintain consistency and linguistic logic.

Figure 2.6   Examples of status changes using the 1-Classifier

Towards a visual poetics

From the late 1980s onwards an explosion occurred in theoretical discourse, according to Keir Elam, that concerns itself with the early modern body, with dissecting and anatomising that body into various parts, functions and metaphors.[21] Stephen Greenblatt's well-known New Historicist reading of *Twelfth Night* in his article titled 'Fiction and Friction' sees the metaphors of sexual friction as the driving 'heat' behind the play – as an energising force and substitution for 'real' coupling and gratification. He writes, 'Shakespeare realized that if sexual chafing could not be presented onstage, it could be represented figuratively: friction could be fictionalized, chafing chastened and hence made fit for the stage, by transforming it into the witty, erotically charged sparring that is the heart of the lovers' experience.'[22] Language for Greenblatt 'chafes' against a metaphoric body, uniting in the verbal wit and repartee that permeates not only *Twelfth Night*, but also most of Shakespeare's comedies. But Greenblatt proposes that with this erotic friction, the body becomes a 'tissue of metaphors or, conversely, that language is perfectly embodied'.[23] Both privilege the oral/aural nature of spoken text or the verbal metaphors that exist in the 'imagination' of the reader/listener. Not so in ASL where visual metaphors are visually realised and enacted on a real body in performance. The sexual body for Greenblatt is transformed into 'verbal wit' rather than the other way round.

Similarly, Dympna Callaghan's materialist feminist analysis of *Twelfth Night* locates Malvolio at the play's centre, where the famous letter scene anatomises the female body through written language:

> The 'graphic' display in *Twelfth Night* is, of course, precisely that, a written representation, linguistic rather than somatic, allowing the

company to be hugely entertained. The elusiveness of graphic display renders female genitalia present in pornographic detail, and absent as 'real' beyond representation. What is palpably present, however, is 'anatomised' femininity. Olivia's 'hand' is both a limb and writing; in this case a blatant misrepresentation, a forgery.[24]

In ASL, such a 'graphic display' is no longer 'elusive', as Callaghan suggests. Rather, with the ability to make somatic what is only verbal, to make explicit what is implicit, and to perform what is only described, ASL reinvents critical discourse with the material presence of the body that no other written or verbal form of language can accommodate. The body is neither transformed into verbal wit nor absent in the translated text, but re-inscribed on the stage and in space through the presence of an individual signer.

Any analysis that places the body within a critical, theoretical, historical or performative discourse can be used to greater extent and with more authenticity in ASL than it can in English or any other spoken/ written/transcribed language. But that discourse must be re-envisioned within a textual *and* performative paradigm. It is no longer possible to separate text from performance as cultural materialists and/or New Historicists can and do when looking only at historical discourse. The translation forces a reading that is both historical and contemporary, textual and embodied, canonical and marginalised simultaneously. As Keir Elam suggests,

> A revised – which is to say historicized and materialized – post-semiotics of Shakespearean drama might offer an analogous space where social history, dramatic history and stage history interrogate each other. But in order to be fully historicized and fully materialized, such an enterprise can only set out from the one historical and material dramatic body we have, the actor's.[25]

In the ASL translation a postmodern critic is able to 'read the body as text', not as one might read, say, urination as 'performance' or a skyscraper as 'text', but through the somatic, corporeal text of ASL.

Combine these visual constructs of class and gender with the simultaneous spoken performance of Shakespeare's text, and the flexibility of ASL in performance presents a semiotically and theoretically complicated theatrical event. In the Philadelphia performance of this translation each character was bifurcated – the voice was separated from the body, meaning that, for the hearing audience, two separate actors comprised one character. The relationship between sign-actor and voice-actor, then, creates for a hearing audience an alienating effect that can be manipulated to greater or lesser degree, depending on the casting of the play and other extra-textual decisions. The division between voice-actor and sign-actor allows for a greater degree of complexity than in traditional theatrical productions.

If I had wanted to emulate a more 'authentically' Elizabethan-era performance, it would have been easy to produce an all-male cast performing in ASL with two women 'voicing' the female roles. This would have further disembodied the female presence, reducing it to only the temporal dimension of sound – an echo, as it were, of female subjectivity. This convention would have allowed the hearing audience to watch a male actor with a 'female' voice – a performance akin to the pre-pubescent boys who portrayed Shakespeare's female characters. I chose instead to cast one female actor who voiced the roles for both Viola and Sebastian, creating an aural 'twinning' for the hearing audience. While they saw two separate actors of either gender on the stage, they heard an identical and unifying female 'voice'. This style of ASL performance generates room for creative combinations of gender, identity and linguistic function in theatrical productions. These examples provide only a few of the ways in which aspects of materialist feminist or New Historicist readings of the play can be, literally, 'incorporated' into the ASL text – where recontextualisation highlights different issues that cannot be foregrounded in the same way through the written text alone.

The significance of the body, specifically the hand, in the ASL translation of *Twelfth Night* might seem obvious if it were not for the complexity of images and meanings related to it throughout the play. 'Hand', or 'hands' are mentioned together thirty-three times in *Twelfth Night* and critics of the play from Geoffrey Hartman to Dympna Callaghan trace the importance of the hand metaphorically within poetic discourse and anatomically as the female body, respectively.[26] Katherine Rowe in her book-length study of images of the hands from the Renaissance to modern literature, relates the particular image of the hand to the body as a whole. 'The body imagined in relation to its hand is shaped by those fictions particular to the hand: the principle of rational organization; the capacity to express, manufacture, and possess; and the dependencies of mutual labor and layered agency.'[27] These fictions are not limited only to those particularly belonging to the hand. Rather, ASL allows for fictions of the body in its entirety, or fictions of specific and individuated bodies particularly.

'Somewhere there is always a device', writes Geoffrey Hartman of *Twelfth Night*, 'or a "hand" that could fool just about anyone.'[28]

The following three examples all centre on the device contrived against Malvolio where body, text and performance exist in a continuum of reflexive signification, all predicated on the hand. In the first example, Maria plans to write a letter in which Malvolio will be gulled into thinking that Olivia is in love with him. 'On a forgotten matter we scarce make distinction of our hands' (2.3, 161–3) she says, while providing a physical comparison between her hand and Olivia's, moving her head to 'read' the similarity of the two hands. The following images from the production illustrate (Figure 2.7) a visual intertextuality in this line with the images Olivia creates in Figure 2.4, where the hand is read as God's plan. Notice Olivia's hand is represented coming from above and stage left, to indicate both Olivia's status and her physical location.

The 'hand' becomes in this instance handwriting, different hands (both Maria's and Olivia's), and the physical embodiment of parchment, all created through the two 5-Classifier images. Maria maintains this signed image throughout most of the interchange, allowing Sir Toby and Sir Andrew to manipulate her body within the dialogue and play on different uses for her hand. The images in Figure 2.8 illustrate Sir Toby using her hand to depict a scent emanating from it, like a perfumed letter, during his line 'I smell a device', while Sir Andrew literalises the image and instead smells Maria's hand directly. Sir Toby ends the series of images by imagining Malvolio 'reading' Maria's hand, and making the signs for 'to fall in love' on her open palm. He concludes by playfully slapping her hand in celebration of the scheme. Maria's hands are manipulated, touched, smelled and read as a letter that exists only on her body. As Michael Neill suggests, 'If the early modern body was a densely textualized site, no part of it was more prominently inscribed than the hand.'[29]

Figure 2.7   Maria compares Olivia's 'hand' to her own

Figure 2.8   Sir Toby and Sir Andrew 'smell a device'

While the body transforms into text in this instance, the action is inverted in the second example when Malvolio actually finds the strategically placed missive. Writing, at least in the western philosophical tradition, has signified absence, as removed from the body, while speech signifies presence, immanence, physicality.[30] Olivia is a constructed entity in the letter, not known through her presence, but by her absence, compounded by its own fiction – the letter is a forgery. Dramatically, we know the purpose of the letter but theatrically, we as 'spectators' can only know *how* it is fashioned if we are allowed to read the letter as well. But there is only one way to know its contents – if Malvolio performs it. Sir Toby's plea reinforces this necessity the moment Malvolio discovers the missive: 'O peace! and the spirit of humours intimate reading aloud to him' (2.5.82). Only if the letter is brought from writing to speech, from 'absence' to 'presence', from text to performance (ASL), does it become actual, does it signify. Sir Toby's 'intimate' here both alludes to physical intimacy and the power of text to suggest without making an explicit declaration. The text requires performance mediated by presence. The ASL translation foregrounds the failure of text alone to adequately convey meaning, and instead renders purely textual moments in physical form. As such, the letter scenes take on greater significance through the performative nature of the translation than they do in Shakespeare's original.

Malvolio is engaged, in this moment of 'reading aloud', in the act of translation. Consider that the letter is written in English since it cannot be a written ASL text. He is, therefore, enacting the translation, mediating between the written text and the performance text. He creates a meta-translation and the cues he receives must be interpreted through his own body. Maria's 'fustian' puzzle, 'M.O.A.I doth sway my life', forces Malvolio to read his own body in order to make sense of it;

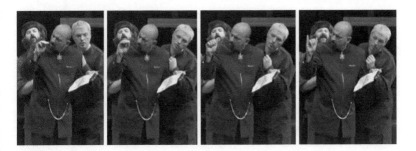

Figure 2.9   Malvolio shows 'M-O-A-I'

re-inscribing the letter onto his own hand and then reading his hand as a text, spelling out the clues of the riddle (Figure 2.9).

Struggling to construct a visually recognisable form, Malvolio contorts his hand into some semblance of himself. Having performed the letter, having articulated it on his own body, Malvolio is fully prepared to believe it.

But Malvolio's visual fantasies also sexually objectify his mistress, Olivia. When Malvolio finds the letter he immediately recognises what he believes to be the physical traces of its author. This letter, unlike Sir Andrew's, remains unsigned. Without a signature, the identity remains elusive, fluid, unsubstantiated. The only way to recognise the author is through her writing: 'By my life, this is my lady's hand. These be her very c's, her u's, and her t's, and thus makes she her great P's' (2.5. 82–4). The joke, of course, is in the vocalisation of the entire word, spelled out for the audience – c-u-n-t ('n' as the weak form of 'and').[31] A joke decidedly for a hearing audience. Reconstructing the joke visually is more complicated. In ASL the sign for 'n' and 't' are similar, and so Malvolio makes a 'slip of the hand' when he spells it out, making the word completely obvious visually. After fingerspelling the letter 'p', for the line 'thus makes she her great P's', Malvolio absentmindedly puts his finger to his mouth, and the suggestion of oral sex is a graphic depiction of his unconscious lust. In fact, throughout the translation, Malvolio's language is the most vividly sexual – his inner concupiscence manifests itself in sexually graphic images.

The letter is the material fulfilment of his fantasies, a contract entered into in secret – the privacy of which is betrayed by such a public demonstration in front of the schemers and on the stage. So naturally, when Malvolio confronts Olivia, obeying the orders of the letter to appear in yellow stockings, cross-gartered, and all smiles, he believes he is fulfilling the requirements of the contract. In this final example, his prurient hopes are met when Olivia commands him to bed, framed within the context of the hand figured as both text and body (Figure 2.10):

> *Malvolio*: It did come to his hands, and commands shall be executed.
> I think we do know the sweet roman hand.
> *Olivia*: Wilt thou go to bed, Malvolio?
> *Malvolio*: To bed? Ay, sweetheart, and I'll come to thee.
> *Olivia*: God comfort thee. Why dost thou smile so, and kiss thy hand so oft?

(3.4.27–35)

It is as if Shakespeare wrote this scene with sign language in mind. Malvolio locates the bed with his left hand and places Olivia on it, facing him. Just as he anatomises her genitalia in the earlier letter scene, he re-figures her body on his own hand and controls the objectified image. Transgressing the boundaries of class in such a blatant display of sexuality, Malvolio's punishment is the dark house.

'Hand' and 'hands' are not empty metaphors in this play, they represent a larger physical presence manifested in the body of the performer. Writing, reading and performing form equal parts along a continuum of meaning in the ASL *Twelfth Night*, all combined in the hands and bodies of the individual performers. It is no longer possible to think of texts as disembodied objects, or of reading without the physical presence of an actor and character. American Sign Language forces a reconsideration of every standard definition of literature, author, writing and reading. Definitions that privilege either the written text and its hold on the primacy of a canon of transcribed literature, or the oral/aural performance of that text, must be re-envisioned in the case of American Sign

Figure 2.10   'To bed? Ay, sweetheart, and I'll come to thee'

Language literature. By combining text and performance we open the possibilities for other definitions of literature, definitions that begin and end with the only material presence we have, the body.

Notes and references

1. I follow the convention in Deaf Studies of capitalising 'Deaf' to signify the culture of people who use Signed Languages as their primary means of communication. Lower case 'deaf' is used to indicate the audiological condition of hearing loss.
2. *Twelfth Night*, trans. Peter Novak, Adrian Blue, Robert DeMayo and Catherine Rush, perf. Adrian Blue, Catherine Rush, Jackie Roth, Amaryllis Theater Company, Prince Music Theater, Philadelphia, 2000.
3. Michael Neill, 'Amphitheaters in the Body,' *Shakespeare Survey* 48 (1995): 33.
4. John Bulwer, *Chirologia: or the Natural Language of the and Chironomia: or the Art of Manual Rhetoric* (London: Printed by Tho. Harper, 1644) 16.
5. Bulwer, *Chirologia* 114.
6. J. L. Styan, *Shakespeare's Stagecraft* (Cambridge: Cambridge UP, 1967) 56.
7. W. J. T. Mitchell, 'Spatial Form in Literature: Toward a General Theory,' *The Language of Images*, ed. W. J. T. Mitchell (Chicago: University of Chicago Press, 1974) 278.
8. *Hamlet*, ed. Harold Jenkins (London: Methuen, 1982).
9. Romy Heylen, *Translation, Poetics, and the Stage: Six French* Hamlets (London: Routledge, 1993) 75.
10. Oliver Sacks, *Seeing Voices: A Journey into the World of the Deaf* (New York: Harper Perennial, 1990) 23.
11. Keir Elam, *The Semiotics of Theater and Drama* (London: Methuen, 1980) 3.
12. Catherine Belsey 'Shakespeare and Film: A Question of Perspective,' in *Shakespeare on Film*, ed. Robert Shaughnessy (New York: St. Martin's Press – now Palgrave Macmillan, 1998) 86.
13. As a result, a better performance of the translation makes for a better translation.
14. See Tom Humphries and Carol Padden, *Deaf in America: Voices from a Culture* (Cambridge, MA: Harvard University Press, 1988) for an example of this epistemological shift in the discussion of the different meanings of the term 'hard-of-hearing' (40).
15. Romy Heylen, *Translation, Poetics, and the Stage: Six French* Hamlets (London: Routledge, 1993) 83.
16. Heylen 97–8.
17. Edward Klima and Ursula Bellugi, *The Signs of Language* (Cambridge MA: Harvard University Press, 1979) 13.
18. Clayton Valli, 'Poetics of ASL Poetry,' in *Deaf Studies IV* (Washington DC: Gallaudet University Press, 1995) 253.
19. Maintaining this intense scrutiny of space was difficult. Keep in mind that Deaf actors memorise their lines physically so that any change in blocking necessitates an actor's re-blocking and re-memorising the lines to account for the change in spatial configuration of the dramatic world.
20. See Edward T. Hall's definition in Elam, *Semiotics* 62.

21. Keir Elam, '"In What Chapter of His Bosom?": Reading Shakespeare's Bodies,' *Alternative Shakespeares* 2, ed. Terence Hawkes (London: Routledge, 1996) 141.

22. Stephen Greenblatt, 'Fiction and Friction,' *Twelfth Night*, ed. R. S. White (New York: St. Martin's Press – now Palgrave Macmillan, 1996) 114.

23. Greenblatt 115.

24. Dympna Callaghan in *Twelfth Night*, ed. R. S. White (New York: St. Martin's Press – now Palgrave Macmillan, 1996) 144.

25. Keir Elam, 'In What Chapter of His Bosom?' 163.

26. Geoffrey Hartman and Dympna Callaghan in *Twelfth Night*, ed. R. S. White (New York: St. Martin's Press – now Palgrave Macmillan, 1996).

27. See Katherine Rowe's *Dead Hands: Fictions of Agency, Renaissance to Modern* (Stanford: Stanford University Press, 1999) xiii.

28. Geoffrey Hartman, 'Shakespeare's Poetical Character in *Twelfth Night*,' *Twelfth Night*, ed. R. S. White (New York: St. Martin's Press – now Palgrave Macmillan, 1996) 25.

29. Neill 27.

30. Lennard Davis, *Enforcing Normalcy* 104. See Davis' discussion of de Man, Rousseau, and Derrida who analyse the privileging of speech over writing in western philosophy.

31. Davis 151–2. Partridge quotes Mr Aylmer Rose who writes that, 'If my suggestion about the innuendo N is correct, it draws attention to the necessity of considering the sound of words and the way in which they are delivered on the stage.' Eric Partridge, *Shakespeare's Bawdy* (London: Routledge, 1968) 151–2.

3
Modernity, Postcoloniality and *Othello*: the Case of *Saptapadi*

Paromita Chakravarti

Othello and the performance of race

The exploration of racial issues in *Othello* has made it a useful and enabling text for racially segregated cultures and more generally for colonial and postcolonial readers, adapters and performers of Shakespeare. Othello's character provides a mouthpiece for the consciousness of a denigrated people in the unequal and exploitative cultural encounter with Europe. But the Moor's status as the voice of a persecuted race remains debatable and deeply problematic. Critics argue that his high social standing in the white Venetian society and his indispensability to the Venetian government and militia largely cancel out the effects of race and colour and make him an exception rather than a typical representative of the oppressed black people.[1]

Whether we see Othello as articulating a black identity or seeking to mask it, whether we believe that Shakespeare was raising the spectre of racism only to erase it, whether we interpret the play as sustaining or questioning racial stereotypes, the polyvalence of the play remains undeniable. The amenability of the text to contrary responses presents interpreters and performers with a vast array of performative possibilities and opportunities. Its rich racial ambiguities can be mined in different ways depending on a particular interpretation or adaptation. The meaning of *Othello*, perhaps more so than other Shakespearean plays, depends on performance, the politics of performance and the politics surrounding performance. We must remember that race, as it is commonly constructed and understood in the nineteenth and twentieth centuries, is predominantly a physically inscribed category inseparable from the material reality of actors' bodies. Factors such as the racial identities of the actors, whether or not Othello is played by a black actor, whether or not Desdemona is white, the racial composition of the audience and where the play is being staged, assume immense importance in terms of our understanding not only of the text but of the cultures which deploy the text in specific ways.[2]

I propose to examine how a performance of *Othello* and the impact it has on the racial politics of a colonised nation is explored tellingly in a postcolonial cinematic negotiation of the play in a specific Indian, Bengali context. I look at an influential and popular Bengali film of the 1960s which is set in British India and uses a performance of *Othello* to question certain racial stereotypes.[3] The focus of interest in this discussion will not be the play and the insights that the performance brings to it but rather how it illuminates the context of playing. The way in which the text is used to construct racial identities and to legitimise interracial contact helps us understand the colonial and postcolonial situation in India and the status of Shakespeare in Indian cultural transactions with British imperialism. For this reason I will explore in some detail the socio-political context of Shakespearean studies, receptions and performances in British India to understand how the colonial legacy is negotiated in a later, postcolonial culture.

The film revolves around the implications and actual repercussions of a staging of the play with a young Bengali actor playing Othello opposite a white Desdemona in British colonial India. This revolutionary stage image of a white girl in the arms of an Indian man challenges both the entrenched notions of racial segregation of the colonialists as well as the Hindu orthodoxies of the traditional Bengalis who looked askance at mixed marriages. It thus becomes an icon of liberal, secular modernity. But this modernity is itself deeply problematic and needs to be located in the larger colonial project of using Shakespeare as a vehicle of disseminating 'modern' and 'civilised' values to a 'benighted' nation.

Shakespeare in colonial India: negotiating modernity

The introduction of Shakespeare to Indians as part of the modernising mission of the colonial government must be studied in the context of the great pedagogical debate of the 1830s between the traditionalists on the one hand, who favoured an Orientalist education for the natives and the Progressivists or modernisers on the other, who supported a western model of instruction.

The debate resulted in the passing of the Indian Education Act (1835) which promulgated that Indians would be educated in English rather than in the classical Indian languages such as Sanskrit, Persian or Arabic, and traditional subjects would be replaced by western sciences and liberal arts. Thus the dissemination of English language and literature was formally acknowledged as the tool to be used by the colonial administration in creating a native élite educated in western ideas and values who would need to be co-opted if British rule was to be consolidated.[4] Thomas Macaulay's 'Minute on Indian Education' (1835) spells out the underlying intentions of this educational programme – to create 'a class of people Indian in blood and colour but English in tastes, in opinions, in morals and intellect' who would serve as 'interpreters between us and the millions whom we govern'.[5]

The black-skinned, white-masked Fanonian colonial subject seems to be under construction here.[6] The study of English literature is adopted as a means of creating such a subject and Shakespeare proves to be a particularly potent tool in this project. The political need was to create a class of anglicised Indians who would help to perpetuate British rule.[7]

Apart from the more cynical reasons for introducing English studies among the natives, there was an altruistic motive of bringing the fruits of a more 'advanced' civilisation to an inferior one.[8] Among the highest achievements of this superior culture were the plays of Shakespeare. As the supreme exemplum of European humanist ideals, Shakespeare became equated with the best values that western civilisation had to offer to the Indians. In pedagogy and performance Shakespearean plays became a conduit for the diffusion of European Enlightenment ideals of reason, liberalism, humanism and progressivism which would become ammunition in the war against Hindu traditionalism, superstition, casteism and what were seen by many as essentially regressive tendencies in native life. As Jashodhara Bagchi points out, English literature in general, and Shakespeare in particular, became 'the *Mantra* for the New India in its fight against obscurantist traditionalism'.[9]

The use of the word 'mantra' is particularly apt because Shakespeare's works acquired a quasi-religious stature as an embodiment of the highest 'human' values. They provided a 'secular' space outside the fold of traditional religion and caste in which young native subjects could formulate their ideas about life. The plays provided them with a language in which they could articulate philosophical, metaphysical and ethical concerns outside the bounds of a Hindu framework. As Bagchi points out, English literature became a 'source of non-denominational spirituality, a harbinger of a secular outlet'.[10] But this space, as we know, was neither secular nor neutral: it was largely Christian and British, yet it had an important contribution in a colonised people's early encounters with modernity.

The ahistorical reading of Shakespeare as an exemplar of a transcendent humanism blinded students to the fact that Shakespeare is indeed *a* writer rather than *the* writer, and English literature is *a* literature of a dominant imperial power, not *the* literature. Universalist assumptions about 'human nature' which underlie colonial Shakespeare studies pose a certain danger by obliterating differences and disparities between the coloniser and the colonised, thus creating a false belief among the Indian élite that they were in fact closer to their European masters than to their fellow countrymen.

On the other hand, these assumptions were also empowering in so far as they offered a certain class of natives a foothold in the coloniser's culture and gave them a common language in which to communicate with the coloniser if not on terms of equality, then at least with some degree of parity. This 'universalism' allowed the Indians to emerge from the confines of Orientalist constructions of the self and acquire the confidence of belonging to a larger, 'modern' community.[11]

Thus English language and literature was not just foisted on the natives as a means of hegemonic control, it also had other effects which were probably not foreseen by Macaulay. A dialectical relationship existed between the colonial government's need to create a class of English-educated loyal administrators and the desire of the Indian élite to use such an education to participate more fully in the workings of the government. While the new learning created a servile 'baboo' class it also helped in the construction of a 'modern', 'secular' identity for the young urban Hindu male and augmented his confidence in himself and his own culture. Thus paradoxically, English education helped to forge a nationalist consciousness and a curiosity about and interest in the wealth of native art and literature. The late nineteenth-century 'Bengal Renaissance' which undertook the revival of a glorious Hindu past was largely a result of the introduction of English education.

This paradox is easily understood if we realise that the Indians' exposure to western modernity was not a one-way process. It involved a complex negotiation in which the interests of the urban élite had to be accommodated and protected. This emerging class required a form of western learning which would not upset the Hindu social hierarchies while offering a means of breaking away from certain orthodoxies. English studies from the beginning had to accommodate the caste, class and gender divisions of this new, urbanised society. This is reflected in the very naming of the new college of 'modernisation' as Hindu College.[12] Thus Indian modernity shaped under colonial rule is an interesting amalgam of both mimicry of and resistance to western paradigms.[13]

Shakespeare and the New Woman

Important texts for understanding this contested colonial modernity are the nineteenth-century Bengali translations of Shakespeare, whose works were seen as the repository of 'modern' western values. The process of linguistic translation was also a process of cultural transaction: issues of loyalty to the original text of Shakespeare became also a matter of political affiliation involving questions of endorsing the imperial project of westernisation or resisting it.

In adapting Shakespeare's works to a Bengali milieu, the translators were forced to transform, indigenise and appropriate western ideals and practices in a distinctively Indian manner. These translations represent early responses of the colonised subject to European culture and his/her attempts to fashion an Indian identity through these encounters with western modernity, not uncritically, but with reference to the subject's own traditions. Bengalis were seeking a self-definition which would allow them to be modern without losing their cultural specificity and dignity.

One area in which Shakespeare's plays provided a rich hunting ground was in the shaping of Bengali womanhood. The heroines of the plays were held up as models to be emulated by the new urban gentlewoman, the 'bhadramahila', who was educated, intelligent, but also dutiful. She was required to be independent and yet subservient to her husband.

These contradictions in the ideals of the Bengali housewife emanate from the larger debate between modernity and tradition of which the New Woman becomes a focus. Colonial paradigms of the 'modern' woman and the Victorian companionate marriage in which the woman is a friend rather than a subordinate triggered off a series of revaluations of and reforms for Indian women. On the one hand, the condition of Indian women was deplored and their degeneration criticised; on the other, elaborate defences were written proving the superiority of traditional Indian womanhood, adducing examples from myth and legend. This insistence on tradition betrays the colonised élite's anxiety about their fast diminishing influence over the only sphere they controlled – the home. It is therefore unsurprising that the fashioning of the New Woman becomes a central concern in the natives' complicated negotiations with western modernity and in the evolution of nationalism.[14]

In the nineteenth-century Shakespeare translations, the heroines are indigenised to become interesting amalgams of western modernity and Hindu tradition. While the native intelligence, efficiency and domestic skills of the Portias and the innocence and intensity of the Mirandas and Juliets are praised as qualities worth emulating, their independence and impulsiveness is toned down to make them into ideal Hindu 'bhadramahilas'. Something similar happens in the treatment of Desdemona's character in the translations of *Othello* and later in its post-colonial negotiation in *Saptapadi*, where the Desdemona character emerges as a perfect combination of the spiritedness of a European heroine and the submissiveness of a Hindu bride.

Gender, race and Indian *Othellos*

In the colonial translations of *Othello* (translated as *Bhimsingha* by Tarini Charan Pal in 1875 and by Debendranath Basu in 1919)[15] Desdemona is represented as the New Woman who defies her father and family to marry the man of her choice, but she is subservient to her husband and dies unprotestingly when accused wrongly of adultery. Thus she is a modern 'sati' who dies to protect her husband's honour.

In an essay entitled 'Shakuntala, Miranda and Desdemona', Bankim Chandra Chattopadhyay, perhaps the most important and prolific writer of nineteenth-century Bengal, compares Shakespeare's heroines to those of the classical Sanskrit poet Kalidasa and finds them to be better 'satis' than their Indian sisters. Both Desdemona and Shakuntala display an independence of spirit in choosing their husbands, but Desdemona scores more points as a 'sati' because she does not lash out at her husband as Shakuntala does.[16] She emerges as a more successful combination of the ancient and the modern than the classical Hindu heroine of Kalidasa. Even in post-colonial adaptations of *Othello*, Desdemona's defiance of her father and the implications it has for the construction of the modern Indian woman's identity assumes the greatest importance. Utpal Dutt, in his book on Shakespeare's social consciousness, includes Desdemona with the spirited and independent heroines of Shakespearean comedy and romance like Hermia, Jessica and Imogen who follow their impulses with charm and aplomb.[17]

Dealing as it does with marriage and love, *Othello* has generic affinities with comedy or domestic drama rather than with heroic or classical tragedy.[18] This could be one of the reasons why in Indian translations, adaptations and critiques, the play is always treated as a text which articulates individual freedom and romantic love against patriarchal dictates and familial pressure. The concerns of gender and women's identity receive much greater prominence than racial issues. In *Saptapadi* too, following the tradition of colonial adaptations of *Othello*, the focus is on the themes of love, romance and marriage. Race is only one component in the romantic plot. This affects the generic expectations of the film, which ends in happy conjugality rather than in the tragic collapse of an interracial marriage.

The silence about racial issues in colonial adaptations of *Othello* was not solely because of the colonial pedagogical strategy which sought to erase the racial context of the play as was clearly the case in South Africa.[19] Nineteenth-century race theories were perhaps also responsible for this silence. Most Orientalist histories traced the origin of both Hindus and Europeans to a common Aryan stock.[20] As such, no racial divide was perceived to exist between the coloniser and colonised. This theory was happily accepted and developed by Indian historians too. Thus, the Indian reader, adapter or translator of *Othello* would more readily identify with the Europeans than with the black character. Othello's predicament in a white society, his alienation and otherness, is not seen as providing a parallel to the situation of the Indian colonised subject. In a few translations, Othello is not even represented as being racially different from the other characters of the play.

So gender issues rather than racial matters assume importance in colonial interpretations of *Othello* in India. However, in performances involving both Indian and English actors the question of race becomes an undeniable reality which demands attention. As I have argued before, it is in such staging that the impact of the racial juxtaposition gains force.

On 17 August 1848, in a landmark performance of *Othello* in colonial Calcutta at the Sans Souci Theatre, for the first time in the history of English professional theatre in India, an Indian appeared on the stage in the lead role among a predominantly white cast. A young Bengali, Baishnab Charan Adhya, played Othello opposite an English woman, Mrs Anderson, as Desdemona.[21] The production created a huge stir. A letter appeared in the *Calcutta Star* which announced the 'debut of a real unpainted nigger Othello' which had set 'the whole world of Calcutta agog'.[22]

The racial identification between the actor and the role had a certain outrage value but certainly not of the same order as the shock and indignation generated by mixed-cast productions of *Othello* in the west.[23] Indian actors do not evoke the same kind of horror. In fact they are commended for their efforts at participating in the 'superior' culture of their colonial masters. Praising Audhya's heroic attempts, the *Bengal Hurkura* said:

Othello was the great attraction on Thursday night...the player however and not the play. Performed by Baboo Bustom Churn Addy...all expectations were of course centred in the young aspirant for dramatic fame, who has gallantly flung down his gauntlet to the rest of the members of the native community...Shakespeare, exiled from the country he honours so much, seeks an asylum on the Calcutta boards...Slim and symmetrical in person, his delivery was somewhat cramped, but under all circumstances his pronunciation of English was for a native remarkably good...The performer had substantial demonstration that the feelings of the audience were fairly enlisted on his side.[24]

Playing Othello becomes not a means of finding a way to articulate the alienation and exploitation of an oppressed people, but of imitating better the highest achievements of European civilisation. This is what happens to the young Bengali hero of *Saptapadi*. Enacting Othello provides him with the opportunity to become more fully a part of European culture which is equated with modernity and progress. But his negotiations with a western paradigm of modernity is neither simple nor easy.

Saptapadi: the seven steps of marriage

A postcolonial film set in colonial times, *Saptapadi* (the seven steps of marriage) is a romantic melodrama about the love of a young Bengali boy for an 'English' girl.[25] The film is structured around a performance of *Othello* which is used as a paradigm to validate this inter-racial romance.

As in colonial readings of the play, marriage, sexual relationships and the role of women continue to be central concerns, but not at the cost of racial issues. In *Saptapadi*, made in post-independence India in the 1960s – a decade which witnessed historic international movements for racial and gender equality – marriage becomes a site for interrogating issues of race, nationalism and Indian identity.

The film is set in colonial India of the early 1940s and begins with shots of the Second World War. This is particularly significant because the war years were a period of British–Indian collaboration when the colonial masters needed to depend on their subjects for survival. This was also a time when Indians realised that the Raj was practically over and the famous Quit India movement was launched in 1942. In the face of the imminent collapse of the Empire and the birth of an independent Indian nation, questions of national identity assumed immense importance.

The film explores these issues through the evolving relationship of the Bengali Krishnendu (literally 'the dark moon') and the 'English'

Rina Brown, who symbolise the changing face of British–Indian interaction. We see a very confident, strident and modern Indian identity emerging in the hero who refuses to allow matters of race, nationality or religion to interfere with his choice of a partner. But this liberal, secular and modern selfhood seems irreconcilable with an indigenous identity and can be achieved only by sacrificing it. *Othello* provides both a precedent and a justification for this process.

The dark son of Kali

Krishnendu and Rina are both students at the Calcutta Medical College and he is infatuated with her. For Rina, however, he is a 'blackie' and thus not even within romantic reckoning. She is in love with an English boy, Clayton, who seems to humour her but is not very enthusiastic about the relationship. The battle lines are drawn between Clayton and Krishnendu, not only over Rina but in the spheres of sports and academia.[26] The Indian is shown to excel in all areas much to the consternation of Rina. He is represented as aggressively and proudly Indian, dressed in dhoti-kurta, defending his nation and race against every calumny. Mischievous, humorous, able and charming, he is a perfect foil to the stiff-upper-lipped, strait-laced Englishman.

But the film makes amply clear that Krishnendu's reiterated 'Indianness' is not an impediment to his participation in a progressive, scientific culture. He is training to be a doctor and wishes to go to England to pursue higher studies. He has differences with his Hindu father who considers going abroad a sin and is opposed to his son's liberal views and lax attitude towards tradition.

Krishnendu's character thus seems to represent a nationalist modernity. He evokes Hindu tropes to defend his culture against attacks from Rina but he is not limited by them. When she calls him a 'darkie', he retorts by saying he is proud to be one since all Indians are sons of Kali, the dark mother goddess of the Hindus. Kali is invoked again as the fierce and exotic protector of the black nations when Krishnendu adeptly sings a 'Shyamasangeet' (a typical devotional song dedicated to Kali) to drown the loud music at Rina's birthday party. He is deeply embedded in the native culture but not blinded by it as his father is. This duality between tradition and modernity is interestingly expressed through the human skull that he carries during the song – although he uses it as if it were an accessory for the tantric rites of Kali, the goddess of death, it is in fact an aid for his medical studies. His insistence from the very beginning that he is an atheist makes nonsense of the charges of heathenism directed by Rina against him. For her, Krishnendu is always the stereotypical 'native' who predictably desires her but is not even worth a glance. It seems impossible that Rina and Krishnendu would ever be able to meet on an equal footing. Such an opportunity is thrown up by an amateur performance of *Othello* at their college where Rina plays Desdemona opposite Krishnendu's Othello.

Othello and the space of the modern

Initially Othello is supposed to be played by Clayton. At the rehearsals he appears awkward and uninspired and Krishnendu steps in to show the Englishman how to put more life into Shakespeare. He tells Clayton that his stilted delivery would horrify Shakespeare had he heard him. Unable to demonstrate the strangling scene with the incensed Rina Brown, he bends over a bearded male friend gingerly and speaks Othello's lines magnificently. Rina expostulates and calls him a buffoon. In response, he breaks a coconut with his bare hands and walks off. This is perhaps meant to convey his strangeness and power, both of which qualities make him a closer kin of the Moor than Clayton can ever be.

On the day of the performance, Clayton does not arrive and Krishnendu has to fill in for him. As he sits at the makeup table, having his face blackened, he simultaneously slips into two roles – those of Clayton and of Othello. Being Othello, paradoxically for Krishnendu, is also being English, or at least finding a voice for himself in the highest reaches of the coloniser's culture. It is less about identifying himself with an alienated black consciousness and more about participating in the exclusive, privileged and charmed circle of white people through appropriating a role which was meant for Clayton. As Othello, Krishnendu can share a stage bed with the white Desdemona, something which appeared impossible in the social space of colonial India. So a performance of the play provides an opportunity for an intimate physical encounter of people otherwise divided by historical and political circumstances.

The murder scene is enacted in a Wellesian melodramatic mode with stark contrasts in black and white. The voices sound very British, particularly Desdemona's. Tellingly, the lines are spoken not by the Bengali actors playing Rina and Krishnendu, both of whose English was heavily accented, but by actors from Geoffrey Kendall's Shakespeare troupe.[27] This ventriloquism and role-playing thus has several layers.

Krishnendu as Clayton-Othello enjoys a certain proximity with Rina on stage. But, initially repulsed by the prospect of a 'native' touching her, she asks Krishnendu to keep a distance. This results in a strange, 'apartheid', *Othello* which is manifested in rather awkward missed kisses on stage. Rina's racial paranoia is an example of what Dympna Callaghan has described as a confusion of 'exhibition' and 'art' resulting in a crisis of mimesis: 'it ceases to be acting, becoming not the representation of the-thing-itself but, instead, *the-thing-in-itself*'.[28] While a white actor can be thought able to represent Othello's blackness, a black or Asiatic actor is considered capable only of demonstrating his own negritude, unable to go beyond what is held to be the undeniable 'reality' of his colour.

But belying Rina's apprehensions, it is art rather than nature which weaves its magic on stage. Through the performance and the physical intimacy it breeds, she falls in love with Krishnendu-as-Othello. The enactment of the murder scene transforms the story of the tragic collapse of a mixed-race marriage into an enabling condition for a mixed-race relationship. The stage provides a secular space which is untouched by Rina's prejudices about 'heathen blackies' and Krishnendu's father's orthodox Hinduism. The physical realities of performance thus challenge racial stereotypes. Shakespeare, not so much textually, but performatively opens up possibilities of a modernity unavailable in other spheres of life.

However, this modernity is severely limited and limiting. It comes at the cost of losing one's indigenous identity. Krishnendu's performance as Othello ends with the curtains but his role as surrogate Clayton continues as he takes up the Englishman's function as suitor to Rina Brown. Soon after mutual declarations of undying love for each other, he converts to Christianity at the insistence of Rina's father and when she deserts him, he ends up adopting the archetypal role of evangelical colonialism – that of the missionary priest.

He is disowned by his Hindu father who is outraged by his son's conversion. In an interesting inversion we see the Othello figure, rather than Desdemona, making the crucial break with the paternal home and culture to further his individual choice in marriage. One wonders whether this can be regarded as a 'feminisation' of Krishnendu's character since it would be considered unmanly to give in to the wife's culture as he does. In colonial Bengal, the most commonly-used epithet for the anglicised Bengali 'baboos' who had sold off their motherland to the English was 'effeminate'. But *Saptapadi* is also trying to create new paradigms of masculinity and gender parity and is challenging these old ideas even while using them. The film uses Othello to construct the modern Indian male as the colonial versions of the play tried to construct the 'bhadramahila' or the New Woman.

Krishnendu renounces the feudal patriarchy and Hindu orthodoxy represented by his father in the interest of a liberal, secular, modern outlook, but manages only to mimic the English uncritically. In his attempts to become an appropriate partner for Rina, he loses his Indian identity and his cheeky resistance against Anglicisation which is evident in the earlier part of the film. The poised balance of modernity and tradition in his character is flattened out.

The 'racial' differences between the two protagonists are deliberately underplayed and erased in the interest of the romantic ending which *Othello* lacks and the popular cinema must provide. The asymmetries of race and gender which characterise the play are too disturbing for *Saptapadi*. In the film, the hero's racial 'inferiority' must be cancelled through his assimilation into white, Christian society and the heroine too must be chastised for humiliating the hero and must occupy a suitably subordinate position. Accordingly, the film reveals that Rina is not a pure-bred English girl. Her mother is a humble Indian servant who was raped by her English father. So she is half Indian after all, which explains her attraction to Krishnendu and diffuses the scandalousness of their relationship somewhat.

Her 'Indianness' also accounts for her subsequent behaviour as a self-sacrificing 'sati' figure. When Krishnendu's father asks her to leave his son alone, she obliges as an obedient Indian daughter-in-law would.[29] Her devotion finally wins over the recalcitrant old man, but by this time she has been devastated by the revelation of her birth details. Her pride in her racial and religious superiority lies shattered. She takes to drinking and is brought in a state of inebriation to the mission hospital which Krishnendu runs as the resident Jesuit priest. Revived by him, she recounts the sordid tale of her disillusionment and loss of faith. Krishnendu tries to restore her belief in humanity. A sermon on the universalism of the religion of Man follows, which is visually reinforced by the images of Hindu prophets alongside those of Christ. But this attempt at transcending religion and opening up a secular space is collapsed in the final scene which shows Krishnendu carrying Rina towards a church with the intention of being united in the eye of a patently Christian God.

The nascent project of forging an Indian secular modernity ends rather disappointingly. It appears that little advance has been made from the nineteenth century which believed that progress lay only in the embracing of western values and religion. Like Othello, Krishnendu has to kill the 'malignant Turk', the Other within the Self, in order to achieve the status of a hero since heroism remains unavailable to the black or the Indian protagonist.

Othello, Hollywood melodrama and the 1960s

I have examined how Shakespeare's *Othello* helps in articulating the colonial subject's encounters with modernity, however restricted the parameters of that modernity might be. In *Saptapadi* it is also apparent how the coming-of-age of Bengali cinema is effected through its interactions with Hollywood and is mediated through *Othello*.

The image of the liberated American heroine who makes independent choices throws up a challenge to Bengali cinema which is answered through a character like Rina Brown, who nevertheless needs to be validated through the authority of Shakespeare. Rina's decision to marry Krishnendu needs to be put in the context of *Othello* to become acceptable on the Bengali screen. The play performs a mediating role in the negotiations of Bengali cinema with Hollywood just as it had provided a template for the emergence of the 'New Woman' in its colonial incarnations.

The popular melodramatic American cinema of the 1950s focused on the individual and on the carving out of an independent domestic space for the central romantic protagonists.[30] Tollygunge responded to these films with its own romantic melodramas which were concerned primarily with heterosexual couple formation.[31] These films characteristically marked a transition from the traditional extended family to conceptions of a new domesticity which was constituted by the couple in exclusion of rest of the society.[32]

The famous shot of Krishnendu and Rina on a motorbike driving for what seems like an eternity and singing the phenomenally popular song 'If this road should never end' articulates the desire for freedom from social and familial pressures of a generation of Bengalis who were witnessing the sexual revolution sweeping the west, but were unable to find an Indian voice to express their own changed perceptions about the relationship of the sexes. This emphasis on the autonomy of the couple and on the conjugal space as opposed to the familial, comes to represent a desire for modernity, for independence from older and cumbrous social structures.[33] This is a modified re-articulation of the colonial subject's attempts to reject Hindu orthodoxy and embrace 'modern', western values without surrendering his/her Indian identity. For both the colonial subject and the post-colonial Bengali of the 1960s, Shakespeare provides a useful paradigm for negotiating western modernity, whether British or American.

By bringing an intensely private bedroom scene onto the public stage, *Othello* creates a space of sexual freedom. The sheer shock of witnessing a consummation-like murder of a white woman by a black man challenges bourgeois morality. It is therefore unsurprising that Hollywood even now can make a sensational, popular thriller out of *Othello*.[34] However problematic the actual implications of the killing are, *Saptapadi* manages to find in it a sexual openness which challenges the conservatism not just of Indian middle-class life, but also the conservatism of screen images or stage performances. Interestingly, one of the characters in *Saptapadi* remarks wonderingly about the *Othello* performance, 'Good Lord, are men and women going to act together then?'

Thus it is not just *Othello* as a text, but the entire culture of Shakespearean performance which clears out an area for a more uninhibited interaction among the sexes and among classes and races. At the cost of glossing over the misogyny and racial prejudices embedded in the text, *Saptapadi* wrests from it a sense of freedom and modernity, which is severely circumscribed but, in its hesitant way, is nevertheless meaningful. The model of this modernity remains essentially western, but it does provide a space for a dialogue between cultures, unavailable elsewhere.

Notes

1. Critical opinion on how far Othello is representative of a black consciousness is divided. Critics like Ruth Cowhig point out the uniqueness of Othello's role as hero on the Renaissance stage which usually portrayed black characters as humorous or comic ('Blacks in English Renaissance drama and the role of Shakespeare's Othello,' *The Black Presence in English Literature*, ed. David Dabydeen (Manchester: Manchester University Press, 1989) 1–25). Leslie Fiedler, in *The Stranger in Shakespeare* (Hertfordshire: Paladin, 1974), contends that despite the many references to Othello's blackness, he ends up as 'colourless: a provincial gentleman warrior, a downright English soldier...' (160). In *Gender, Race, Renaissance Drama* (Manchester: Manchester University Press, 1989) 48, Ania Loomba however disagrees with Fiedler and sees Othello's character as effecting a passage from 'an honorary white to a total outsider.'

2. Ben Okri recounts how the experience of watching Othello in a theatre with a predominantly white audience permanently changed his perception of the play ('Meditations on Othello,' *West Africa* (23 and 30 March 1987) 562–3). In ' "Othello was a white man": Properties of Race on Shakespeare's Stage,' *Shakespeare Without Women: Representing Gender and Race on the Renaissance Stage* (London: Routledge, 2000) 75–96, Dympna Callaghan points out how the convention of having white actors play Othello has influenced not just our understanding of the play but also of racial politics. Theatrical experiments such as the 1997–98 Lansburgh Theatre (Washington) production of the 'photo-negative' *Othello*, directed by Jude Kelly, with an all-black cast with the exception of the title role, which is played by the solitary white actor (Patrick Stewart), testify to the abiding importance that performance and the visual impact of colour politics still has on our readings of *Othello*.

3. *Saptapadi* belongs to the era of black-and-white films featuring Uttam Kumar and Suchitra Sen which started in 1953 and continued into the late 1960s, creating the most popular star couple and a series of films which enjoyed unprecedented success. The films have become classics and continue to live in people's imaginations through revivals on television, video circulation and reruns of the audio cassettes of their music.

4. For the ideological underpinnings of the introduction of English studies in colonial India see Gauri Vishwanathan, *Masks of Conquest: Literary Study and British Rule in India* (London: Faber and Faber, 1989).

5. Thomas B. Macaulay, 'Minute on Indian Education,' 1835. Reprinted in *Thomas Babington Macaulay: Selected Writings*, ed. J. Clive and T. Pinney (Chicago: Chicago University Press, 1972) 729.

6. Frantz Fanon, *Black Skin, White Masks*, trans. Charles Lamm (New York: Grove Press, 1967) 1–80.

7. The English had in fact successfully created the kind of 'hybrid' subject envisaged by Macaulay in the Bengali 'baboos'. This was a class of English-educated bureaucrats, loyal to the government, critical of their own culture, in whom the British administration had implicit faith and who actually made the functioning of the colonial government possible even in the face of bitter nationalist opposition.

8. Jyotsna G. Singh, 'Shakespeare and the Civilising Mission,' *Colonial Narratives/Cultural Dialogues* (London: Routledge, 1996) 124–7.

9. J. Bagchi, 'Shakespeare in Loin Cloths: English Literature and the Early Nationalist Consciousness in Bengal,' *Rethinking English: Essays in Literature, Language, History*, ed. Svati Joshi (New Delhi: Trianka, 1991) 151.

10. Bagchi 150.

11. Ania Loomba describes this new English education as offering a 'programme of building a new man who would feel himself a citizen of the world while the very face of the world was being constructed in the mirror of the dominant culture of the West.' *Gender, Race, Renaissance Drama* 21.

12. Bagchi 148.

13. Homi Bhabha, 'Signs Taken for Wonders: Questions of Ambivalence and Authority under a Tree outside New Delhi – May 1817,' *Critical Inquiry* 12: 1 (1985) 162.

14. Dipesh Chakravarty, 'The Difference–Deferral of a Colonial Modernity: Public Debates on Domesticity in British Bengal,' *Subaltern Studies VIII*, ed. David Arnold and David Hardiman (Delhi: OUP, 1994) 52–88: 'It was thus that the idea of the "new woman" came to be written into the techniques of the self that nationalism evolved, which looked on the domestic as an inseparable part of the national. The public sphere could not be erected without reconstructing the private' (58).

15. Subir Raychaudhuri ed., *Bilati Jatra theke Swadeshi Theatre* (Calcutta: Jadavpur University, 1972) Appendix I.

16. Bankim Chandra Chattopadhyay, Brajendranath Bandyopadhyay and Sajanikanta Das eds, *Bijnan-rahasya, Samya, Vividh Prabandha* (Calcutta: Bangiya Sahitya Parishad, 1938) 86–7.

17. U. Dutt, *Shakespeare-er Samaj Chetana* (Calcutta: M. C. Sarkar and Sons, 1986) 11.

18. Barbara Heliodora C. deMendonça, '*Othello*: A Tragedy Built on a Comic Structure,' *Shakespeare Survey* 21(1968): 31–8.

19. Martin Orkin, 'Othello and the "plain face" of racism,' *Shakespeare Quarterly* 38 (1987): 166–88, and *Shakespeare Against Apartheid* (Craighall: A. D. Donker, 1987).

20. Thomas R. Metcalf, *Ideologies of the Raj* (Cambridge: CUP, 1998) 66–92; Peter Robb ed., *The Concept of Race in South Asia* (Delhi: OUP, 1995) 165–218; 282–303.

21. For a detailed discussion of this production see Jyotsna Singh and Sudipto Chatterjee, 'Moor or Less: The Surveillance of Othello, Calcutta, 1848,' *Shakespeare and Appropriation*, ed. Christy Desmet and Robert Sawyer (London: Routledge, 1999) 65–82.

22. Kironmoy Raha (*Bengali Theatre*, New Delhi: National Book Trust, 1978) as quoted in *Shakespeare on the Calcutta Stage: A Checklist*, ed. Ananda Lal and Sukanta Chaudhuri (Kolkata: Papyrus, 2001) 22.

23. Dympna Callaghan mentions nineteenth-century American performances in which white actresses like Ellen Tree played Desdemona opposite black actors and created great distress and concern to the white community who did not want 'their' women to be 'pawed' by black men. The spectre of miscegenation is raised by the visual impact of seeing a mixed race couple on stage. See ' "Othello was a white man": Properties of Race on Shakespeare's Stage,' in Callaghan, *Shakespeare Without Women* (London: Routledge, 2000) 90–1.

24. *Bengal Hurkura*, 19 August 1848. Quoted in Lal and Chaudhuri 22.

25. Alochaya Productions, 1961, black and white, direction and script, Ajoy Kar, lead roles, Uttam Kumar and Suchitra Sen.

26. The shots of the football match in which Krishnendu ousts Clayton deliberately echo scenes from nationalist sporting history, particularly the match between Mohunbagan, a 'native' Calcutta team who could not even afford football boots, and a team of well equipped 'Goras' or whites, which ended in an Indian victory. The recent Hindi film *Lagaan* (dir. Ashutosh Gowariker, perf. Aamir Khan, Gracy Singh, Paul Blackthorne and Suhasini Muley. India: Aamir Khan Productions, 2001) explores these issues through a colonial cricket match played between a British and an Indian team.

27. Othello is dubbed by Utpal Dutt who started his career in Kendall's troupe and then went on to found the Indian People's Theatre and to translate and produce several Shakespearean plays.

28. Callaghan 91.

29. *Saptapadi*'s heroine carries resonances of Bankim Chandra's characterisation of Desdemona as 'sati'. She is like the reconstructed 'New Woman' who can be both modern and traditional.

30. Thomas Elsaesser, 'Tales of Sound and Fury: Observations on the Family Melodrama' (1972), *Movies and Methods*, Vol. II, ed. Bill Nichols (Berkeley: University of California Press, 1985) 165–89 and Peter Brooks, *The Melodramatic Imagination* (New York: Columbia University Press, 1985).

31. Tollygunge is the name of the area in which the Calcutta film studios are concentrated. Like Hollywood, the name has become a metonymy for Bengali films.

32. Moinak Biswas, 'The Couple and Their Spaces: *Harano Sur* as Melodrama Now,' *Making Meaning in Indian Cinema*, ed. Ravi Vasudevan (New Delhi: OUP, 2000) 122–42.
33. Madhava Prasad, 'Cinema and the Desire for Modernity,' *Journal of Arts and Ideas* (1993): 25–6.
34. The Oliver Parker film made in 1995. For an excellent discussion on the sensationalism of the film see Pascale Aebischer, 'Black Rams Tupping White Ewes: Race vs. Gender in the Final Scene of Six *Othellos*,' *Retrovisions: Historical Make-overs in Film and Literature*, ed. D. Cartmell *et al.* (London: Pluto, 2001) 59–73.

4
Reading 'Other Shakespeares'

Poonam Trivedi

Not for nothing has Shakespeare been named the writer of the millennium – his works are translated, published and performed in more languages all over the world than those of any other author. This Shakespeare diaspora, earlier part of the spread of the English language in the wake of the Empire, now rides the crest of a postcolonial and post-modern libertarianism. While in earlier days Shakespeare's name was a touchstone for an Englishness of language and literature, today it is not so much the 'English-language Shakespeare' that is making waves but a hybrid Shakespeare in sundry accents and hues. Shakespeare today exists throughout the world in a state of constantly renewed 'otherness': in recensions/appropriations/translations/parodies and rewrites which, more and more, are demanding a serious critical attention. In fact, the more Shakespeare is cannibalised, the more he seems to flourish. What is also distinct about this second wave of the spread of Shakespeare is that nowhere is this otherness more manifest than on the stage. Performance, in the global consumerist culture, is now more central to the spread and popularity of Shakespeare than classroom study ever was. (It is a well-known fact that all over the colonies of the English Empire Shakespeare was introduced as part of the English language curriculum in schools and colleges – as early as 1814 in India.)[1] Just as the translation of Shakespeare used to be seen as a measuring-rod of another language's potency and maturity, the performance of his plays today is a sign of a culture's cosmopolitanism.

Yet the very celebrated 'otherness' of the diasporic Shakespeares has challenged critical practice. Issues of 'authenticity' particularly bedevil criticism. Which, what and who is the 'real' Shakespeare? How are we to judge translations in foreign tongues and, even more intractably, in foreign performance vocabularies? Can there be one and the same yardstick for understanding adaptations in diverse cultures and locations? If not, do we then relinquish the assessments and the pleasures of these 'other' Shakespeares to the local auditors only? Will the canon of performed Shakespeare continue to be confined, inevitably, to the Eurocentric or should we not attempt to expand definitions to embrace the rich hybridity and 'otherness' of Shakespeare too; definitions which not merely acknowledge alterity but see it as equal? Though a sustained effort to analyse the implications of this phenomenon has not yet been undertaken, what has found expression is the discomfiture at the fracturing of a received interpretative system. Reactions ranging from hostility to a cautious scepticism to strong caveats reveal the disruptive effects of the 'Other Shakespeares'. Inga-Stina Ewbank, for instance, in an essay entitled 'Shakespeare Translation as Cultural Exchange', in which she speaks from the point of view of the English, finds 'a somewhat embarrassing kind of inverse colonialism' in translated/adapted Shakespeare and wonders whether there is not 'a kind of cultural collusion to turn Shakespeare into something he isn't?' producing 'a kind of pollution of Shakespeare?'[2] Kate McLuskie in '*Macbeth/Umabatha*: Global Shakespeare in a Post-Colonial Market' alerts attention to 'the discourses which articulate the intersection between performances of Shakespeare in the theatre and successive movements of cultural politics...includ[ing] the opposition between art and commerce, between the authentic and the fake and, in this case between the metropolitan and the third world.'[3] It is Dennis Kennedy, however, who in 'Shakespeare without Shakespeare' sounds the alarm about the current dis-appropriation – an appropriation in which Shakespeare virtually disappears. Pointing to the current packaging of Shakespeare, he says,

> Commodity culture doesn't want Shakespeare; it wants Shakespeare without Shakespeare. Taking a cue from contemporary marketing, we might call this phenomenon 'Shaxä.'...At the commercial end Shaxä is a sales gimmick, an elegant package for almost any commodity presentation. At the elite end Shaxä has become a blank or empty vessel for our obsessions and desires. Shakespeare has at last become a 'universal' figure – not as humanists mean the term but as it is meant in the millennial marketplace.[4]

At the furthest extreme is the hangover from colonialism and consequent demonisation of the Other which was articulated in response to the critical study of Shakespeare translation and performance in regional Indian languages. In opposition to the translation into English of 'regional' texts which supposedly 'opens vistas', this view proposes that 'bringing English texts, even of the stature of Shakespeare, to the Indian readers through regionally confined languages or theatre... [is] imposing closures on a world resource'.[5]

This essay aims to revoke such prejudices and fulfil the need to centre 'Other' Shakespeares. Through a discussion of the problems of reading those performance texts, I want to signal towards an alternative logic and practice of assessment. Key productions from India of varying interaction with Shakespeare will be examined as templates of 'otherness' to focus attention on three central areas through which Shakespeare is being expanded today and which remain the critical foci of performance study: (a) 'other texts', i.e. Shakespeare in translation, (b) 'other bodies', i.e. the embodiment of Shakespeare in alternative performance styles and (c) 'other sites', i.e. the shifting cultural locations and their specific re-contextualisations of Shakespeare. This investigation of 'Other' Shakespeares will locate itself in the complex of associations accruing to the term 'Other', as evolved from Hegel, Heidegger, Sartre and Lacan and given currency by feminist and postcolonial theory.[6] It will narrow the focus to Shakespeare in India, grounding the discussions in a brief history of the performance of Shakespeare in India, its colonial and postcolonial implications, and its aesthetic ramifications.

Non-Anglophone Shakespeares, particularly, have until recently suffered a position of 'othering' and been denied a subjectivity of their own. They have received little critical estimation and have languished in a master–slave relationship, relegated to a subordinate, inassimilable and extraneous position. Though they may seem to represent a rupture from the parent text, 'Other' Shakespeares, in an extension of the Lacanian paradigm, become the differential which constitutes the subject, a site of the signifier; worldwide Shakespeare which incorporates the 'Other' becomes the whole. Shakespeare, the man of the millennium, must be appreciated in his global avatar. The very proliferation of the 'Other' Shakespeares reveals them to be, like the female Other of feminist theory, objects of desire that nevertheless threaten the unity of the purist Shakespeare canon. Like the postcolonial Other, they challenge the power of the authentic with their staged mimicry and hybrid alterity. The tensions of the oppositional and the essential are intrinsic to their condition. The 'Other' by its breakaway but mirror nature both re-inscribes the engendering text and constitutes a split from it. 'Other' Shakespeares locked into this complex circulate the canon even as they simultaneously 'play', take liberties with and radicalise it.

A conspicuous focus on this 'otherness' was programmed into the Seventh World Shakespeare Congress (18–23 April 2001) at Valencia, Spain, on 'Shakespeare and the Mediterranean'. 'Otherness' was explored in Shakespeare's play world and in the position of Shakespeare in the world today. More than half of the seminars dealt with 'otherness' seen variously as non-European, or non-Anglophone, or simply in the person of a stranger. Within a broad perspective, they saw 'otherness' through a re-framing, mediation, appropriation, negotiation of boundaries, while more specifically, it was explored within the subsumed geopolitics of the Mediterranean. A wealth of documentation emerged, debates were conducted, but no consensus on assessment emerged. Questions remained hanging over the interpretation of these 'versions' of Shakespeare. The 'Creative and Critical Appropriations of Shakespeare' Seminar, whose mandate was precisely to discuss these issues and of which I was a member, repeatedly returned to the question of how far you could stretch the texts, but ended with the caveat that it is not the function of criticism to police appropriations. 'Are the plays infinitely malleable, able to accommodate diverse performative and cultural transformations?' was another issue that came up for discussion. Or how do auditors the world over begin to unravel codified performance styles like *kathakali* or *kabuki*? With participants from nine countries, not just aesthetics, but the question of history and contextualisation too assumed a piquant challenge, as in relation to *The Merchant of Venice* for instance. Can cultures without the background of Semitism continue to meaningfully play Shylock as an example of the money-lender, a type as old as Roman comedy, or has the recent past foreclosed this option? Whose history, asked the seminar, for whom and by whom and how is it to be inserted into or extracted out of the performance text? Reinscriptions or resistances, it emerged, are not necessarily binary opposites but sliding positions on the appropriative scale.

A similar paradox was articulated at a micro/local level at the 'Shakespeare on the Indian Stage' seminar and theatre festival held just before the Shakespeare World Congress, 24 February–2 March 2001 at Kasargode (Kerala, India), where eight widely differing productions were mounted but were received with equally diverse responses. This event, unique in its singular focus on Shakespeare, had performances challenging critical response. Two 'straight' productions, two adaptations, two an eclectic mix of folk and realism and two plays in indigenous folk forms had the audience divided and somewhat confused about how to 'read' these different Shakespeares. In the absence of a theory of 'Other' Shakespeares, the challenge of commensurate response is not just a Eurocentric issue; 'other' auditors, often the very targets of the 'Other' Shakespeares, too, need to suspend their conditioned and colonised mindsets. Several generations of Indians who were taught to look upon Shakespeare as their literary bible still cannot stomach any deviations from the text. This is so in spite of the fact that Indians especially could advantageously take a leaf out of their own indigenous literary tradition where translation, adaptation, rewriting and transformation have been sanctioned practices of literary creation. Unlike the western tradition in which even translation is a 'fall' from the origin and a condition of 'exile', the Indian literary tradition recognises these practices as legitimate modes of alterity. The Indian theory of literary growth and evolution through translation and adaptation is best seen, as formulated by Harish Trivedi in *Post-Colonial Translation*, in terms of a Banyan tree, where a central tradition, author or text ramifies and puts down shoots which take root and become free-standing 'original' texts in their own right.[7] Adaptation and re-vision of a literary text are thus neither parasitic nor transgressive but rather a norm which, in fact, serves to uphold the centrality of the 'mother' text. (The words used for literary creation, representation and translation in Sanskrit literary theory, which forms the classical base of all Indian literatures, *anukriti, anukaran* and *anuvada*, all share the same root *anu* = to come after, underlining not just an equivalence of the three processes, but also the view that even the very act of literary creation is a re-scription, an imitation.)[8] Recreations of Shakespeare the world over can be reassessed in this light as a complex network of intertwining but also independent, organic offshoots. Adaptations and appropriations would then hold, in critical discourse, a space equal to the original text, and 'Other' Shakespeares would figure equally in local and global valuation. The task now is to move beyond a critical compartmentalism; if 'other' literatures are happy to adopt and adapt Shakespeare it would not be amiss to take a leaf out of 'other' theoretical systems to assess those (performance) texts.

Other texts

The Lacanian 'Other' also represents language, the symbolic order. 'Other' Shakespeares have a particularly tendentious relation with the text, the extended site of the signifier. In India at the Kasargode seminar, as in Spain at the World Congress, the chief obstacle to the evaluation of these 'Other' Shakespeares was, despite the well-known interventions of performance theory, the authority of the text and the consequent authenticity of the 'tradaptation' in performance. All appropriations inevitably continued to be judged according to the extent of their departures from the text. But which texts/editions/translations? With the published sanction of not just multiple editions, but also differing textual versions of the same plays (e.g. *Lear*), variant spellings and even names of characters (Falstaff/Oldcastle), is it at all possible to speak of an authoritative 'text' of any Shakespeare play? Critics need to accept what editors have done for some time now, that the texts of Shakespeare's plays, revised and improvised upon by the playwright himself, are fluid and plural. Any attempt to stabilise them is contingent upon a host of contextual factors. The boundaries between texts, pretexts, subtexts and play-texts are continually fusing into each other. Performance texts, therefore, need to be read on their own terms, on par with other 'texts' and not in ultimate submission to a notional authenticity of 'the text' on the page. Performance theory has long argued for the acceptance of text-as-work, text-as-process, text-as-textuality and text-as-performance.[9]

The tyranny of 'the text' was experienced in a particularly piquant fashion with a 'straight' production (i.e. the unadapted and unedited text in a realistic rendering) at Kasargode, of *King Lear* in a Marathi verse translation by the well-known poet Vinda Karandikar, presented by the Pratya Theatre of Kolhapur and directed by Sharad Buthadia. This performance played almost the full text in a quasi-Elizabethan costume. It chose a broadly realistic mode with minimal symbolic props eschewing any localisation. It was a production which had been acclaimed in its own state of Maharashtra and was being revived for the all-India festival as the best Shakespeare production of its region. It was played by enthusiastic amateurs (the director is a medical doctor by profession) from an area which has a long tradition of playing Shakespeare, both in the amateur and commercial spheres. Further, the production used a text which is seen as the acme of sensitive and supple translation of Shakespeare in Marathi and, what is more, of the spoken performance texts of the Marathi stages. It should have been a walkover success. But in the changed locale of Kerala, without the privilege of an audience familiar with Marathi, it fell flat. The problem, I want to suggest, lay in the text: the very polished and perfected poetry which had inspired the performance had blocked the suiting of the action to the words.

To enter into the intricacies of text, performance and reception in this particular case and to generalise therefrom, it might be useful to take a brief look at the history of Shakespeare performance in India, and especially, in Maharashtra, or the 'Bombay presidency', as it was called in the colonial period. Of all the major eighteen languages in India, Marathi bears the widest and deepest impress of Shakespeare. It has the largest number of translations, was the first to produce the *Complete Works* in translation (Apte, 1985) and has the highest number of performances. Though it was not the first to begin staging Shakespeare (performed first in Calcutta in 1775 and in Bombay in 1808, by an English troupe for the benefit of the English traders), its modern drama and theatre developed in reactive and assimilative response to western theatre. Élite Indians invited to witness these shows were so captivated by the illusionist realism and formalism of this eighteenth-century western theatre, totally removed from their indigenous forms of performance, that they were eager to imitate and participate in the building of the first public theatres in both Bombay and Calcutta. The inclusion of Shakespeare in the English-language curriculum in the early 1800s resulted in the performance, initially, of scenes and then full plays by Indian students in English, the earliest recorded instance being scenes from *The Merchant of Venice* in Calcutta in 1824 and, in 1861, *The Taming of the Shrew* in Bombay. Elphinstone College, Bombay University, was the first to establish a Shakespeare Society in 1864, after which date an annual Shakespeare production became a norm which later spread to other colleges all over India and continues in some today. The very first performance in India of Shakespeare in translation was in 1852 at Gujarati in Surat, when *The Taming of the Shrew* was performed. The first production in Marathi was an *Othello*, performed in 1879. Marathi playwriting, like that in other parts of the country, was impelled to borrow conventions like the soliloquy, the five-act structure, the tragic framework, the psychologised characterisation from Shakespeare. It is not surprising then to find modern Marathi theatre being characterised in a new authoritative history as one which accords 'paramount importance to the text' and in which 'the position of the playwright has never been seriously challenged, not even during the most experimental phase of the parallel theatre',[10] features entirely western since traditional Indian drama based on myth and legend is oral and improvisatory.

Emerging out of such an inheritance, the textual emphasis and authority of the *King Lear* translation staged in Kasargode was carried into performance. Even though translation into contemporary speech may be the site of disruption and revision, and may, as argued by John Russell Brown, transmit the spirit of Shakespeare's play better than the original Elizabethan verse,[11] here the close equivalence of the translation to the original was paradoxically its downfall. 'This is the very best translation of *Lear* in Marathi,' explained the actor-director, Sharad Buthadia (who played Lear) in a discussion after the show, 'and we were concentrating on getting that across to the audience'.

Some of us who were familiar with the high estimation this production was held in Maharashtra were surprised to find how literal, stilted and even stereotyped this performance seemed. To those freed of the straight-jacketing of 'the text' – without any inwardness with the language of translation (most Indian languages share a common fund of Sanskrit derivatives and similarities of syntax, so that other language speakers can follow them to an extent but cannot appreciate the finer points) – the very merits of the production came through as severe drawbacks. The actors' careful articulation of the nuances of the translation seemed a literalism which hampered their movement. Their absorption with the words and images of the linguistic text blocked their translation into a performative lexicon of gesture and movement. With an exclusive attention to the words on the page, action was missed out. The sincerity of the acting became a *naïveté* and the 'straight' untouched rendering felt banal and predictable. Without the privilege of a knowing audience, the attempt to play the uncut, unmediated text floundered, and drama lost out to poetry. Is it possible that the 'faithful' enactment of Shakespeare today seems predicated upon an informed and tutored audience and that the logo-centrism of Shakespeare's plays may in fact block and not facilitate performance? Does a close reinscription in translation resist performance?

Other bodies

The 'Other' is also a refracted embodying of the self, and some of the most notable 'Other' Shakespeares re-configure the textuality of the canon in 'Other', particularly, actor-centred, physicalised and non-illusionist languages of the stage. Linguistic and cultural translation introduce their own shade of otherness, but the performative vocabularies of especially the Asian stage threaten to transmute and subsume the logocentric world of Shakespeare. This representation in the 'body' of the actor has been, after the question of the authenticity of the text, the focus of the next key debate in performance studies. What is the loss and/or gain when Shakespeare is bodied forth in performative and non-logocentric styles? Two new productions at Kasargode adapted Shakespeare into the indigenous folk forms of their own regions: *Charudattam* (*Julius Caesar*) in *kathakali* from Kerala and *Iruthiattam* (*Lear*) from Tamil Nadu which adapted not just the play but also the local folk form, *theerukoottu*, for a particular interpretative effect. They form acute examples of 'Other Shakespearean bodies' and the transgressions incumbent upon such transformation.

While *kathakali* Shakespeare has become something of a minor tradition, with three full plays (*Lear*, *Othello* and *Julius Caesar*) and scenes (*Macbeth* and *A Midsummer Night's Dream*) in its repertoire, the *theerukoottu* Shakespeare was a novelty. The transfiguration of a canonical author usually stems from a double intent, that of a political appropriation as well as a domestication for the sake of greater acceptability. But more than this, it was the cultural need for an aesthetic validation of their own traditional forms against the global authority of Shakespeare that led to these particular productions. Indian folk theatre forms which emerged in the fifteenth and sixteenth centuries declined with the development of modern theatre along western lines in the nineteenth century. Since the Independence, there has been a concerted move to revive and experiment with these decaying folk forms in an effort to go 'back to the roots' in search of a new postcolonial identity. Hence, it is the performative aesthetic of these forms which has been fore-grounded. *Kathakali* is primarily a dramatic dance form and while *theerukoottu* is more strictly theatre – allowing for speech and improvised dialogue by some character types – it is the dance, music and gestural element which is predominant in these forms. In such actor-centred, mimetic styles, the literary 'text' is not erased, rather it is meshed in a polysemous textuality of gestural, kinetic and musical scores. Words, sung in accompaniment to the movement, along with tonal and rhythmic variations, interpret the emotional nuances and enhance the mood. All these forms are based on the Indian dramatic theory of *rasa* (essence), as elaborated in the *Natyashastra*,[12] which aims to invoke, in the spectator, the experience of a quintessential mood or state of being. These are to be made concrete for the audience's delectation through four primary modes of representation or *abhinaya*, which are the *vachika* (verbal), *angika* (gestural), *aharya* (dress and makeup) and *sattvika* (permanent states of being). In effect, performance is meant to focus on the sensuous and the affective aspects through the physicalised stylisation of the actor. Indian performance theory becomes, as pointed out by Hobgood and Mitchell, the opposite of the 'coldly intellectual (not to say bloodless) structural diagnosis' of Aristotle's *Poetics* 'of an art we know to be charged with passion and sensuousness'.[13] Thus much of the debate around the first *kathakali* Shakespeare, the Annette Leday/David McRuvie *Lear* was misplaced, for it chiefly revolved around the changes to Shakespeare's text and *kathakali*'s hallowed conventions.[14] The transposing aesthetic of 'em-body-ment' of dramatic structure and narrative through key moods, the primary trajectory of *kathakali*, was hardly given critical attention. In *kathakali*, especially, the actor's body is of central significance, each bodily muscle (including some whose presence we do not normally suspect, on the forehead and on the cheek bone for instance!) is rigorously trained over years to expressively enact subtle nuances of mood. Action develops more through reiteration and elaboration than through conflict or debate. Thus new areas of intensity and differing levels of sensitivity are discovered. In fact, it is the actor's body which textualises the play and therefore it is what Antony Dawson has termed the 'bodiliness' or the affective power of the body that needs to be examined.[15] In the codified stylisations of *kathakali*, affect and effect work in conjunction and the critical challenge is to discursively extend this emotive power.

Charudattam was scripted, directed and sung by Sadanam Harikumar and presented by Satwikam, of Kalasadanam, from Palakkad, North Kerala. Harikumar, a young *kathakali* master, is not averse to experimentation; he was one of the singers in Annette Leday's *Lear* and now for his own venture took up the challenge to extend his own art form with an adaptation of *Julius Caesar*. The plot was reduced to ten main scenes incorporating the main episodes: conspiracy, women's forebodings, murder and vengeance. Changes necessitated by the philosophical underpinning of all traditional Indian performing arts, which sees art as an enactment of the heroic and the moral, emphasised Caesar as a benevolent, alms-giving monarch whose murder had to be avenged by Mark Antony, made up as a *minukku* (golden-hued) morally upright character. His lament over Caesar's body was the emotional centre; the verses sung as a mournful dirge to pellucid gestures of grief have rarely been more moving, nor his gradual outrage and decision to avenge more convincing and heroic. The performance ended with Antony slaying both Cassius and Brutus. Antony the loyalist, and not the machiavell, became the hero. 'Shakespeare has to be rewritten, not just transcreated,' said the director Harikumar in a discussion after the show, 'and the reading should be a form of resistance'. In this case, a resistance not to the essence of the play but to the traditions of interpretation and performance coalescing around it. This recreation also challenged the conventions of *kathakali* and those of staging Shakespeare. Cassius presented the main difficulty: an ambiguous, 'in-between' character, he did not fit the types of the traditional *kathakali* repertoire and an entirely original *aharya* – make up/costume – representative of his status, along with a new choreography, verses and rhythms had to be devised for him. Often overshadowed by Caesar and Brutus and rendered anomalous in mainstream performance, Cassius in the *kathakali* *vesham* (characterisation), neither *pacca*, green-faced, heroic nor *katti*, of mixed attributes, acquired a more individualised persona. This was specially reflected in the playing of his death: he was given a heroic battle with Antony and not an ignominious suicide, yet his dying gasps, played out with consummate virtuosity over several long minutes, with tongue hanging, eyes bulging, breath rasping, and limbs a-twitching, left no doubt about his diabolical nature and the moral equity of his end. Mimetic theatres like *kathakali* have the resource to articulate the unspoken, to embody and concretise the subtext and thereby lift the performance into another realm of imaginative involvement. John Russell Brown, who in his *New Sites for Shakespeare* has called for radical changes deriving from eastern performative traditions in the staging of Shakespeare, particularly points to the final scenes of Shakespeare's tragedies and histories which he feels can benefit from the performative techniques of *kudiattam*, a theatre form akin to *kathakali*. These scenes he says, 'all end with some simplification of expressive means...In each case the dramatic reality that holds the audience's attention cannot depend on the text alone and will require further substantiation by the actor, his imaginative creativity and the audience's ability to share in that creativity' and advocates a kudiattam-like immediacy and imaginative 'transfer of consciousness' in their staging.[16]

Iruthiattam (*Lear*), directed by R. Raju, and presented by Arangam of Pondicherry, on the other hand, deconstructed and played around with the text and conventions of both Shakespeare and its own base theatre form. It was for many the most successful production of the festival. Its success derived from the inherent subversiveness and spontaneity of the *theerukoottu*, a popular street theatre form of Tamil Nadu, South India, which is traditionally performed by socially underdeveloped rural groups. Its performative lexicon is more acrobatic than stylised, broad and melodramatic rather than lyrical, full of earthy banter which is diametrically opposed to the classical and polished form of *kathakali*. Though it shares many of the features of the more sophisticated forms of traditional theatre, like prologue, typed characterisation, song and dance, its difference lies in its practice of interpolating social critique into its set narratives.[17] *Iruthiattam* was adapted from a Tamil adaptation of *King Lear* by the reputed dramatist and novelist Indira Parthasarathy, and attempted to match the vitality of Shakespeare's poetry with strong dramatic effects. It interpreted the play in terms of a power struggle, kept the sub-plot to make an ideological feminist point that sons too can be cruel (the director and others of the group had had their training in an experimental drama school), and ended the play with the storm scene at the end of which Cordelia appeared to rescue Lear and lead him off to safety. This, of course, was not the first *King Lear* with a 'happy' ending, and the chief interpretative insight and theatrical innovation of this production was the introduction of Lear as an unkingly earthy clown who entered playing a flute, giggled and demanded that his fool literally scratch his back! This persona made better sense of Lear's whimsical and foolish egotism, for when Goneril and Regan lavished praise, massaging his ego, he giggled again. The production's 'otherness', manifest in the strongly physicalised action deriving out of the actors' training in *theerukoottu*, was integrated into the Shakespearean text through a contrapuntal relationship established between the Fool and Lear, who had purloined not just the mannerisms, but also some of the accoutrements of the folk fool (the *vidushaka* of classical Indian theatre and the *komali* of the *theerukoottu*), like a conical cap, a pot belly and a flowing beard. In the stock folk stage business the fool mocked and mirrored, provoked and led his master, the king. The fool/*komali* is the main instrument of improvisatory energy and critique in *theerukoottu*: he not only has the freedom to speak out, but also doubles up as a *sutradhara*, a choric master of ceremonies. Here, in a complex interactive by-play the fool performed somersaults, cart-wheeled and stood on his head in critical response to his master's doings. Here was a production which did away with much of 'the text', but improvised with its own 'otherness' to embody with a physicalised wit and style the central themes of the ill-treatment of the old and the calculated opportunism of the young.

Other sites

Inevitably, different audiences will react and judge performances according to their own contexts and imperatives. The audience of the small coastal town of Kasargode was evenly split between those inculcated with a reverence towards the canonical poet and the Marxist iconoclasts who wanted class struggle justified through Shakespeare (since 1957, Kerala has had more democratically elected left-wing governments than any other state in the Union of India). The festival itself was occasioned by a phenomenal postcolonial event: the translation, editing and publication, in April 2000, of Shakespeare's *Complete Works* in a new Malayalam translation under the general editorship of K. Ayyappa Paniker. This three-volume edition was undertaken and completed in five years and unexpectedly sold 5,000 copies within three months. Kerala, on the southwestern tip of the Indian peninsula, has been exposed to foreign traders and influences, especially in its coastal regions, since the beginning of the Christian era. Even though Christian missionaries were relatively more successful in their conversions (the state has 20 per cent Christians as opposed to the 2.3 per cent national average), Kerala as a whole escaped the ravages of cultural colonialism, so that its regional dance, music and literature have a longer continuity than in many other, especially north Indian, regions. In the recent past, the Kerala Communist Party has promoted theatre as a means of propaganda: annual state-supported drama festivals at the school and college level are hugely popular. In this context, this resurgence of interest in Shakespeare was exceptional. Though the earliest Shakespeare transla-tions in Malayalam were made around the same period (1866) as in the other major Indian languages (excepting Bengali and Marathi, which saw earlier translations), the track record of the performance of Shakespeare in Kerala, especially before independence, is undistin-guished. Without the example of the English amateur theatre to emulate as in the colonial settlements of Calcutta and Bombay, modern theatre and Shakespeare remained largely confined to the school and college stage. The continuation of enlightened Hindu rulers in the Kerala princely state of Travancore on the other hand provided the patronage for the traditional performative arts to flourish. Today, Kerala is charac-terised by a unique and paradoxical blend of Marxism and Hinduism, of the modern radical with the ancient traditional. Not surprisingly, one of the contested issues of debate in the seminar held alongside the festival was that of adjudicating the popularity of Shakespeare and his influence on Malayalam drama. Opinions remained divided, for many could not conceive of considering appropriated and popularised Malayali Shakespeare – a melodramatic *Othello*, for instance, sung by Sambhasiva, an itinerant priest, over 200 times in a bowdlerised devotional form, the *harikatha*, for the edification and entertainment of vast crowds in temple complexes – as 'proper' Shakespeare or even 'proper' Malayalam theatre.

The 'Other' ultimately is not an oppositional, antinomical identity but a palimpsest combining changing ways of accommodating differ-ence. The final performance of the Kerala festival was *Kodumkattu* (storm) (*The Tempest*) which appropriately encapsulated the multi-layered nature of the Kerala literary and theatre world. This was a pro-duction commissioned in conjunction with the *Complete Works* – it was based on a Malayalam translation done by the director K. N. Panikkar himself, for the *Complete Works*, and had been first staged as part of the book launch. Panikkar is one of the most innovative exponents of the 'back to the roots' theatre movement. A playwright and director, he has not so much revived a folk form as evolved a style of performance which is a blend of several theatre forms, martial arts, yoga and music. He is one of the few artists who have been consistently successful in re-enacting classical Sanskrit drama for contemporary audiences. His productions of Sanskrit dramatist Bhasa's plays have won him recognition all over India and abroad. His dramaturgy derives largely from *kudiattam*, the oldest of the extant Indian theatre forms (*c.* 10th century), said to be closest to the classical Sanskrit drama and now surviving as a living tradition only in Kerala. For someone like Panikkar to take on a western text, and one as logocentric as Shakespeare, speaks for his creative experimentalism. *Kodumkattu* thus became part of both the ancient Indian and the contemporary trends, the traditional and the experimental in Kerala today.

Panikkar speaks of the 'cruelty of the text' which he effaces with the creation of a 'parallel visual text'.[18] For the performance of *Kodumkattu* he developed a pared-down text, supported by a sub-text of stylised movement and vocalisation evolved to give, according to Panikkar, 'the rigidity of the text a mellowy run...and translate the *avasthas* (states) depicted in the text into action'.[19] *Kudiattam*, as a theatre form, is defined by its intensive explorations of the sub-texts of the story. Panikkar located the key to *The Tempest* in nature: 'the elements of nature – earth, water, and wind, with fire and the ethereal expanse above and their interaction with human and supernatural beings create a sense of belief and disbelief', he explained in his programme note. For him the turbulence of the play was part of nature's cycle, now a tempest, then a calm; he added a brief verse on the omnipresent roar of the ocean's waves around the island which was sung as a choric chant to emphasise the ebb and flow of human fortune. Storm and calm, sailors and spirits, bewilderment and self-recognition therefore all seemed to meld together, especially when acted in a choric mimed dance. Panikkar's is also a theatre of 'transformation' (*pakarnnattam*), a concept which goes back to the *Natyashastra* and which refers to the ritualistic process of the actor becoming the character as opposed to the actor pulling the character into him (as in realistic drama). Panikkar has been interested in stories which extend this inherent transformative dimension of theatre. *The Tempest* with its magical changes was particularly suited to this dramaturgy. The doubling of the actors became not just a practical convenience but part of the artistic process: the Milanese, through a quick change of head-gear, transformed themselves into spirits. Avenging Prospero, too, learned through his travails and, prompted by the freedom-loving Ariel, reached a state of reconciliation and tranquility. This production integrated Shakespeare not just into the Indian theatrical but also into the philosophical traditions: Shakespeare's magic illusion became *maya* (the illusory nature of reality) the abjuration of which brings a spiritual salvation. It was only when Prospero was ready to break his 'charms' and 'rough magic' that he could assume the 'nobler reason' of virtue rather than vengeance. The colonial dimension, suggested through the presence of a native tribal Sycorax, was also seen as part of the cycles of time, when Prospero exited waving to Caliban, now centre stage. Relocations, too, become resistant, for they challenge the given readings of a text, even as they may reinscribe, in their different ways, the essence of the same text. However, many of the left-wing members of the Kasargode audience, who had expected a direct political interface, were dissatisfied with this 'essentialising' of Shakespeare even though relocation in another philosophical and aesthetic tradition may be equally charged with the political.

It may be useful at this point to briefly look at another production which tried to be both intercultural and political, but failed to be either. This was *Sturm* (*The Tempest*), performed during the German festival in Delhi (2000–01), directed by Annette Leday (of the *kathakali Lear* fame) in collaboration with the Bremer Shakespeare Company. It had many similarities with Panikkar's *Kodumkattu*: both used a reduced text which was nonetheless 'faithful' to the original. They used stylistic and performative relocations into similar forms: *kathakali* in the German play and *kudiattam* in Panikkar's. They interpreted the island as a world of magical transformation. They were both thus examples of interculturalism, but while Panikkar's *Tempest* assimilated the play into a different perspective of an alternate dramatic and philosophical system, the German *Sturm* remained a superficial imposition of 'exotic' styles upon the play which ultimately was found to be disturbingly regressive. It used German actors, English subtitles and *kathakali* dancers in a polarised manner. It cast tall white Anglo-Saxon males as the Milanese and short dark-skinned *kathakali* dancers as the native spirits of the island, reifying the most stereotyped racial categories. To undercut this racial charge, it had a white German as Caliban, but in today's postcolonial context when 'colour-blind' casting has almost become mandatory, this 'coloured casting' was disturbingly insensitive to Indian sensibilities. Leday's production, appreciated in the west, fell flat in India. Even though she has said 'I believe in difference', her deployment of the *kathakali* dancers to represent 'a magical island rich in colour and sound, inhabited by strange powerful spirits',[20] came through as facile Orientalising, in which (unlike her *Lear* where a western text was immersed in an eastern form) the mere form was borrowed without respect for its deep structure. Further, the physicalised virtuoso and witty performances, played against the grain by Miranda, Trinculo and Antonio, had, in contrast to the mellifluous *kathakali* dancers, the effect of distancing rather than drawing the audiences in. It was not a matter of an 'othering' by Indians; though showcased in the official panoply of a cultural festival (it was billed as the opening event) the production became an example of an exploitative, not an integrated interculturalism. Rustom Bharucha's critique of the 'borrowing' of eastern forms and conventions as cultural tourism is well known.[21] Different sites will create different Shakespeares but sometimes it seems at the expense of the 'Other'.

What then is Shakespeare and when does he stop being Shakespeare? Do we need to be judgemental and to police between Shakespeare and not Shakespeare? Or rather, do we need to investigate what it is that draws different cultures across time to perform Shakespeare and how and why they do it? And, most crucially, how do we, as critics, receive and perceive this phenomenon? In this protean proliferation of a millennial Shakespeare,[22] the act of reading, attending to and centering 'Other' Shakespeares acquires seminal significance. 'Other' Shakespeares which manifest themselves through 'other texts', 'other bodies' and 'other sites', as we have seen, need a decoding and a familiarisation to enable a negotiation with the processes which seem to be leading to an 'othering' of Shakespeare himself. We need to develop a taxonomy of difference in which a new identification and relation between the Self and the Other is worked out. What is clear is that no one paradigm or theory will do justice to the multiple complexities of 'Other Shakespeares'. While it is time to move beyond what is called the 'real' Shakespeare, the original canon, the central trunk of the 'Banyan Tree Shakespeare', will continue to provide the anchoring root and the source of creative energy for all offshoots, as it will also let them stand independently, with their own spacial right and merits. Micro and macro studies attentive to the layers of inflexions will have not only to co-exist but also to interosculate. They will show that 'Other' Shakespeares, through their intercultural expansion, threaten not the unity of the canon but the fixity of response; that their hybridities need to be seen not as desecrations, but as renewals, inspiring proto-renaissances in diverse cultures. And belying fears, they are in fact pollinating, not polluting: the more Shakespeare is re-written, the greater becomes the debt to the original text(s). Resistance implies reinscription and Shakespeare's name can function as a trade mark precisely because his works have become a world resource. The translation and performance in different languages the world over is, then, not imposing closures but opening up a mediation across boundaries of history and culture. Demarcation lines between us and them are being muddied over by 'Other' Shakespeares.

Notes and references

1. [Ed.: for a fuller discussion of this issue, see Chakravarti's discussion of 'Shakespeare in Colonial India: Negotiating Modernity,' in 'Modernity, Post-Coloniality and *Othello*: The Case of *Saptapadi*' in this volume, pp. 40–2.]
2. Inga-Stina Ewbank, 'Shakespeare Translation as Cultural Exchange,' *Shakespeare Survey* 48 (1995): 2.
3. Kate McLuskie, '*Macbeth/Umabatha*: Global Shakespeare in a Post-Colonial Market,' *Shakespeare Survey* 52 (1999): 165.
4. Dennis Kennedy, 'Shakespeare without Shakespeare,' Paper at the Seventh World Shakespeare Congress seminar, 'Shakespeare in Non-Anglophone Countries,' Valencia, 20 April 2001.
5. Anonymous Reader's Report for Oxford University Press (India) on a collection of essays I am editing on Indian interactions with Shakespeare. It goes on to add: 'yet the editor expects these exercises to be of interest to English knowing [*sic*] readers.'
6. See Elleke Boehmer, *Colonial and Postcolonial Literature* (Oxford: OUP, 1995) 21, 79–89, and *passim*, and Toril Moi, *Sexual/Textual Politics* (London: Methuen, 1985) 100–1.
7. Harish Trivedi, Introduction, *Post-Colonial Translation: Theory and Practice*, ed. Susan Bassnett and Harish Trivedi (London: Routledge, 1999) 10.
8. V. Y. Kantak, 'On the Mis-reading of Kalidasa and Shakespeare,' *Perspectives on Indian Literary Culture* (Delhi: Pencraft, 1996) 116–17.
9. W. B. Worthen, *Shakespeare and the Authority of Performance* (Cambridge: CUP, 1997) 1–18.
10. Shanta Gokhale, *Playwright at the Centre: Marathi Drama from 1843 to the Present* (Calcutta: Seagull Books, 2000) Preface xi.
11. John Russell Brown, 'Foreign Shakespeare and English-speaking Audiences,' *Foreign Shakespeare: Contemporary Performances* (Cambridge: CUP, 1993) 29.
12. *The Natyashastra*, the ancient Indian treatise of theatre practice, said to have been compiled between 2 BC to AD 2 by Bharata Muni.
13. Burnet Hobgood and Thomas Mitchell, 'The Sensuous Dimension of Theatre,' *Rasa: The Indian Performative Arts in the Last Twentyfive Years*, Vol. II Theatre and Cinema, ed. A. Lal and C. Dasgupta (Calcutta: Anamika Kala Sangam, Research and Publication, 1995) 30.
14. For a critical Indian perspective, see Suresh Awasthi, 'The Intercultural Experience and the Kathakali *King Lear*,' *New Theatre Quarterly* IX 34 (May 1993) 178. For a supportive view see Philip B. Zarelli, 'For Whom is a King a King? Issues of Intercultural Production, Perception, and Reception in a Kathakali *King Lear*,' *Critical Theory and Performance*, ed. Janelle G. Reinelt and Joseph R. Roach (Ann Arbor: University of Michigan Press, 1995) 16–40. For a discussion of the kathakali *Othello* in the larger perspective of Shakespeare performance in India see my 'Re-locating Shakespeare: Acting and Reacting to *Othello* in India,' *Shakespeare in China: Performances and*

Perspectives (Shanghai: Shanghai Theatre Academy, 1999) 65–74; 'Interculturalism or Indigenisation: Modes of Exchange, Shakespeare East and West,' *Shakespeare and his Contemporaries in Performance*, ed. Edward J. Esche (London: Ashgate, 2000) 73–88 and 'Folk Shakespeares: the Performance of Shakespeare in Traditional Indian Theatre Forms,' in Poonam Trivedi and Dennis Bartholomeusz (eds), *India's Shakespeare: Translation, Interpretation and Performance*, forthcoming. For a postcolonial critique of the kathakali *Othello* see Ania Loomba, ' "Local manufacture made-in-India Othello fellows": Issues of Race, Hybridity and Location in Post-colonial Shakespeares,' *Post-Colonial Shakespeares*, ed. Ania Loomba and Martin Orkin (London: Routledge, 1998) 143–63.

15. Antony Dawson, 'Performance and Participation: Desdemona, Foucault, and the Actor's Body,' *Shakespeare, Theory and Performance*, ed. James C. Bulman (London: Routledge, 1996) 30.

16. John Russell Brown, *New Sites for Shakespeare: Theatre, the Audience and Asia* (London: Routledge, 1999) 84, 85.

17. Kapila Vatsyayan, *Traditional Indian Theatre: Multiple Streams* (New Delhi: National Book Trust, 1980) 48–64.

18. Interview with the author, July 2000.

19. Programme note.

20. Programme note.

21. Rustom Bharucha, *The Theatre and the World* (New Delhi: Manohar, 1990) 15.

22. Gary Taylor, 'Afterword: The Incredible Shrinking Bard,' in *Shakespeare and Appropriation*, ed. Christy Desmet and Robert Sawyer (London: Routledge, 1999) 197–205, argues for a decline in the cultural authority of Shakespeare in the twentieth century and an inevitable diminishing in the future. However, his opinions are based solely on Anglo-American examples. He does not take into consideration anything from continental Europe or the larger world beyond.

5

Othello's Travels in New Zealand: Shakespeare, Race and National Identity

Catherine Silverstone

Othello has, in recent years, been read as an originary text of race, both inside and outside the academy. As with appropriations and revisions of *The Tempest*, *Othello* has received its most vigorous reworkings in the hands of postcolonial writers, such as Salman Rushdie and Tayeb Salih. Inside the academy, Thomas Cartelli observes that '*Othello* is well on the way to replacing *The Tempest* as a favored field of debate and contention both for scholars and critics of Shakespeare, and for the increasingly numerous workers in the field of postcolonial studies.'[1] In an attempt to expand the postcolonial *Othello* archive, which tends to focus on *Othello* in terms of a black Africanist presence or the way the text resonates in the Indian subcontinent, I want to focus on two recent productions of *Othello* in New Zealand and to explore what happens when a text with *Othello's* racial loading is performed in a settler culture riven with the effects of its former colonial status.

Inhabited by the indigenous population of the Maori, New Zealand was colonised in the early nineteenth century by the British.[2] In 1840 the Treaty of Waitangi was signed between many (but not all) Maori chiefs and the British Crown. Notoriously, the Treaty exists in two versions: English and Maori. The English version promises that in return for yielding their sovereignty to Queen Victoria, the Maori would be guaranteed the rights of British subjects and access to fisheries and forests. The Maori version denotes the same range of protection and access but, crucially, states that *kawanatanga* (governance) rather than *tino rangatiratanga* (absolute sovereignty) was to be surrendered.[3] Much of New Zealand's recent history has been concerned with disputes over the Treaty. As with other settler cultures, such as Australia and Canada, where the main colonising culture also became the dominant cultural and political force, New Zealand eventually asserted its political independence from Britain.

New Zealand today also has significant immigrant populations from the Pacific Islands and Asia and still bears the legacy of its former colonial status, particularly with respect to often fraught race-relations between Maori and Pakeha (New Zealanders of European descent).[4]

Just as Shakespeare's works first travelled to India on board an East India Company voyage in 1607, Shakespeare arrived in New Zealand, some 160 years later in 1769, on another British voyage of imperial exploration: this time as part of Sydney Parkinson's library on board the *Endeavour*.[5] Gradually taking root in New Zealand, Shakespeare – that most identifiable of global brand names – has become an integral part of my culture. Beginning in the nineteenth and early twentieth centuries, there is a history of British Shakespeare troupes touring to New Zealand as part of their Australasian itinerary; a phenomenon which survives today in recent visits by the Royal National Theatre and the Royal Shakespeare Company to New Zealand's International Festival of the Arts. Shakespeare's texts also pervade the fiction of many New Zealand writers, notably that of Ngaio Marsh and Janet Frame.[6] With respect to education, Shakespeare is the only compulsory author for final year high school students and studying Shakespeare continues to form part of New Zealand undergraduate degrees in English. Perhaps most curiously, the tapestries that hang in Shakespeare's Globe theatre in London were stitched by some 500 New Zealand needle-workers, embodying what Mark Houlahan describes as a 'material legacy of this late-twentieth-century Shakespearean zealotry'.[7] In this article I focus on two recent productions of *Othello* in New Zealand: a storyline from the local soap opera, *Shortland Street* (1997) which I read in conjunction with high school exam questions on Shakespeare, and Theatre at Large's politically controversial appropriation of *Othello* entitled *Manawa Taua/Savage Hearts* (1994). By addressing the specificities of each production I want to argue that New Zealand is in a state of flux with respect to Shakespeare and the imperial legacy his texts embody. Attracted to Shakespeare, New Zealand both embraces and resists his texts as commodities of British culture, and, most compellingly, is also capable of redeploying Shakespeare to construct trenchant local narratives about our history.

In noting New Zealand's status as a settler culture, where the British colonisers remained in the country following the ceding of 'imperial authority', I wish to draw attention to the difference (and problematics) this marks in terms of cultural analysis. My use of the words 'settler' and 'settler culture' ostensibly privileges Pakeha New Zealanders and parts of my analysis do focus on Pakeha 'settler' subjects in particular. However, as my analysis also pays attention to Maori and Pacific Island cultures, my use of 'settler culture' functions more broadly as a way of denoting countries like New Zealand as sites of interaction between various cultural groupings resulting from successive waves of immigration. I do not, however, intend this demarcation to diminish the political efficacy of identifying oneself as belonging to an 'indigenous' population, and the later part of this article is especially attentive to issues surrounding this subject position. Alongside recent work on settler cultures, this article attempts to fill a gap created by much postcolonial criticism – Shakespearean and otherwise – which, for the most part, avoids considering settler cultures as appropriate material for 'postcolonial' investigation, even though they offer an opportunity to similarly examine processes of colonisation and identity formation in a postimperial world.[8] This is not to deny important differences between 'settler' and 'postcolonial' cultures or differences within these groupings but, rather, to suggest a set of shared concerns which demand attentive, culturally specific readings. In the settler situation, then, this means being particularly attuned to relationships between indigenous peoples, settlers and the settlers' culture of origin and, as Daiva Stasiulis and Nira Yuval-Davis suggest, to view 'the histories of indigenous and migrant peoples as interdependent'.[9]

The productions discussed here have received very little or no critical attention.[10] Shakespeare and New Zealand is a neglected research topic, both in New Zealand and in Shakespeare studies more generally. Like work on most non-mainstream productions this is partly because such research is often hampered by the ephemeral nature of the archival material which is rarely catalogued. Further, New Zealand's relative geographic isolation from the academic metropolises of the United Kingdom and the United States means that the archival research on which my reading depends is expensive and time-consuming for scholars outside New Zealand to undertake. In addition to the logistical problems of such research, New Zealand literature is currently not as popular within the metropolitan academy as other 'postcolonial' literatures, such as those from India, the Caribbean or Africa. The constraints of the archive and minimal academic 'demand' thus mean that the international market for academic work on Shakespeare and New Zealand, despite a wealth of material and the commitment of a small number of scholars, has yet to flourish. While this article cannot do justice to the broader topic of Shakespeare in New Zealand, by writing about New Zealand productions of *Othello* I seek to show how such a discussion might add to an understanding of New Zealand culture, and to think through how performances of Shakespeare in a settler culture might be read. This article, then, aims to use performances of *Othello* to engage with questions of race and national identity, especially in relation to New Zealand's negotiation with a history of British cultural imperialism.

If performances of *Othello*, particularly in postcolonial or settler cultures, are haunted by Shakespeare as a marker of British cultural authority, they are also insistently haunted by ideas about race and race-relations. As I illustrate in later parts of this discussion, the actor's body is forced to engage with both these spectres.[11] To be haunted by race is to be haunted by some 400 years of theories, histories of identity formation and violence. The etymology of the term 'race' has changed substantially over the last 400 years. Patricia Parker and Margo Hendricks write:

> 'race' as that term developed across several European languages was a highly unstable term in the early modern period... At the beginnings of this era... [race] variously designated notions of lineage or genealogy... even before its application in Spain to Moors and Jews or its eventual extension to paradigms of physical and phenotypical difference that would become the basis of later discourses of racism and racial difference.[12]

It was not until the late eighteenth and early nineteenth centuries, influenced by the work of the French anatomist Georges Cuvier, that 'race' became widely associated with genetic characteristics, with skin colour hailed as the most obvious marker of racial difference. This epidermal taxonomy has persisted to the present day, with Lynda E. Boose suggesting that in the twentieth century it is 'generally presumed that skin colour is... [race's] determining factor'.[13] However, as Peggy Phelan argues, 'Race identity involves recognizing something other than skin and physical inscriptions. One cannot simply "read" race as skin-color. The tendency to do so leads to the corollary proposition that all people with the same skin color believe the same thing.'[14] Partly in an effort to dislodge these associations, 'race' has more recently been theorised as denoting a shared cultural identity which is not necessarily predicated on biological characteristics. To mark this shift 'race' is often placed in inverted commas or replaced with 'ethnicity' to emphasise its status as a cultural construction which has been used to assert political and/or cultural supremacy and to oppress and radicalise disadvantaged peoples. But as the destructive effects of racism make all too clear, uneasy race-relations often tend to coalesce around visible markers of difference, such as skin colour.[15] More positively, as Kobena Mercer has shown, 'ethnic' identity can also be represented and celebrated through corporeal signifiers such as hairstyle.[16] It seems, then, that at this historical juncture 'race', and to a lesser extent, 'ethnicity', still retain something of their historical valence as indices of biological difference. By acknowledging this history, I am not proposing a regressive critical and political return to equivalences between biological and cultural difference or suggesting that 'racial' identity is fixed or immutable. Instead, my analysis seeks to engage with both the conceptual and corporeal aspects of the 'racialised' body in order to explore how often stereotypical ideas about 'racial' or 'ethnic' difference are made to impress upon the performing body.

As recent scholarship on race and the early modern period has shown, it is far from clear what Shakespeare meant by designating Othello as the 'Moor of Venice'. Kim F. Hall contends that in early modern England, 'Moor' signified all that was non-European. Nearly 400 years of stage productions and criticism reveal that Othello's colour and racial origins have been the subject of much speculation; he has been described variously as a sub-Saharan African, an 'Oriental', or even white.[17] Rather than adding to such speculations I am concerned with exploring how productions negotiate or address the matter of Othello's racial otherness. In terms of performance, academic debates about race, colour and *Othello* are reflected and refracted in multiple ways when confronted with the materiality of the actor's body. Always, though, no matter how the character is cast, the body of Othello is racially marked. As Sudipto Chatterjee and Jyotsna G. Singh argue, 'we cannot extricate the tragic resonance of the moment [at the end of the play] from *the racialized body of the Shakespearean* actor, black, or white-in-black face, who must confront and play the European stereotypes...at the moment of his horrific suicide.'[18] Focusing primarily on the rhetoric and practices surrounding the casting and performance of Othello, in the following discussion I aim to consider Othello's political 'colour' in contrast to the hegemonic 'white' culture that surrounds him and to explore how gender is figured in this racial dynamic. In an attempt to investigate how Shakespeare in the settler culture 'plays' out, this discussion will turn now to an analysis of a storyline from the local soap opera, *Shortland Street*, in the context of the high school English syllabus.

Othello at school: *Shortland Street* (1997) and the Bursary English exam (1998)

Broadcasting its first episode in 1992, *Shortland Street* went on to become an extraordinarily successful New Zealand serial drama. Set in and around a fictional Auckland accident and emergency clinic, *Shortland Street*, from its inception, prided itself on its local content, actors and accents. Interestingly for what follows, several of the *Shortland Street* storylines written for the teenage characters attending a local high school have involved Shakespearean references. In the rather unsubtle way of soap operas, these storylines are used thematically to comment on other aspects of the action. For instance, one student ended up as Romeo's understudy in an attempt to win the affections of the student playing Juliet. Another character performed Hamlet's 'O that this too too sullied flesh' soliloquy in a techno-punk style, strapped Christ-like to a cross. Here the student used his performance to protest against what he perceived as his mother's hasty involvement with another man following his father's death. Similarly, using an *Othello* storyline, Iago's Machiavellian plots were enacted by both the student assigned to play him and the clinic's resident doctor of evil.

How then might these Shakespeare stories in the *Shortland Street* school be accounted for? One answer to this question revolves around the fact that Shakespeare is a staple feature of New Zealand high school English and Drama classrooms. I do not want to read *Shortland Street* as a 'real-TV docudrama' which authentically represents the New Zealand high school experience. However, by reading the *Othello* storyline in conjunction with final year school exam questions on Shakespeare, I suggest that the soap opera's storyline can be read as symptomatic of some of the issues that surround the teaching and performance of Shakespeare in New Zealand high schools, particularly in relation to local content and race.

The New Zealand high school classroom seems, for the most part, resistant to both Shakespeare's local significance and recent critical approaches. Bursary, the final year school exam in English, requires students to write one essay on a Shakespeare play. Shakespeare is the exam's only compulsory author, thus demonstrating his prestigious position in the New Zealand high school English syllabus. A relatively narrow canon of plays is rotated, giving students a choice of writing on a comedy, history or tragedy. Influenced by A. C. Bradley and New Criticism, most school Shakespeare studies are grounded in analyses of character, theme, plot, imagery, setting and genre, and are pervaded by notions of universality and coherence. In 1998 an essay question on *Othello*, with an unusually topical critical emphasis, asked students to 'discuss some of the ways in which race contributes to the tragedy of Othello'.[19] This prompted several angry responses from teachers of English, one of whom wrote to the chief examiner:

> Of course race is an issue but it is not a vital enough issue to allow Bursary/Scholarship students to write essays of depth in content, thought and argument. In other words, to do themselves justice. One wonders why the venerable BBC cast Othello as European.[20]

Here race is acknowledged only to be sidelined and subsequently 'whited-out' in the body of Anthony Hopkins, the BBC's 'Mediterranean magnifico' Othello.[21] As Houlahan suggests, the rhetoric '"vital", "depth", and "venerable", opens out instead into a Leavisite past'.[22]

Initially, the *Shortland Street* storyline looks to tacitly counter the real-life teacher's lack of interest in race by using *Othello* and the politics involved in casting the play for a school production to comment on race-relations in a New Zealand context. In terms of the production concept, the fictional drama teacher says that they will set the 'play very much in the present' and that it will be 'right up to date'.[23] The story, then, opens with auditions and the casting process. The drama teacher feels unable to cast the play because he has not found the 'right' Othello, so he invites a neighbouring school to participate (1318.3, 11). At the new auditions, James, the Pakeha boy passed over as Othello, surveys the competition. As the camera slowly pans around the drama room, the Maori and Pacific Island faces of the new actors are registered on screen. James is outraged at what he sees as the 'blatant discrimination' involved in casting a Pacific Island student as Othello (1318.11). In a surreal parody of Laurence Olivier's buffed blacked-up body, James blacks up his face and interrupts the auditions (Figure 5.1). He steals the Pacific Island student's line and, with his protest literally smeared onto his body, asks the drama teacher why he did not tell him he was 'the wrong colour' (1318.15). Thus he seizes on skin colour, and the attendant racial difference which it marks, as the primary signifier of difference between himself and the other students. James then asserts that Othello was a Moor and that the Pacific Island boys are no more racially 'right' for the part than he is, before concluding that the auditions are 'a racist farce' (1318.17). At this point, the teacher suggests that James's make-up could be considered racist and says he has given Othello to the best actor, the Pacific Island student, Eli.

Despite their differences of opinion, both James and the drama teacher appear to be working out of a colour-blind casting tradition. The central premise of this approach is that the best actor for the job should be employed, regardless of colour. At its most politically challenging, colour-blind casting, like the cross-gender casting in Caryl Churchill's *Cloud Nine*, has the potential to disrupt audience perceptions about the biological basis of categories such as race and to challenge 'straightforward' associations between the performer and the role.[24] However, the *Shortland Street* storyline does not seem much interested in such work. Rather, like the casting of Jonathan Pryce, a white British actor, as the Eurasian Engineer in the Broadway première of *Miss Saigon* in 1991,

Figure 5.1   Video still of *Othello* scene in *Shortland Street*

the drama teacher's casting seems to assume, in Dorinne Kondo's words, 'that the individuals involved are shorn of history and beyond or outside power relations'.[25] This kind of thinking suggests that an actor can be cast in any role as though his or her body were a hollow vessel waiting to be filled and 'coloured' by the character. This denies the effect that an actor's body can have both on the role and the culture in which it is performed. In addition, in the drama teacher's assertion that the play deals with universal human emotions and his refusal to address either the racial otherness of Othello or the actor he has chosen to play him, his colour-blind casting effectively 'whites-out' the play. This results in a situation where all the characters are played to the default 'white' setting of the dominant culture.

Although the drama teacher works to offer a 'whited-out' and delocalised production of the play, the bodies of the actors confound this narrative, inscribing *Othello*'s concerns with race within a New Zealand context. The blacked-up body of James, his accusations of racism, and the conflict between him and the Pacific Island students invite their bodies to be read metonymically as a reference to racial tensions in New Zealand culture more generally. Further, the casting of the Pacific Island boy in preference to the similarly well-qualified Pakeha boy touches on debates about affirmative action policies in operation in some New Zealand institutional settings, such as medical and law schools. A similar anxiety surrounded Sam Mendes's RNT production of *Othello* which toured to New Zealand as part of the Festival of the Arts in 1998. Here, reviewers, focusing on design, costume and voice work, were silent on the matter of what it might mean for *Othello* to be performed in the context of New Zealand's racial milieu. However, writing about the casting of David Harewood, a British-born black actor, as Othello, local columnist Denis Welch asked whether white actors should be forbidden from playing Othello and whether a ban of this sort would be 'taking political correctness too far'.[26] Welch's comments, like James's reactions in the *Shortland Street* storyline, are symptomatic of some of the discomfort circulating in New Zealand about 'political correctness', or the practices of equal opportunities and affirmative action, which were instituted in order to effect social and economic improvements for groups who have been disadvantaged.

The *Shortland Street* storyline also refers to the way in which cultural difference can be exoticised and exploited as a commodity. Minnie, the Pakeha character cast as Desdemona, is interested in Eli. While Eli reciprocates her feelings, James initially derails their relationship. He tells Eli that Minnie only likes boys if they go with her 'look' and suggests that 'she's keen on all things Polynesian – style, music'. At this point Minnie enters the scene and announces her plan to give the play a 'Pacifika' setting whereby she envisages they will 'throw up tapa cloth and run some funky pacific music' (1323.13). Thus Pacific Island culture is reduced to a set of consumable aesthetic signifiers. However, rather than exploring a relationship between violence and the exoticised, consumable 'other', the storyline steps outside this paradigm. It does this by including a narrative of abuse where the Pakeha drama teacher sexually harasses the Pakeha student Minnie. This removes the focus from a narrative of murderous miscegenation played out between a Pacific Island boy and a Pakeha girl: strikingly, the threat to Minnie comes from within Pakeha culture.

To cast a Pacific Island student in this role does, however, seem to reinforce disturbing negative stereotypical associations between racial 'otherness' and violence. Indeed, in his choice of Eli, the teacher's colour-blind casting seems shadowed by a more insidious desire to equate ethnic 'otherness' with the violence that the play demands.

This trend in the soap opera was (no doubt inadvertently) repeated at the 1998 Sheilah Winn 7th National Festival of Shakespeare in Schools. Partly due to *Othello*'s inclusion on that year's Bursary syllabus, the play was a popular choice for scenes selected for presentation at the Festival. Here the majority of the students cast as Othello were of Maori or Pacific Island descent and also included, as one reviewer noted, 'an African student from Malawi in a traditional production, with the Moor as the only black in the cast'.[27] Strikingly, in one entry, designed around a 'Maori Othello with a bone carving replacing the handkerchief',[28] the actor playing Othello wore a *moko* or traditional Maori facial tattoo and carried a *mere*, a Maori warrior club. Here the body of Othello was localised and reinscribed, literally with the moko, in a New Zealand context. This reinscription, however, seems to trade on the idea of the 'noble savage' chief who ultimately regresses to a figure of violence at the end of the play.

Most searchingly, though, James's reactions in the *Shortland Street* storyline can be read as embodying some of the anxieties and sense of ambivalence that are attendant upon being a settler in a country with a relatively short 'postcolonial' history.[29] He is both of, and not of, Europe and New Zealand. James is displaced from his culture of 'origin' and not of the 'indigenous' (read: Maori) culture of his place of birth, yet his primary cultural, geographical and legal affiliations are to New Zealand. The second- or third-generation settler has no other home than that of his or her birth, even if this home is shadowed by a sense of dislocation. In his assertion that he is no less right for the part than the Maori and Pacific Island boys, James recognises the distance they all share from the Shakespearean text he seeks to co-opt. For James, Shakespeare writes about an ethnic otherness which is outside the experience of each one of them. Simultaneously, in his relentless Machiavellian quest to be Othello – he is cast as Iago – he acts as though he had a prior claim to Shakespearean (read: British) culture. In staking a claim on his 'English' inheritance it is as if James were attempting to short-circuit a sense of alienation, which, ironically, asserts itself in his desire to act out Othello's position of otherness.

While it is possible to mine the episodes for comments on the settler condition, within the televisual diegesis these issues are quickly closed down. Instead, they give way to a liberal humanist understanding of acting and casting and Bradleyan notions of character and theme. As the drama teacher tells his students: 'Mister Shakespeare is a very challenging writer who deals with big issues. Love, hate, jealousy, betrayal' (1320.12). This type of analysis has also occurred in professional productions of

Othello in New Zealand, exemplified by Michael Hurst's comments about his 1995 production of the play for Auckland's Watershed Theatre. For Hurst, Shakespeare is a universal genius whose ideas transcend time; he is a writer of 'acute psychological reality' and 'His plays are inevitably intense observations of the human condition.'[30] This view of *Othello* was supported by reviewers who talked of how the play represents 'today's issues' of 'trust, of treason, of the green-eyed monster jealousy, and of the ultimate loss of reality and reason'.[31] Considering how the local might impact on his production, Hurst said that 'At no time did I think of setting the play in New Zealand. I did not want any Tangata Whenua [indigenous people's] references or Treaty of Waitangi business or Gang-related stuff. I wanted the play only.'[32] In his eyes, 'Racism is . . . a bit of a sop to the story' and 'to relate the play to racial politics in New Zealand would be to diminish in some respects the central concerns of love and jealousy'. Comparable to Hurst's valorisation of 'universal' human themes and denial of (local) racial dynamics, by the time the opening night arrives in the *Shortland Street* production, the play is almost completely shorn of local significance, racial or otherwise, with the only such traces being the rugby-style costumes of the soldiers (1331.16, 19).

The *Shortland Street* storyline, then, like the Bursary English exam, shows the institution of Shakespeare in New Zealand high schools as a marker of universal human truths. However, the casting debate, which highlights tensions between Maori, Pacific Island and Pakeha students and which creates space for a consideration of the settler, does suggest the potential for *Othello* to be read as a commentary on contemporary New Zealand culture. Whereas *Shortland Street* attempts to defuse tensions between *Othello* and race-relations in a New Zealand context, Theatre at Large's *Manawa Taua/Savage Hearts* politicises these issues by embedding them in a history of colonisation and miscegenation.

Theatre at Large's *Manawa Taua/Savage Hearts* (1994)

In the settler cultures of Australia and Canada, *The Tempest* has provided a convenient narrative template for cross-cultural encounters or issues relating to settler populations. By contrast, one of the most trenchant rewritings of Shakespeare in terms of race-relations in New Zealand has been Theatre at Large's *Othello*-inflected *Manawa Taua/Savage Hearts*. This choice of a tragedy to explore these issues, rather than the romance of *The Tempest*, can be read speculatively as representative of a climate of 'black' comedy and (dis)ease which permeates much New Zealand literature, film and pop music. Theatre at Large, formed by Anna

Marbrook and Christian Penny in 1990, was a New Zealand theatre company with a commitment to developing and performing improvised theatre. *Manawa Taua* was a collaborative project devised by writers David Geary and Willie Davis, directors Anna Marbrook and Christian Penny, and a cast of five actors. In what might be described as a post-colonial/postmodern pastiche, the resulting performance made use of a range of performance styles and texts including Shakespeare, music hall routines, melodrama, Maori performance arts and French-influenced improvisational theatre. Thus Shakespeare was implicated in a discourse of cultural exchange between Maori, Pakeha, British and other European cultures, networking between the component cultures of the settler situation. In the resulting performance, *Manawa Taua* critiqued some of the issues involved in casting *Othello* and inquired into the cultural and somatic effects of performing Shakespeare in a settler culture.

The production and performance history of *Manawa Taua* is notable for the fact that, as Michael Neill records,

> bitter divisions opened up which left the two playwrights at odds with the directors and with each other, and the cast itself divided along broadly ethnic lines. In the end these divisions seem to have been resolved only by an extraordinary agreement to suppress the play at the end of its highly successful run, so that it would neither be published nor made available for further performance.[33]

I am interested in examining how this narrative of suppression both informs the practice of writing about performance and how it might be read back into the cultural politics of the performance itself. The act of suppression points to one of the central problems of writing about performance: how to write about that which, following the moment of performance, is always and forever absent and permanently disembodied. *Manawa Taua*'s production history and afterlife 'embodies' this proposition. Substantially reworked in and between performances, the resulting 'theatre events' are textually unstable, resulting in a situation where *Manawa Taua*'s performing bodies resist analyses that attempt to fix them. Further, the conventional archival traces of final script copy and video or sound recordings are unavailable – those ephemera either never existed or are lost.[34] Ironically, it is the absence of ephemera and the presence of trauma which provides the most compelling lens through which to consider the play. The resulting traumas, both corporeal and psychic, are bound up in the production's insightful critique of race-relations and the processes of colonisation.

Whereas the *Shortland Street* storyline and Hurst's production seemed disinterested in the concept of a 'New Zealand *Othello*', *Manawa Taua*, like Cathy Downes's recent 2001 Court Theatre production in Christchurch, which set the play in the context of the 1860s New Zealand Wars, sought to explore the play in relation to New Zealand's history of racial conflict. Also set on the eve of the 1860s New Zealand land wars between the indigenous population of the Maori and the British colonial settlers, *Manawa Taua* detailed the fictional story of Tupou, a Maori chief who journeys to London to meet Queen Victoria and gain her protection for his people. Victoria promises to help him, provided he agrees to play the part of Othello in a touring Shakespeare troupe which is about to embark on an expedition to the colonies. Forcing aside the company's usual Othello, the blacked-up Roy Folly, Victoria wants to cast Tupou as Othello because she thinks it 'would seem most apt, in that Othello deals with the savage heart. No offence' (1.12). Resonating with the entry in the Shakespeare in Schools Festival where Othello was presented as a Maori chief, here *Manawa Taua* can be read as a comment on casting conventions which seek to close the gap between the performer and the role.

This convention of selecting ethnically 'appropriate' actors for 'integrity' or 'authenticity' – which is as prevalent in twentieth-century theatrical practice as its opposite of colour-blind casting – expresses a desire to represent, or indeed, recover the 'real'. But, as I suggested above, not only do we have no clear idea what Shakespeare intended his Moor to look like, but the 'authentic' Shakespearean Moor on the Elizabethan stage was most likely a white man in black make-up. In effect, the 'authentic' or 'real' Othello is always absent. Rather than representing the 'real' character, casting a coloured actor in the name of authenticity can have the effect of collapsing the difference between performer and role in the assumption, as Paromita Chakravarti suggests, that a non-white actor is 'capable only of demonstrating his own negritude, unable to go beyond what is held to be the undeniable "reality" of his colour' (p. 49). In this way the performer is taken for the 'real' and represents as 'authentic' whatever racial stereotypes the character embodies. With respect to Othello, the coloured body of the actor is forced to engage with images which equate such a body with violence. So, whereas casting a white actor opens a production to charges of stereotypical racial impersonation, casting a black actor for reasons of 'integrity' or 'authenticity' implicates productions in a different, but perhaps no less destructive, set of racist issues.

Far from simply a 'humorous' fable, the casting narrative in *Manawa Taua* has a 'real' history in the casting of several black Othellos.

Thus Francesca T. Royster observes that Ira Aldridge's 1836 audiences 'insisted on seeing his savage passion as "real", as the authentic and essential sign of his blackness'[35] and Dympna Callaghan notes that in the 1930s Paul Robeson was thought to be 'better suited to the part because...he [supposedly] possessed primitive black emotions'.[36] The 'truth effect' produced by black actors playing Othello, such as Laurence Fishburne in Oliver Parker's 1995 film and David Harewood in the Royal National Theatre's 1998 production, frequently produces the black body as sexually threatening, muscular and violent, images which are confirmed in the play's violent ending.[37] The way in which these images function is consistent with what Mercer terms 'Classical racism'. This involves 'a logic of dehumanization, in which African peoples were defined as having bodies but not minds: in this way the superexploitation of the black body as muscle-machine could be justified'.[38] It is this act of objectification which was made explicit in the meta-theatrical space of *Manawa Taua*. *Manawa Taua* thus used the casting story to suggest that the British constructed their colonial subjects as 'savage' others. In effect Victoria was represented as a consumer of western cultural fantasies, eloquently identified by Frantz Fanon in *Black Skin, White Masks*, of the black man as sexually powerful and aggressive.[39] As the narrative progressed, *Manawa Taua* continued to play with the relationship between performer and role. Thus within the narrative Tupou and Lottie, the actor playing Desdemona, fell in love with one another, a device which proved to be the catalyst for the conflict which the play produced.

By charting the changes in Tupou as he rehearsed *Othello*, fell in love with Lottie and returned to New Zealand, his body was used by the production to register his colonisation and attendant alienation from his culture, a process in which Shakespeare played a central part. His clothes changed from a traditional Maori cloak to European garb. More tellingly, he lost his capacity to speak Maori; instead all he could do was speak 'Shakespeare'. Despite the 'comic', 'happy' ending, in which a member of Folly's company was punished for appropriating Maori land, the play dramatised issues concerning Maori cultural alienation as a result of the process of British colonisation of New Zealand through Tupou's corporeal transformations while playing Shakespeare.

In the casting of Maori actor Cliff Curtis as Tupou, a link was forged between Tupou's victimisation as a result of colonial processes and the effects these processes continue to have at the end of the twentieth century. At the time of *Manawa Taua*'s performance Curtis had received national media exposure for his work in Lee Tamahori's 1994 film

Once Were Warriors.[40] In the film he played Uncle Bully, a Maori man whose rape of a teenage Maori girl contributed to the seemingly unrelenting misery of her life, ultimately resulting in her suicide and the film's traumatic portrayal of its aftermath. Curtis asserted post-*Warriors* that he was 'sick of playing angry, confused Maori men who don't know how to bring aspects of Maoridom and their changing circumstances together', and that he knows 'other stories' and 'plenty of Maoris [sic] who succeed despite the difficulties'.[41] While Curtis appears to have chosen Tupou in order to counter stereotypical images of Maori men, I suggest that his body unavoidably carries the freight of his former role as a sexual abuser. The body of the actor thus becomes a palimpsest, accumulating previous roles which seep, however imperceptibly, into those which follow. As Barbara Hodgdon elegantly demonstrates in her 'Hamletic' readings, the performing body carries cultural memories. In this way, *Manawa Taua*'s representation of Tupou as a victim of colonialism was meshed with *Once Were Warriors*'s grim depiction of Maori culture as alienated, economically deprived and torn by abuse: a chilling reminder of the worst effects of New Zealand's colonial legacy.

Central to *Manawa Taua*'s narrative of cultural alienation was Shakespeare's narrative of miscegenation. The action of *Othello* became the template for the main drama concerning Tupou's relationship with Lottie. Through a series of regressive frames, that narrative of miscegenation, in turn, became the impetus for dividing the directors, cast and writers, ultimately resulting in the traumatic act of suppression. In a pre-production article on the play, Linda Herrick wrote:

> The relationship – between a Maori nobleman and a pakeha woman – is historically unheard of, and the portrayal has created a dilemma for Curtis. 'I've found it almost impossible to play a chief who would sacrifice everything for a pakeha woman, especially in that historical context,' says Curtis. 'I just don't think it would happen. To play and make it believable has been very hard for me.'[42]

Writer David Geary confirms that the split was to do with the representation of the interracial love affair, saying that:

> Very broadly, from what I could gather, it hung on whether a chief would sacrifice the good of his tribe for the love of a white woman . . . I guess it did highlight just how volatile race relations can be over how our 'history' is presented.

Needless to say the arguments weren't over the appropriation of Shakespeare.[43]

With his last comment, Geary notes the way in which *Manawa Taua* subsumed (or perhaps consumed) Shakespeare under the broader issue of cross-cultural encounters and the politics of historical representation. This sidelining seems to offer one way of negotiating the performance of Shakespeare in New Zealand towards the end of the twentieth century: the influence of the imperial text is overwritten with the concerns of the local and a history of colonisation. In the act of suppression, though, what is lost or sidelined is not Shakespeare or *Othello*, which are scarcely in need of protection. Rather, we lose access to a striking local narrative which embodies some of the ways in which Maori and Pakeha might, together, negotiate an understanding of our (post)colonial history. Thus, while the trauma itself offers an incisive comment on racial tensions, its suppression does little to assist the reparative work to ease these tensions. Such reparative work is, however, formally codified in the government's creation of the Waitangi Tribunal in 1975 as a permanent commission of inquiry to make recommendations relating to the practical application of the Treaty, and the Office of Treaty Settlements in 1995 in order to address Maori claims for land compensation. Further, in 1993 the position of Race Relations Conciliator was established to arbitrate in race-relations disputes.

In detailing the specificities of these productions I have attempted to use *Othello* to think through some ways in which the performance of Shakespeare localises issues relating to New Zealand's relationship with Britain, ideas about race, race-relations, colonial processes and the politics of casting practices. The productions' lack of engagement with ethnicities other than Maori, Pakeha, Pacific Island and British does, however, replicate one of the biases involved in thinking through racial and national identity issues in New Zealand. That is, such work tends to figure New Zealand as bi- rather than multicultural, focusing on Maori and Pakeha at the expense of its 'other' settler and immigrant populations. While the productions perpetuate this gap, which marks an area for further work, it is clear that *Othello* is a text which seems, always already – and all too readily – to instigate a sometimes painful assessment of intercultural relationships. The status of Shakespeare in New Zealand is clearly far from 'settled'. The performance of Shakespeare on our shores is, then, to some extent, bound up in the cultural work of establishing what it might mean to live in a settler culture. In this cultural work, New Zealand is haunted by Britain and a history of colonisation, situated at the edge of the world, far from the metropolis which introduced Shakespeare into our national psyche.

Notes and references

My thanks to Playmarket Wellington, South Pacific Pictures©, David Geary, Margaret Healy, Mark Houlahan, Michael Hurst, Michelle Keown, Lindsey Moore, Ruth Payne and Judith Pryor.

1. Thomas Cartelli, *Repositioning Shakespeare: National Formations, Postcolonial Appropriations* (London: Routledge, 1999) 124.
2. The issue of New Zealand's 'first' inhabitants is controversial. The Chatham Islands, which lie to the east of the South Island of New Zealand, were inhabited by the Moriori and it is possible that the Moriori may also have made landfall on the South Island. For an extended discussion of the Moriori and their encounters with Europeans and the Maori see Michael King, *Moriori: A People Rediscovered* (Auckland: Viking, 2000).
3. For an extended discussion of the Treaty and the differences between the two versions, see Claudia Orange, *The Treaty of Waitangi* (Wellington, NZ: Allen and Unwin, Port Nicholson Press, 1987). A web version of the Treaty can also be found at: *http://www.govt.nz/en/aboutnz.*
4. The 2001 Census recorded New Zealand's population at 3.79 million, comprising: 80% Pakeha – this group originates primarily from the British Isles but also includes peoples from the Netherlands, Yugoslavia, Germany and other European nations; 14.7% Maori; 6.6% Asian; 6.5% Pacific Islanders; and 0.7% constituting 'other' ethnic identities. These figures include the results from census participants who identified with more than one ethnic category. (2001 Census, Statistics New Zealand/Te Tari Tatau, *http://www.stats.govt.nz.*)
5. Mark Houlahan, 'Shakespeare in New Zealand,' *The Oxford Companion to New Zealand Literature*, ed. Roger Robinson and Nelson Wattie (Melbourne: OUP, 1998) 489.
6. See for example, Janet Frame, *Owls Do Cry*, 1958 (Auckland: Vintage, 1991), Frame, *Faces in the Water*, 1961 (London: Women's Press, 1982) and Ngaio Marsh, *Light Thickens* (London: Collins, 1982).
7. Houlahan, 'Shakespeare in New Zealand' 490.
8. I do not mean to imply that there is no academic work on settler cultures. Rather, I want to suggest that although much work is produced such analyses tend to be marginalised or elided from dominant academic *postcolonial* discourse. Robert J. C. Young's seminal new work, *Postcolonialism: An Historical Introduction* (Oxford: Blackwell, 2001) is a case in point. In the course of his analysis, which runs to nearly 500 pages, Young makes only passing reference to settler cultures such as Australia, Canada and New Zealand.
9. Daiva Stasiulis and Nira Yuval-Davis, 'Introduction: Beyond Dichotomies – Gender, Race, Ethnicity and Class in Settler Societies,' *Unsettling Settler Societies: Articulations of Gender, Race, Ethnicity and Class*, ed. Stasiulis and Yuval-Davis, Sage Ser. on Race and Ethnic Relations 11 (London: Sage, 1995) 5.
10. Exceptions include Michael Neill's brief analyses of *Manawa Taua/ Savage Hearts* in 'Post-colonial Shakespeare? Writing Away from the

Centre,' *Post-Colonial Shakespeares*, ed. Ania Loomba and Martin Orkin (London: Routledge, 1998) 181–4 and 'Shakespeare Upside Down,' *World and Stage: Essays for Colin Gibson*, ed. Greg Waite *et al.*, Otago Studies in English 6 (Dunedin, NZ: Dept. of English, Univ. of Otago, 1998) 150–1. For other work on Shakespeare and New Zealand see Houlahan, 'Shakespeare in New Zealand' 489–91, and 'Shakespeare, Hegemony and Assessment in New Zealand High Schools,' *For All Time? Critical Issues in Teaching Shakespeare*, ed. Paul Skrebels and Sieta van der Hoeven (Kent Town, South Australia: Wakefield Press, 2002) 6–16.

11. In referring to race as a 'spectre' I do not intend to deny, as will shortly become clear, the way race and racism tend to be materially worked out on the bodies of subjects.

12. Margo Hendricks and Patricia Parker, Introduction, *Women, 'Race' and Writing in the Early Modern Period*, ed. Hendricks and Parker (London: Routledge, 1994) 1–2.

13. Lynda E. Boose, '"The Getting of a Lawful Race": Racial Discourse in Early Modern England and the Unrepresentable Black Woman,' Hendricks and Parker 35.

14. Peggy Phelan, *Unmarked: The Politics of Performance* (London: Routledge, 1993) 8.

15. For further discussion of these issues see Homi K. Bhabha, 'The Other Question: Stereotype, Discrimination and the Discourse of Colonialism,' *The Location of Culture* (London: Routledge, 1994) 66–80.

16. Kobena Mercer, *Welcome to the Jungle: New Positions in Black Cultural Studies* (London: Routledge, 1994), especially Chapter 4 'Black Hair/Style Politics' 97–128.

17. Kim F. Hall, *Things of Darkness: Economies of Race and Gender in Early Modern England* (Ithaca, NY: Cornell University Press, 1995) 7. For a more detailed etymological study of the term 'Moor,' see Anthony Gerard Barthelemy, *Black Face, Maligned Race: The Representations of Blacks in English Drama from Shakespeare to Southerne* (Baton Rouge: Louisiana State University Press, 1987) 6–17. For discussions of the stage history of *Othello* see, for example, Marvin Rosenberg, *The Masks of Othello: The Search for the Identity of Othello, Iago, and Desdemona by Three Centuries of Actors and Critics* (Berkeley: University of California Press, 1961) and Virginia Mason Vaughan, *Othello: A Contextual History* (Cambridge: CUP, 1994).

18. Sudipto Chatterjee and Jyotsna G. Singh. 'Moor or Less? The Surveillance of *Othello*, Calcutta 1848,' *Shakespeare and Appropriation*, ed. Christy Desmet and Robert Sawyer (London: Routledge, 1999) 66. Italics in original.

19. English, University Entrance, Bursaries and Scholarship Examinations, New Zealand Qualifications Authority, 1998: 16.

20. Letter to the Chief Examiner, University Entrance, Bursaries and Scholarship English, Dec. 1998. Authorship details withheld by request.

21. Jonathan Miller, *Subsequent Performances* (London and Boston: Faber and Faber, 1986) 159.

22. Houlahan, 'Shakespeare, Hegemony and Assessment' 12.

23. *Shortland Street*, videocassette, South Pacific Pictures©, 1997, episode 1320, scene 12. Dialogue is quoted from South Pacific Pictures©'s *Shortland Street* scripts. All further references will be given in the text in the form (episode. scene).

24. For a discussion of some of the issues involved in colour-blind casting see Richard Schechner, 'Race Free, Gender Free, Body-Type Free, Age Free Casting,' *The Drama Review* 33.1 (1989): 4–12. A recent high profile example of colour blind casting is the casting of black actor David Oyelowo, in the title roles, in the RSC's productions of *Henry VI Parts I, II* and *III* in 2001.

25. Dorinne K. Kondo, *About Face: Performing Race in Fashion and Theatre* (New York: Routledge, 1997) 230.

26. Denis Welch, 'Black is Back,' *Listener* 7 March 1998: 42.

27. Dawn Sanders, rev. of Sheilah Winn 7th National Festival of Shakespeare in Schools, *Shakespeare Globe Centre Newsletter* 25, July 1998: 4.

28. Sanders 4.

29. For a discussion of the ambivalent position of the settler subject see, for example, Alan Lawson, 'Postcolonial Theory and the "Settler" Subject,' *Essays on Canadian Writing* 56 (1995): 20–36.

30. Michael Hurst, 'Othello,' e-mail to the author, 19 Sept. 2000. All quotations from Hurst are from this document.

31. Bernadette Rae, rev. *Othello*, dir. Hurst, *New Zealand Herald*, 14 July 1995, 19.

32. With respect to Hurst's reference to gangs, New Zealand has a number of well established gangs, at least two of which, 'Black Power' and 'The Mongrel Mob,' have a predominantly Maori membership.

33. Neill, 'Post-colonial Shakespeare?' 182.

34. In the absence of any audio or videotapes of a performance or a 'final' copy of the script, dialogue is quoted from the following document: David Geary, Christian Penny and Anna Marbrook, *Savage Hearts*, unpublished first draft (Wellington: Playmarket, 1994). This document is held in the archive of Playmarket in Wellington and was substantially reworked in performance. References will be given in the text in the form (scene.page).

35. Francesca T. Royster, 'The "End of Race" and the Future of Early Modern Cultural Studies,' *Shakespeare Studies* 26 (1998): 64.

36. Dympna Callaghan, *Shakespeare Without Women: Representing Gender and Race on the Renaissance Stage* (London: Routledge, 2000) 95.

37. *Othello*, dir. Oliver Parker, perf. Laurence Fishburne, Irene Jacob and Kenneth Branagh, Castle Rock, 1995. See Royster's discussion on the way Fishburne is produced as a violent, sexy black body (65–8).

38. Mercer 138.

39. Frantz Fanon, *Black Skin, White Masks*, trans. Charles Lamm Markmann (New York: Grove Weidenfeld, 1967). See especially Chapter 6 'The Negro and Psychopathology' (141–209). In a controversial move, Fanon also offers a comment 'on the psychosexuality of the white woman,' saying that 'when a woman lives the fantasy of rape by a Negro, it is in some way the fulfilment of a private dream, of an inner wish' (179).

40. *Once Were Warriors*, dir. Lee Tamahori, perf. Rena Owen, Temuera Morrison, Mamaengaroa Kerr-Bell, Communicado, 1994.

41. Cliff Curtis qtd. in Bernadette Rae, 'Theatre Company Sweats it Out,' *New Zealand Herald* 13 Oct. 1994: 2.2.

42. Linda Herrick, 'Clash of Cultures Aims for the Heart,' *Sunday Star Times* 23 Oct. 1994: D4.

43. David Geary, '*Manawa Taua/Savage Hearts*,' e-mail to the author, 10 Oct. 2000.

6
'Alas poor country!': Documenting the Politics of Performance in Two British Television *Macbeths* since the 1980s

Susanne Greenhalgh

In his study of postmodern culture Fredric Jameson nominates video, 'so closely related to the dominant computer and information technology' of globalisation, as the 'hegemonic art form *par excellence* of late capitalism' in both its commercial and experimental forms.[1] It is now evident that paradigms of performance and theatricality have replaced those of textuality and canon within British television's representations of Shakespeare since the completion of the BBC and Time/Life Complete Works in 1985. It is equally evident that our experience and understanding of performance are themselves increasingly mediated, re-contextualised, by the conventions of film and television, recorded and at hand for research or review in our homes, public libraries or local video stores. This essay seeks to examine some of the ways in which Shakespeare is being retextualised by these new hegemonic forms; the extent to which, as Michèle Willems suggests, 'postmodern re-presentation of Shakespeare, with its self-referential system of echoes, allusions or even visual quotations, is in part at least the product of our new video culture'.[2] There is certainly a dialectical relationship between, on the one hand, the proven potential of videos to become objects in permanent and 'authoritative' archives of fixed television interpretations and performances (epitomised by the BBC Shakespeare), re-enshrining textuality at the centre of Shakespeare studies; and, on the other, the enabling of diverse interpretations through the creation of new texts which juxtapose extracts from different versions. Willems has argued that video-tapes are becoming both theatre's history and its memory, as well as the chief means by which films, television drama, and recordings of theatrical performance are experienced in

93

educational or domestic settings, a development which blurs boundaries, definitions and codes in ways with which critical practice is still trying to keep pace.[3] Jameson, who considers that video, unlike the modernist medium of film, structurally *excludes* memory,[4] does make an exception of documentary video. Whilst video typically 'does not project fictive time, and does not work with fiction or fictions', documentary video 'still projects a kind of residual fictionality – a kind of documentary constructed time – at the very heart of its aesthetic ideology', a 'simulacrum of fictive time',[5] and thus of history and memory. When these 'documents' are digitally encoded onto computer memory, whether by the Open University or MIT, the audience can *play with* rather than simply *re-play* the memory of performance.[6]

Video culture not only changes performance but can make it disappear. Although Richard Eyre's television survey of modern British theatre *Changing Stages* (BBC2 2000) opened with a homage to Shakespeare as its 'theatrical DNA', it deliberately used made-for-TV or film clips instead of performance recordings which, Eyre argued, could never catch the snowman-like ephemerality of the theatrical moment.[7] Here, paradoxically, theatricality is celebrated by its absence, performance becomes the ghost in the machine of another medium (as the image of Eyre himself is digitally inserted or removed from a succession of filmed auditoria). When performance does appear directly in the 'nearly unbroken chain' of British televised Shakespeare it is now most often anchored in the context of educational programmes,[8] in which performance or film extracts illustrate or enliven commentary and interviews, or in arts documentaries where they provide visual evidence of the former, present, and future cultural dominance of Shakespeare.[9] These are further contextualised by most often being scheduled in special seasons such as BBC2's *Bard on the Box* (1994) or BBC Knowledge's day-long, non-stop Shakespeare transmissions *A Day in with Shakespeare* (2000) alongside other documentaries and made-for television adaptations of the plays. The latter are now infrequent, in line with the overall decline in single plays produced for television and the recent steady supply of Shakespeare from the cinema. The Shakespeare television documentary, however, thrives (if only by comparison), targeted as it is at both the educational and culture market, at the international as well as British audience, and increasingly capable of transposition into a variety of broadcast and digital media. How this 'turn' to documentary recontextualises the performance and politics of television Shakespeare in the video and digital age is the main focus of this essay.

Documentary can be defined as 'the loose and often highly contested label given, internationally, to certain kinds of film and television...which reflect and report on "the real" through the use of recorded images and sounds of actuality'.[10] As such video-recordings of theatre productions might appear to authenticate the 'real' of performance through their documentation of its actuality. Such documentations can never be neutral mirrorings however, but rather report from the scene of an event, providing either a 'historically relevant "reading"' of the performance, an *illustration* of ways in which a spectator might have focused on the performance stimuli,[11] or 'recording as *analysis*' offering 'a deliberately partial and partisan reading of the theatrical happening'.[12] These distinctions, between preservation of a hypothetical 'audience view' and analytical reinterpretation in terms of the new medium, can in turn be mapped onto the duality intrinsic to all documentary work – 'its character as both artifice and evidence'.[13] Stella Bruzzi's concept of *performative documentary* is helpful here: 'a mode which emphasises – and indeed constructs a film around – the often hidden aspect of performance, whether on the part of the documentary subjects or the film-makers'.[14] In this formulation the dual characteristics of documentary as artifice and evidence are kept continuously in play, reality is constantly re-staged, destabilising any claims to absolute authenticity or fixed meaning. This is very different from the kind of relationship between documentary and performance in drama which adopts a documentary *style*.

> Within such a realist aesthetic, the role of performance is, paradoxically, to draw the audience into the reality of the situations being dramatised, to authenticate the fictionalisation. In contrast to this, the performative documentary uses performance within a non-fiction context to draw attention to the impossibilities of authentic documentary representation. The performative element within the framework of non-fiction is thereby an alienating, distancing device, not one which actively promotes identification and a straightforward response to a film's content.[15]

Two versions of *Macbeth*, originally transmitted on British public broadcast television, provide a useful context in which to examine the radical potentialities or otherwise of these shifting relationships between documentary and performance. *Macbeth on the Estate* (BBC2 1997) was directed by the documentary maker Penny Woolcock, as a sequel to her award-winning film, *Shakespeare on the Estate* (BBC2 1994), which recorded Michael Bogdanov's work on Shakespeare with inhabitants of an inner-city housing estate in Birmingham.[16] Her *Macbeth* mixed professionals and locals in the cast, and to date has had one repeat broadcast and is unavailable on commercial video. Gregory Doran's television film of his own acclaimed RSC production for the Swan in 1999 starred Antony Sher and Harriet Walter and was produced by Illuminations for the RSC and transmitted on Channel 4 in January 2001. Subsequently it was used in the pilot project for the British government's proposed *Culture Online*, featuring in the demo storyboard available on the government web-site, and will appear in video and DVD format in due course, as well as being available for RSC web casts in the future.[17]

In his study of national and postcolonial appropriations of Shakespeare, Thomas Cartelli draws attention to the tension 'between the different and the same, the general and the specific, the global and the local', out of which the contemporary recontextualisation of Shakespeare emerges.[18] Both these versions, like many recent *Macbeth*s, are modern-dress productions which, though not set historically, might qualify as what Graham Holderness calls 'social tragedy', in which social problems and contradictions can be rendered visible and fully intelligible.[19] Both reposition the play in a devastated urban landscape to suggest an overall concern with contemporary realities, and even share some directorial devices, such as mixed-race casting. In both, as at the time of the play's first performances, Scotland is England's Other, a mirror in which to glimpse a future Britain. But whereas Doran's interpretation fits comfortably into what Cartelli terms a 'tributary relationship'[20] to the original work, Woolcock's film can best be seen as a *'transpositional'* appropriation: one which 'identifies and isolates a specific theme, plot, or argument in its appropriative objective and brings it into its own, arguably analogous, interpretive field to underwrite or enrich a presumably related thesis or argument'.[21] These distinctly different ideological orientations are also in part produced by their different mediations of performance, film and television, and, most significantly, their use of the documentary genre. Woolcock's fiction film *Macbeth on the Estate* retains many of the features of her previous performative documentaries, employed as 'alienating, distancing' strategies which complicate audience response. Doran's adaptation of his RSC production, on the other hand, mainly uses its documentary style to authenticate the fiction of the play and draw its audience closer into its 'reality'. Through its employment of 'reality TV' techniques, however, this style also produces its moments of performative dislocation. My analysis thus has parallels with that of Ramona Wray, who, in her discussion of Kenneth Branagh's *Love's Labour's Lost* in this volume, detects a 'confused amalgam, a screen product hesitating between modes of intertextual communication...and collisions of generic and national identification' (p. 167). In these television *Macbeths*, too, stylistic and generic choices, as well as their self-positioning as local or global texts, point us to the political unconscious encoded in their documenting of performance.

Restaging locality: Penny Woolcock's estate Shakespeare

Penny Woolcock is now widely recognised as a leading experimental documentary film-maker. Writing of an earlier film *When the Dog Bites*,[22] which depicted the town of Consett after the closure of its steel mills, Corner applauds her 'bravura use of different documentary styles' to depict a community in the process of change and the quest for a new identity.[23] This combined interview sequences (often filmed in a non-conventional *mise-en-scène*), observational footage with a clear symbolic as well as naturalistic force, and, most significantly for my purposes, innovative and controversial use of dramatisation in the form of scenarios improvised by some of the film's subjects.[24] Documentary realism is also enriched by a bizarre and carnivalesque associative mode, especially in sequences set in a drag cabaret, creating 'a "space" upon which certain parodic forms both of masculinity and national identity can be projected...an energy of the grotesque which the film is able to juxtapose with the more conventional (if nevertheless variously displaced) naturalisms it uses elsewhere'.[25] However, Corner suggests, such a degree of 'postmodern reflexivity', ironising and stylisation of the film's participants, and overall 'documentary playfulness', runs the risk of both 'losing' the popular audience and calling into question the film's trustworthiness as documentary.[26]

These issues of aesthetics, agency, and accountability were equally crucial in *Shakespeare on the Estate*, which also made use of a complex structure of interviews, observation and performance. When she was invited to provide the BBC Bristol contribution to the *Bard in the Box* season Woolcock argued hard, in the face of strong opposition, against the proposed subject of Shakespeare teaching in secondary schools and in favour of further investigating the world of the 'sink estates' explored in her previous films set in Consett and Rhondda, 'people who were completely outside civil society in many ways'.[27] The Ladywood estate in Birmingham was chosen both for its racial mix and the ironies of its proximity to the city's famous repertory theatre, and a month was spent in painstaking liaison with the residents prior to a week's filming, following the arrival of Bogdanov, who selected scenes thought suited to those who wanted to take part. All this seemed to promise the 'radical potentialty' that Graham Holderness had viewed as exemplary in an earlier television programme, Bogdanov's 1980s rehearsal workshop-cum-lecture series *Shakespeare Lives!* (Channel 4, 1983).

> In place of the monumental stability of a definitive version, the cultural authority of an institutional production, solidly flanked by the apparatus of special occasion, publicity promotion, ancillary introduction, linked publications; we have the provisional, tentative, unfinished debate of the practical rehearsal, and the spectacle of people trying to make meaning out of Shakespeare.[28]

Whereas *Shakespeare Lives!* utilised the talk show format, with professional actor-demonstrators performing (confessing?) in front of a studio audience, *Shakespeare on the Estate* at first sight appears to adopt the familiar investigative mode of much television documentary (which has its roots in journalism, sociological enquiry and ethnography). A middle-class outsider ventures into working-class *terra incognita* to shed light on the strange customs of its inhabitants. But Bogdanov is more a missionary than an anthropologist. Often seen – and probably seeing himself – as both maverick and marginalised in the English theatre establishment, for many years he has preached a political Shakespeare: feminist, subversive and, more recently, multicultural. The quest documented by *Shakespeare on the Estate* – to find out what Shakespeare meant to the residents and to popularise his work – was quixotic, perhaps contradictory, and completely in character with Bogdanov's long-held theatrical goal to bring Shakespeare to 'the people'.

> The object was to gather evidence as to the impact of Shakespeare on the lives of the greater part of our population, while at the same time examining to what extent this myth of Shakespeare, the popular writer of and for the people is true. I worked on ideas and extracts with a group of Asian youths, various representatives of the large black community, drunks, homeless, unemployed – the majority. Battered wives, thieves, drug addicts. Sometimes re-writing in Punjabi, West Indian patois and street English. Composing in rap, bhangra, raga and rock, in an attempt to find a point of contact with those who showed interest. More often than not looking and making a patronising prat of myself.[29]

Although Bogdanov presents himself here as an impartial investigator of the Shakespeare myth, his syntax is revealing in the way it implicitly erases the differently raced others 're-writing' and 'composing' Shakespeare to make himself the subject of the sentence. Like that master of the colonialist project, Prospero, Bogdanov not only seems reluctant to relinquish his command of language, the 'point of contact' between explorer and explored, but succeeds in appropriating its magical powers of transposition to himself alone.

In contrast to *When the Dog Bites*, Woolcock permits Bogdanov a seemingly authoritative, sometimes reflective, voiceover charting his journey through Ladywood. This sense of someone merely passing through is also carried by the opening tracking sequence from a moving car, followed by high-angle locating shots of the estate, counter-pointed by the soundtrack of 'Mr William Shakespeare's Blues', which strings his best-known lines together in improvised jazz style. A number of key locations are quickly identified, chief among them the pub outside which Bogdanov has his first encounter with the locals. This area is bounded by a mesh perimeter fence, introduced by a resident as 'the Great Wall of Ladywood', which protects a building site beyond, variously connotative of progress and renovation, the ripped-out heart of the neighbourhood, or a playground for its children. The other main public spaces are a grassed recreation ground where many of the rehearsals take place, the interior of the pub, used in particular, in another echo of *When the Dog Bites*, for a 'Lady's Night' complete with drag act, and sequences shot in the Ladywood Evangelical Mission, which include a baptism.

The narrative falls into three parts: recruitment and audition, rehearsal, and performance. First Bogdanov persuades the residents to get involved despite their good-natured lack of interest: 'Who was Shakespeare? Who knows? Who cares?' These sequences include an edgy meeting with local black activists wary of Shakespeare, the white man's writer, and a more relaxed session in the mothers' drop-in centre, where the camera lingers on the luminously expectant face of one young woman in particular, later seen attending the evangelical service. Conversion apparently accomplished rehearsals begin, and there is a strong sense that Prospero's project is failing when Bogdanov accidentally blacks someone's eye whilst teaching him stage fighting. Order returns with the allocation of roles suited to the 'character and personality' of the would-be actors and a shot of a tidy line of scripts on the rehearsal room table. Although rehearsal still takes place in homes, the pub, and the open air, Bogdanov appears to have reasserted his directorial authority and the last sequence is a series of acted speeches and scenes 'on location' in the estate introduced by title captions. The first performance, by an actor who would go on to play Seyton in *Macbeth* (earlier he is seen attempting the 'Tomorrow' speech) is Caliban's from 1.3 of *The Tempest*, 'This island's mine',[30] a possible acknowledgement, by Bogdanov as well as Woolcock, that his role is indeed open to the charge of neo-colonialism. The last speech, by the same actor, framed against the mesh fence, is from the same play: 'Our revels now are ended. These our actors...are melted into air...We are such things as dreams are made on' (4.1.148–58). As the blues soundtrack, played by black musicians, overlays the words of 'Mr William Shakespeare' the 'Shakespeare experience', it appears, is no more than midsummer madness, leaving no trace behind in Ladywood or its actors.

Nonetheless, after winning awards for the film, Woolcock was invited by the BBC to adapt and film *Macbeth* on the same estate and cast some of the same actors (notably several black actors who had performed scenes from *Romeo and Juliet*) along with any residents who wished to be extras, and a majority of professional actors, including Andrew Tiernan (Banquo) who had grown up on the estate and, as a walk-on, his brother who still lived there. An avowed theatre-hater, Woolcock found in *Macbeth* an 'ideal metaphor' for the 'different legal and economic system which operated on council estates' which she had observed in her previous films and was to be the subject of her later *Tina* series, one which would allow her to explore the criminality which could only be hinted at in the documentaries.[31] In many respects Woolcock's investigation of the 'estate' of contemporary society parallels that of feminist writer Beatrix Campbell, whose 1993 study of the 'dangerous places' of Britain challenged the then influential theories of an 'underclass', caused by the break-up of the traditional family, to argue that many working-class areas were 'colonized' by male-dominated riots and criminality, under the disabling pressures of unemployment and the Conservative government's withdrawal of support systems from women left to fend for themselves and their children in 'sink estates'.[32]

> The word that embraced everything feared and loathed by the new orthodoxy about class and crime was *estate*: what was once the emblem of respectability, what once evoked the dignity and clamour of a powerful social constituency, part of the body politic, but which now described only the edge of a class and the end of the city. 'Estate' evoked rookery, slum, ghetto – without the exotic energy of urbanity...Single mothers become represented as a contagion, their

children become aliens, their neighbourhoods become colonies contained in the imagery of big dogs, smoking women, wall-to-wall TV, snotty children who learn to say 'fuck off' before they can say 'please'.[33]

Woolcock organised her drastically cut and reordered script in two main ways. One thematic strand focused on mothers and children, following the imagery of the play, but also perhaps responding to the public anxiety and debate around young people that followed the trial of two ten-year-old boys for the murder of the toddler James Bulger:[34] 'What happens when children are neglected, impoverished and under educated?'[35] The witches were seemingly feral street-wise kids (originally played by even younger children) who had created a play space decorated with discarded toys in an abandoned apartment-block where they prophetically constructed Diana-like shrines a year before her death. Lady Macbeth, played with a Scottish accent by Susan Vidor, was first seen carrying the Macduff baby, kept her dead child's room intact (this was the location for her first soliloquy) and tried to save the Macduff family from death. Fleance and Donalbain dealt drugs in the pub toilets, and the final degradation of Macbeth came when he battered Macduff's youngest daughter to death in her pram.

Made in the last full year of Conservative government and broadcast less than a month before the May election that brought New Labour to power, the film's other thematic strand was political, dealing, like many other 1990s television dramas, with the state of the nation reflected variously in the estate's racial diversity (though it was notable that the Asian presence was much less conspicuous than in *Shakespeare on the Estate*), its (fictional?) criminalised drug culture, and the juxtaposition of dereliction and violence with the sporadic pleasures of dope, alcohol and stolen consumer durables. Half-demolished tower blocks became the site for meetings with the witches, a pristine flat was the upwardly mobile Macbeths' Glamis where Duncan and his girlfriend were murdered amid the co-ordinated decor of the guest bedroom, and Malcolm and Macduff found asylum in a disused mental hospital (now a prospective green field site for redevelopment). *Macbeth* is a play seldom conceived of in racial terms, but in Woolcock's version the racial identities of actors were as crucial as in the Bengali 'postcolonial cinematic negotiation' of *Othello* documented by Paromita Chakravarti, or the performances in New Zealand discussed by Catherine Silverstone. The casting, as Duncan, of Ray Winstone, an actor who has frequently played small-time, often racist, villains, not only linked the film with other contemporary treatments of gangster lowlife and the 'noir' television police dramas then dominating the schedules. It also fore-grounded the themes of race relations and incipient conflict. Although shown with both a black wife and girlfriend, Duncan's choice of Malcolm as heir over his brother seemed as much to do with his lighter skin as with his age or suitability for the role. Duncan's counterpart was Macduff, played commandingly by the black actor David Harewood. Often seen wearing Nation of Islam shirts, and portrayed as a caring father, he was clearly the moral centre of the film, concluding it with Ross's lines from Act 4, 'Alas poor country!/ Almost afraid to know itself' in direct address to camera on a pile of demolition rubble.

But despite this constant intertextuality with social realist film and television drama, like Consett in *When the Dog Bites* and the picture of the estate that emerged in Woolcock's previous Shakespeare film, Ladywood/Scotland was also a shifting dreamlike place, similarly full of grotesque, exotic energies. A tartan-clad reveller turned up at the 'banquet' in the pub (now called the Forres) to lead Macbeth into a drinking contest delirium out of which Banquo's ghost appeared. At the end of the film, in a surreal moment (reminiscent stylistically of another 'performative documentary' *Signs of the Time*) the sofa on which the dead bodies of the Macbeths sat was transferred to the sylvan green setting where Banquo was killed.[36] Woolcock's *Macbeth* is an unsettling blend of artifice and evidence centred on the juxtaposition of amateur and professional actors and their recorded performances. As we watch we become aware that even the Birmingham accent is natural to some, more or less skilfully imitated by others. At times we cannot know whether the appearance of someone in shot is part of a scene's planned storyboard or a confirmation of its documentary 'truth'. Often it is both, just as many of the performers – like Macbeth – are and are not actors.

Although the last part of *Shakespeare on the Estate* showed the residents acting in their own mini Shakespeare films their performances remained bounded by their everyday realities – indeed Bogdanov had ensured this by casting them in roles as near their 'real' situations as possible (a single mother as Lady Macduff, a black bartender speaking Shylock's 'Has not a Jew' speech). In *Macbeth* the relationship between the 'real' of Ladywood and that of the film was much more complex. By turning the estate into the troubled state of 'Scotland' and casting the residents as its hapless people, silent witnesses to gang warfare and murderous rivalry between crack dealers, the adaptation unfixes our reading of its politics as it complicates our sense of what performance is and is not in this context. After Lady Macbeth has jumped to her death from a tower block,

Macbeth speaks the 'Tomorrow' speech to an audience of impassive residents. The lines not only express the nihilism to which Macbeth's actions have brought him but evoke a specific mode of documentary film, particularly associated with the 'staged' wartime documentaries of Humphrey Jennings, which employs a heightened or poetic text as voiceover to the unspoken (unspeakable?) thoughts behind the blank faces panned by the camera.[37] In a play that uses its theatrical metaphors to such effect to image the dissolution of identity, performative documentary's power to unsettle our conventional reception of television acting is apt and haunting, but it also leaves ambiguous whether we are witnessing silence or silencing, a fatalistic foretelling of the political powerlessness and apathy evidenced by diminishing voter turn-outs in the 1997 and 2001 General Elections, and the simmering violence that would erupt again in urban unrest in 2001.[38]

According to Campbell, the young men she interviewed were 'soaked in globally transmitted images and ideologies of butch and brutal solutions to life's difficulties...schooled in unprecedented displays of personal and public force'.[39] *Macbeth*, with its obsessive concern with misogyny, masculinity and violence, unexpectedly proved the ideal text for transposition to explore what made such estates 'dangerous places'. Like Consett, Ladywood is constructed as 'a "space" upon which certain parodic forms both of masculinity and national identity can be projected', a location of vitality as well as viciousness.[40] The hybrid genre of performative documentary, which enabled critique, not simply ethnographical documentation, of Bogdanov's neo-colonialist enterprise, also turns *Macbeth* into a mirror which can project the colonial gaze back upon itself. Documentary infuses the film to make it more than just a documentarised drama. It is rather a dynamic generic mix of social realist drama, the crime thriller genre, with its 'globalised' imagery and ideology of macho violence, and the aesthetically stylised 'new documentary': something 'wild and unworkable' from the conventional BBC perspective.[41] Woolcock, who herself grew up in the expatriate anglophone community of Argentina, plays with televisual genres to *reposition* Shakespeare: interrogating the politics of location, re-staging locality and challenging the British audience to know 'our' country by looking at it as though through foreign eyes.

'Like a movie camera': Gregory Doran's reality *Macbeth*

Gregory Doran's production of *Macbeth* (RSC 1999) was haunted by both the theatre and television productions of Trevor Nunn's version starring

Ian McKellen and Judi Dench in The Other Place in 1976 over twenty years earlier.[42] After eight years of Adrian Noble's leadership of the RSC there was general critical consensus that there had been a marked falling-off since the glory days under Nunn, a legend of which his *Macbeth* was a key part. In its day and subsequently, Nunn's production was praised for heralding a new RSC openness to performance in intimate, stripped-down studio spaces. If the RSC needed to find a new sense of purpose and direction, Doran's production just might show the way.

Of course a major reason why Nunn's twenty-year old production retained such currency is its continued circulation on video and on television in the equally critically-acclaimed television adaptation.[43] Few commentators dissent from Kenneth S. Rothwell's judgement that this was arguably 'one of the greatest successes in the history of televised Shakespeare . . . adapted without loss to either theatrical or telegenic values',[44] but its interpretation of the theatre performance, a ritual in a timeless setting creating a seance-like exploration of good and evil, was scarcely radical.[45] Its engagement with contemporary politics was limited to McKellen's appropriation of Idi Amin, then the despotic ruler of Uganda, together with Hitler, as sources for his characterisation of Macbeth.[46] Played on the thrust stage of the Swan, part of the success of Doran's production was the way it updated what was essentially the same universalist reading of *Macbeth* for a different stage and a new millennium, one which could be charged with an equally opportunistic use of the imagery of current events.

Sher records that, after originally visualising a 'Jacobean' approach to explore the experience of fear and darkness which Doran considered central to the play, the TV documentaries about 'violence and warfare' watched as background research became the key to their interpretation: 'we remind one another of images we've seen on TV recently: earthquakes in Turkey, the war in Kosovo – again and again images of modern societies made primitive, modern societies with the electricity gone, modern societies in deepest darkness.'[47] In rehearsal these were collaged into 'a modern world but one you can't easily identify. Everything and everyone will be caked in soot, oil, grime, dried blood, uniforms and weaponry will be a hotchpotch – people grab anything to fight – soldiers and witches look the same, and you can't say which war this is either: Flanders, Vietnam, Balkans?'[48] This concept, as well as the mode of pre-production research, had had a trial run in Doran's modern-dress production of *Titus Andronicus* with a cast of black, white and coloured actors at the Market Theatre in Johannesburg in 1996.[49] This was a sincere but often clumsily naïve attempt to turn ancient Rome into the recent past of South Africa – 'a world, not elsewhere but else*when*'[50] – fed, like *Macbeth*, by television documentaries of violence and massacres under Apartheid. Although Sher (characteristically) interviewed convicted murderers in preparation for the role, his final view of Macbeth was as 'one of those NATO commander-in-chiefs we see on the telly all the time, very hands-on, one of the lads, liked by the troops, matey with fellow officers, happier at work than at home'.[51] It was also in some ways a younger version of the brutal Africaaner patriarch which he had created for his homecoming *Titus*, itself based in part on Nicholas Broomfield's 'performative documentary' on the South African white supremacist Eugene Terreblanche.[52]

Given these televisual inspirations, *Macbeth* was surprisingly faithful both to the theatrical conventions of the play's originating Jacobean moment and to the RSC's 'patented Shakespeare Lite formula – all speed and swishing greatcoats, drums and dry ice'.[53] Its minimalism required few props other than cigarettes, torches, a galvanised bucket and towel, a clothes-horse, guns, the inescapable daggers and finally tree branches for Malcolm's invasion. The first item of furniture – a table – came on only with the banquet scene. Royalty, arrayed in mediaeval splendour, entered from a back-lit drawbridge, the drunken Porter of Hell Gate from the trapdoor. Actors were positioned symmetrically on the Swan thrust stage, though much use was also made of the theatre gangways and stairs. Played at speed without an interval, the running time virtually achieved the legendary two hour's traffic. Whenever possible the dimly-lit stage was restored to a murkiness in which sound, whether the sighs, coughs and gasps of the weird sisters, the explosions of battle or the percussive music, took on added potency. In this shell-shocked world the military approach dominated Sher's alternately ferocious, introspective and ironic 'action man' Macbeth partnered by Harriet Walter's febrile upper-class Lady. As many critics noted, the weird sisters (potential asylum seekers rather than witches) were side-lined as observers rather than agents of destiny. The powers of good, represented by Joseph O'Connor's pensive Duncan and a morally tortured Malcolm, were finally restored, even though threatened by Fleance, who fingered the sisters' talisman at the end of the play. Local and topical recontextualisation was provided nightly by Stephen Noonan's Porter whose ad libs always included a take-off of Prime Minister Tony Blair's 'equivocation'.

Given the way the production was hailed as a restoration of powers often thought to be failing (Doran began to be talked of as a possible successor to Noble)[54] it was hardly surprising that the RSC made a quick decision to further market its millennial hit. Although Channel 4 put up some of the money for screening rights, the televising was essentially an RSC project. The modest budget of £310,000 was made viable only because actors and the production company were willing to accept lower than standard fees and residuals.[55] Illuminations had earlier filmed the Royal National Theatre's production of *Richard II* directed by Deborah Warner and starring Fiona Shaw as the king for BBC2.[56] But whereas this was studio-shot, the location for *Macbeth* activated both theatrical and filmic memories. The Roundhouse in Camden is famous as a venue for innovative theatre in the 1960s and 1970s, including Tony Richardson's 1969 *Hamlet*, with Nicol Williamson, which was subsequently filmed there.

Whilst Nunn's *Macbeth* was transferred to the small screen by an established television director, Doran was directing his own first film under the care of a team of experienced technicians. The stated intention was to make a 'reconceived' version rather than an archive recording. In any case the change of location to a theatre space famous for its in-the-round productions ensured that the thrust stage performance dynamics would be abandoned. Adrian Noble had described the Swan to Sher as being 'like a movie camera. We can see into your head. We can enter your thoughts,'[57] but Doran also had a specific *televisual* look in mind, which would heighten what was for him the central premise of the play, its setting in a time of war. The footage of Gulf War smart missiles and Bosnian carnage which had fed his original concept of the production would become the overall style of the television version, combined with an 'observational documentary style' modelled on globally franchised, fly on the wall programmes such as *Big Brother* and *Survivor* in order to achieve what he considered to be a Shakespearean 'edgy complicity and intimacy'.[58] Despite filming on videotape, use of the industry-standard DigiBeta allowed the auto-conformed master to be graded to give the accustomed warm tones of video a steely metallic quality before 'film-effecting' it to achieve a grainier feel, most dramatically in the weird green 'night vision' of the opening sequence which substituted for the pitch darkness of the theatre.[59]

Like the recently released film *The Blair Witch Project*, whose 'staged reality', constructed out of faked documentary, was a clear influence, *Macbeth*'s style is marked out as skilful pastiche rather than probing reinvention of genre.[60] A similar adroitness is evident in the way Doran added *mise-en-scène* to his minimalist theatre production. The brick walls and metal stairs and pillars of the Roundhouse successfully suggested the cellars and air-raid shelters of a bombed-out city.

However this realism was undercut, dislocated, by a bleached, odd-angled surrealism reminiscent of such films as *Trainspotting*, especially in the high-angled shot of Lady Macbeth's soliloquy, framed by the white walls of a bathtub and partly spoken (in voiceover) under water, or the row of 'worst toilets in Scotland' that replaced the trapdoor hell mouth.[61] Derek Paget has detected a particular kind of 'Britishness' articulated in *Trainspotting* which makes it akin to the local concerns of Woolcock's estate films yet also 'readable' by international audiences: 'It focused on a social group marginalized in almost all senses, and its drug-taking "schemies" from the Edinburgh estates became metonymic of young, ghettoized and dispossessed city-dwellers everywhere.'[62] As with the borrowings from *The Blair Witch Project* it is this 'transnational' intertextuality, as well as the film's modish stylisation, that seems dominant in Doran's *Macbeth*, bleached as it is of more specific national or local connotations. Unlike Branagh's *Love's Labour's Lost*, in which, as Wray argues, the mix of film genres reveals the faultlines of a doomed modernist project to harmonise irreconcilable national and cultural difference, *Macbeth*, the product of video culture, sidesteps all such uncomfortable questions. Although the film's visual text imitates the immediacy of war footage, it is closer in genre to the kind of glossy television commercial that authenticates its multinational product through shots of the more photogenic wretched of the earth. Shakespeare is relocated in a postmodernist version of No Man's Land, constructed from the newly emerging conventions of reality TV.

The production's stated aim, to conscript Shakespeare as our contemporary, must be examined in this light. In Sher's words, it wanted to force its audience to become a witness: 'Accessories to the deed, you're complicit, you're involved, this is about you, about us.'[63] According to Corner, 'documentary minimalism' used in television drama can indeed powerfully position an audience, but rather as 'vicarious viewers to events... providing them with the *frisson* of social voyeurism'.[64] In many ways the television version's urgency of pace, achieved by its nervy camera work and editing, provided a successful equivalent to its intended main theatrical effect of fear, in a way comparable to the in-the-round intimacy captured by the circling camera and unlocalised setting of Nunn's *Macbeth*. But the sense of performance was very different. Where the Other Place *Macbeth* created a ritualistic circuit of power into which actors and audience were insidiously drawn, Doran's employment of reality TV conventions trapped the play's characters in a labyrinth of corridors and dead ends reminiscent of a game show maze, competing for a prize less and less worth the cost of the contest, constantly aware of a hidden mocking audience. When Macbeth spoke in direct address to the camera he had the mixed cynicism and bravado of a contestant about to be voted off the show. In the theatre Sher left the stage on the line 'signifying nothing', sometimes almost walking right out of the auditorium. In the film he opened a fire door letting a shocking burst of natural light and traffic noise into what had become, despite its initially realist feel, an artificial world. But this was achieved as much by film intertextuality as by televisual means – or rather its filming reflected the hybrid styles and blurred genres of current documentary television in which, with the resources of digital 'film-effects', the video camera can film 'like a movie camera'.

It thus marks a significant development in what Robert Shaughnessy has termed 'the mutating RSC's house style' under the influence of a 'sustained preoccupation with film-culture'.[65] If, as Cynthia Marshall argues of Matthew Warchus's 1997 *Hamlet*, this cinematic emphasis strips away political meaning to advance 'a universalized human subject with whom the majority of his viewers would identify',[66] Sher's *Macbeth* is equally, though differently, depoliticised. Doran's preferred model of tragic subjectivity is no longer the hero of classic Hollywood narrative but anyone fleetingly captured by the surveillance cameras that police our streets and spy on and record our peaceful or violent encounters. As Jameson observes, 'mechanical depersonalization (or decentring of the subject) goes even further in the new medium, where the auteurs themselves are dissolved along with the spectator'.[67] Doran's *Macbeth* is so saturated by the spectrum of media images and genres that flicker and hybridise across our screens worldwide, that there can be no 'collision', no distancing, finally no history. Instead the play is recontextualised, not in the 'real' of the contemporary political violence it claims to represent and seek to make its audience witness, but rather in Baudrillard's realm of the simulacrum, where wars never really happened.

Recontextualising Shakespeare in a globalised culture might seem to require a cartography in which Britain takes its place at the edges rather than the centre of any new map of the Shakespearian world. Nonetheless it would be politically naïve to ignore the impact that 'British Shakespeare' can still exercise far from its own shores through the export of its cultural products, especially those of its national broadcasting institutions. Globalisation not only sets local and international identities and needs in constant, sometimes catastrophic, collision, but requires that we consider how these identities are re-played by the developing connections of new and old technologies. If video has helped construct postmodern Shakespeare, we can also identify two versions of postcolonialism in Woolcock's and Doran's *Macbeths*. In Woolcock's films, as Catherine Silverstone suggests of 'settler Shakespeare' in New Zealand, 'local' performances open the route to an interrogation of the colonising force of Shakespeare within his 'native' culture, but also provide the means by which the Shakespearean text is transposed in the service of a project to illuminate the social and political forces at work in 'darkest' Britain. Like Branagh's *Love's Labour's Lost*, Doran's *Macbeth* reflects metatelevisually on 'the shift from staid, televisual productions of Shakespeare to looser, more inventive and restless modes of appropriation'.[68] But since it sources its politics from the imagery of the international media market, it ultimately offers the same view as that articulated by the Home Office Minister, Paul Boateng, speaking of the Histories.

> I came across the plays when I was growing up in Ghana and they seemed relevant there... English people should celebrate the fact that they have not needed to have the flag-waving patriotism of more historically repressed countries. We should be proud that England has always been outward-looking and proud of the fact that Shakespeare is a global figure.[69]

This Blairite vision of Shakespeare as peace ambassador for the new world order is enacted in the controversial policy for the RSC's future development unveiled by Adrian Noble in the autumn of 2001. The performance spaces of the Barbican in London and The Other Place in Stratford will give way to virtual theatre.

> If RSC directors in the future want to use a found space in London or warehouse in New York, I want people to be able to access that experience in Stratford. If we want to film productions, or use performance in webcasts as part of our education work, I want us to use one of our Stratford auditoria... This new morphing is crucial if a new generation of artists is to keep it fresh and innovative.[70]

As the RSC prepares to colonise the brave new world of interactivity now may be the time to stop and ask which performances will be memorialised and 'morphed' through video and digital documentation. It is clear that the recording of the RSC's new television *Macbeth* is likely to have as long a video shelf-life as its predecessor. Perhaps it will be longer if the British government ever goes ahead with the proposed *Culture Online*, which promises to schoolchildren and adults alike open (and international) access to, and interaction with, the riches of the British cultural treasure-house.[71] The RSC's need and readiness to be globally entrepreneurial will lead it to turn more and more of its performances into virtual products and *Macbeth*, with its rent-a-war look, surface contemporaneity, and fashionable postmodern reflexivity is likely to fare well in the world market. Yet this scarcely seems to be what Bogdanov meant when he called for the capture of the Internet for political Shakespeare.[72] The deliberate localism and generic hybridity of *Macbeth on the Estate* may make it closer to what both he and Holderness would view as potentially radical television Shakespeare. But as broadcast drama in a documentary mode (as opposed to 'documentarised drama'), one which deliberately locates itself in the specifics of British multiculturalism, rather than the generalities of media culture, and also offering a level of violence likely to be deemed unsuitable for the educational market, this production is unlikely to reach a worldwide audience, either by video or webcast. Here, as much as in the interpretations and generic choices offered by the versions discussed, we can observe the global politics of performance at work.

Notes and references

I am grateful to Penny Woolcock, Seb Grant of Illuminations and my colleagues Jeremy Bubb, Jen Harvie and Jeremy Ridgman for their assistance in providing information used in this paper.

1. Fredric Jameson, *Postmodernism, or, The Cultural Logic of Late Capitalism* (London and New York: Verso, 1991) 76.
2. Michèle Willems, 'Video and its Paradoxes,' *The Cambridge Companion to Shakespeare on Film*, ed. Russell Jackson (Cambridge: Cambridge University Press, 2000) 45.
3. Willems, 'Video' 41, 42, 45.
4. Jameson, *Postmodernism* 73.
5. Jameson, *Postmodernism* 75.
6. The Open University/BBC Shakespeare Multimedia Research Project has produced a video based on performances of *As You Like It*, together with an interactive CD-ROM on which some of the video material has been re-edited to allow 'the student/user to reorder and re-edit video sequences from live performance, in the process of learning about the distinction between live theatre and theatre on video' (see the Project web-site at *http://www.open.ac.uk/OU/Academic/Arts/shakespr.htm*). The Shakespeare Electronic Archive at the Massachusetts Institute of Technology originated in a project to link a variety of electronic texts of the plays with film versions on

CD-ROM or other local storage media, enabling students to produce multimedia essays and presentations combining text, video and other media. Work is continuing to expand this 'locally-delivered' archive whilst also exploring the 'Web's potential to make accessible Shakespearean materials that reside at different institutions around the world' to bring together texts, recorded performances, films and artwork related to Shakespeare in a 'virtual institute.' See Lee Ridgeway 'Teaching an Old Bard New Tricks: Shakespeare Electronic Archive,' *i/s* 15:1 (September/October 1999), *http://htf-puppy.mit.edu/research/shakespeare/index.html*.

7. *Changing Stages*, directed by Richard Eyre (UK, BBC2 2001).

8. Kenneth S. Rothwell, *A History of Shakespeare on Screen* (Cambridge: CUP, 1999) 122.

9. See Gary Taylor, 'Afterward: The Incredible Shrinking Shakespeare,' *Shakespeare and Appropriation*, ed. Christy Desmet and Robert Sawyer (London: Routledge, 1999) 201, for the view that this reliance on the 'dreary' education market is evidence of the inexorable decline of Shakespeare's global prestige.

10. John Corner, *The Art of Record: a Critical Introduction to Documentary* (Manchester: Manchester University Press, 1996) 2.

11. Marvin Carlson, 'The Theatre Event and Filmic Documentation,' *Degrés* IV: 48 (Winter 1986) 12.

12. Marco de Marinis, 'A Faithful Betrayal of Performance: Notes on the Use of Video in Theatre,' *New Theatre Quarterly* 1:4 (November 1985) 348.

13. Corner, *The Art of Record* 2.

14. Stella Bruzzi, *New Documentary: a Critical Introduction* (London: Routledge, 2000) 153.

15. Bruzzi, *New Documentary* 153–4.

16. *Shakespeare on the Estate*, directed by Penny Woolcock (UK, BBC2 1994), *Macbeth on the Estate*, directed by Penny Woolcock (UK, BBC2 1997).

17. *Macbeth* directed by Gregory Doran (UK, Illuminations for the RSC and Channel 4, 2000). Illuminations was co-founded by the media theorist and practitioner John Wyver and reflects his longstanding commitment to aligning the arts with digital technologies. Wyver, who co-produced *Macbeth* with Seb Grant, was a consultant for the specially commissioned Report by Charles Leadbeater, in which the *Culture Online* project was first proposed. See Charles Leadbeater, *Culture Online: the Vision*, report written for the Department for Culture, Media and Sport (2000), available online at *http://www.gov.org.uk*.

18. Thomas Cartelli, *Repositioning Shakespeare: National Formations, Postcolonial Appropriations* (London: Routledge, 1999) 13.

19. Graham Holderness, 'Radical Potentiality and Institutional Closure,' *Political Shakespeare*, ed. Alan Sinfield and Jonathan Dollimore (Manchester: Manchester University Press, 1985) 191.

20. Cartelli, *Repositioning Shakespeare* 15.

21. Cartelli, *Repositioning Shakespeare* 17.

22. *When the Dog Bites*, directed by Penny Woolcock (UK, Trade Films 1988).

23. Corner, *Art of Record* 139.

24. Corner, *Art of Record* 140. This last device would also be at the heart of Woolcock's later films *Tina Goes Shopping* (UK, Channel 4 1999) and *Tina*

Takes a Break (UK, Channel 4 2001) which build dramatic narratives around the real lives of inhabitants of a Leeds housing estate.

25. Corner, *Art of Record* 144.
26. Corner, *Art of Record* 142, 143, 149, 150. There was much hostility to the finished film from some of the inhabitants of Consett (see Woolcock, interviewed in Corner, *Art of Record* 153–4).
27. Penny Woolcock, personal correspondence with the author (September 2001).
28. Graham Holderness, 'Boxing the Bard: Shakespeare and Television,' *The Shakespeare Myth* (Manchester: Manchester University Press, 1988) 182.
29. Michael Bogdanov, 'Shakespeare is Dead' Lecture, *Shakespeare for The Millennium* series, BBC Radio 3 and the Literature Department of the Royal Festival Hall (1999), see *http://www.bbc.co.uk*. The initial idea of planting a 'Shakespearian expert' in an estate was Woolcock's own, and she chose Bogdanov 'because he was the only one who was prepared to "fail" and seemed genuinely interested in how people might react' (Woolcock, personal correspondence).
30. All quotations from Shakespeare are from *The Riverside Shakespeare*, ed. G. Blakemore Evans (Boston: Houghton Mifflin, 1974).
31. Woolcock, personal correspondence.
32. Beatrix Campbell, *Goliath: Britain's Dangerous Places* (London: Methuen, 1993).
33. Campbell, *Goliath* 319, 321.
34. The killing of three-year old James Bulger by Robert Thomson and Jon Venables in 1993 had a huge impact on the British public imagination, not least because the abduction from a Liverpool shopping centre was captured on security cameras. At the subsequent trial both the media and the judge made much of the possible influence of their viewing of horror films on the boys' actions. Controversy over the length of sentencing kept public debate about the case alive after the Conservative Home Secretary, Michael Howard, increased the tariff imposed by the trial judge. After appeal to the European Court of Human Rights, and a consequent ruling by Lord Chief Justice Woolf in 2000, Thomson and Venables were granted permission to seek parole, rather than being transferred to a Young Offenders' Prison, and were released from secure accommodation in 2001 and given new identities. They now live under constant threat of death from vigilantes, with a legal injunction in place which prevents the British media from publishing anything that might identify them. There are many web-sites devoted to the case but for a thoughtful account of the trial and public reaction in the context of a broader concern with childhood in contemporary society see Blake Morrison, *As If* (Cambridge: Granta, 1997).
35. Woolcock, personal correspondence. Campbell suggests that a 'new myth about children as criminals' displaced awareness of masculinity as a factor in the riots and estate crime of the early 1990s. See Campbell, *Goliath* 204.
36. Nicholas Barker's documentary series *Signs of the Time* (UK, BBC1 1992) interrogated the taste and interior design of selected individuals with forensic minimalism, characterised by 'a fetishistic intensity, mesmerised by superficialities, appearance and detail.' The 'sofa shot' was a feature throughout. See Bruzzi, *New Documentary* 158.

37. See, for example, *Words for Battle* (UK, Crown Film Unit 1941) and *Diary for Timothy* (UK, Crown Film Unit 1945), which has a commentary written by E. M. Forster.

38. In the summer of 2001 rioting broke out in several towns in Yorkshire and Lancashire where there were large Asian minorities. There were conflicting views at the time as to whether the causes were racial or religious conflict, or the disaffection of young working-class males of all ethnic groups, or a mixture of all three.

39. Campbell, *Goliath* 323.

40. This projection became literal in *Shakespeare on the Estate* when the 1936 film of *Romeo and Juliet* was beamed onto a tower block wall as the balcony scene was replayed in the contemporary argot of the young actors.

41. Woolcock, personal correspondence. She also describes how uneasy the BBC was with the film's stylistic innovation right up to the final edit.

42. Antony Sher, *Beside Myself* (London: Hutchinson, 2001) 334.

43. *Macbeth*, directed by Phillip Casson (UK, Thames Television, 1979).

44. Rothwell 101.

45. See Barbara Hodgdon's analysis of the 'Bradleyan moral characterology' underlying Ian McKellen's 'Leavisite' reading of his own performance of the 'Tomorrow' speech on the documentary arts programme *The South Bank Show* (Channel 4 1979), in 'The Critic, the Poor Player, Prince Hamlet, and the Lady in the Dark,' *Shakespeare Reread: the Texts in New Contexts*, ed. Ross MacDonald (Ithaca: Cornell University Press, 1994) 272.

46. Amin was popularly associated with grisly quasi-magical acts of cannibalism, and the use of 'voodoo' signifiers in Nunn's production suggests a disquieting unconscious equation of evil, blackness and Africa.

47. Sher, *Beside Myself* 336–7, 340.

48. Sher, *Beside Myself* 341. This 'war for all seasons' was also invoked in the Programme Notes by the BBC journalist Fergal Keane, who is best known for studied and personalised 'radio essays' from and on the war-zones of the world.

49. Despite being an unpopular and controversial choice with Johannesburg audience, due equally to its unfamiliarity, provocative violence, and above all the use of local accents rather than 'British Shakespeare,' *Titus Andronicus* was filmed for South African television. See Antony Sher and Gregory Doran, *Woza Shakespeare! Titus Andronicus in South Africa* (London: Methuen, 1996).

50. Gregory Doran, *Woza Shakespeare!* 88.

51. Sher, *Beside Myself* 342.

52. *The Leader, His Driver, and the Driver's Wife*, directed by Nicholas Broomfield (South Africa, 1991). See Bruzzi, *New Documentary* 175–8.

53. Nick Curtis, Review of *Macbeth* at Stratford 17 November, repr. *Theatre Record* 1–18 (November 1999) 1524.

54. On the crisis at the RSC, see for example Lyn Gardner, 'Now buy the T-shirt ...,' *Guardian* (27 February 2001), Fiachra Gibbons, 'Dramatic changes afoot as RSC looks to the stars,' *Guardian* (25 May 2001), and 'RSC director defends changes,' *Guardian* (26 May 2001). On Doran as a possible successor to Noble see Michael Billington, 'The Bard's biggest fan,' interview with Gregory Doran, *Guardian* (27 April 2000).

55. Seb Grant, interview with the author, 14 July 2001.

56. This was transmitted in the same *Performance* season as *Shakespeare on the Estate* in March to April 1997. This season was billed as consisting of televised versions of theatrical hits and Woolcock's film was the only exception to this rule.

57. Sher, *Beside Myself* 346.

58. 'C.A.', 'Macbeth the Movie,' *Soho Independent* (January 2001) *http://www.sohoindependent.com*.

59. Grant, interview with the author.

60. *The Blair Witch Project*, directed by Eduardo Sanchez and Daniel Myrick (USA, Haxan Films 1998).

61. *Trainspotting*, directed by Danny Boyle (UK, Miramax 1996).

62. Derek Paget, 'Speaking Out: The Transformations of *Trainspotting*,' *Adaptations: from Text to Screen, Screen to Text*, ed. Imelda Whelehan and Deborah Cartmell (London: Routledge, 1999) 129.

63. Sher, *Beside Myself* 348.

64. Corner, *Art of Record* 32–3.

65. Robert Shaughnessy, 'The Last Post: *Henry V*, War Culture and the Postmodern Shakespeare,' *Theatre Survey* 39:1 (May 1998): 45, 46.

66. Cynthia Marshall, 'Sight and Sound: Two Models of Shakespearean Subjectivity on the British Stage,' *Shakespeare Quarterly* 51 (2000): 357.

67. Jameson, *Postmodernism* 74.

68. See Ramona Wray, 'The Singing Shakespearean' in this volume, p. 154.

69. See Vanessa Thorpe, 'The Bard slays St George as national symbol,' *Observer* (22 April 2001).

70. Adrian Noble, 'All's Well,' *Guardian* (3 October 2001). Other controversial plans included demolishing the 1930s theatre at Stratford and building a 'Shakespeare village' alongside a new 'audience friendly' auditorium. In April 2002, after much criticism of his project, and the successful opening of his musical *Chitty Chitty Bang Bang* in the West End, Noble announced his resignation as artistic director of the RSC. It was suggested by a number of commentators that Noble was leaving in order to be free to undertake the worldwide directing commitments demanded by a globally franchised musical.

71. Leadbeater, *Culture Online: the Vision*.

72. Bogdanov, 'Shakespeare is Dead.'

7
Julius Caesar in Interesting Times

Jean Chothia

Orson Welles' notoriety as a showman has tended to blur the political and theatrical significance of *Caesar*, his 1937 Mercury Theatre adaptation of Shakespeare's play.[1] As part of the enquiry into the remaking of Shakespeare's plays in different media and performance conditions, I want to explore the circumstances and effects of Welles' adaptation and to make some comparisons with the next notable American transposition of the play, Joseph L. Mankiewicz' 1953 Hollywood film *Julius Caesar*.[2] As well as their origin in Shakespeare's play, these two versions have in common John Houseman, as their producer. Collaborator with Welles in the 1930s on a number of avant-garde productions for Project 891 of the Federal Theatre Project, Houseman founded Mercury Theatre with him to enable their work to continue independently when, in 1937, under government directive, Federal Theatre withdrew support for the Project 891 production of Marc Blitzstein's political musical *The Cradle Will Rock*.[3] *Caesar* was their first Mercury production. In 1953, alienated from Welles since *Citizen Kane* (1941), and now in Hollywood as a senior producer with MGM, Houseman was instigator and very closely involved in the making of Mankiewicz' film. He is one of the chief sources of information about both productions.[4]

Presented at very different moments in American public and political life, the one in the context of the American New Deal and the rise of European totalitarianism, the other in full Cold War, these adaptations offer vivid demonstrations of ways in which a revival of a classic text might reflect on and itself be shaped by the emotional currents and political preoccupations of the specific time and place in which it is produced. They raise sharply questions of what is being probed, over-simplified or avoided in a given production. My focus is on the staging of the crowd scenes, and, in particular, 3.3, the killing of Cinna the poet.

Not played between 1719 and the end of the nineteenth century, and often eliminated since, the inclusion or omission of this scene and, if played, how it is played, is one of the prime indicators of the kind of reading of the play a modern director is offering. Bridges Adams' Stratford production, for example, three years before Welles', was one which, despite John Ripley's description of it as 'the first uncut version since the Restoration',[5] omitted the Cinna scene.

Discussing the film in *Sight and Sound* in 1953, Houseman wrote:

> While never deliberately exploiting the historical parallels, there were certain emotional patterns arising from political events of the immediate past that we were prepared to evoke – Hitler, Mussolini and Ciano at the Brenner Pass; the assemblage at Munich; Stalin and Ribbentrop signing the Pact... These sights are as much part of our contemporary consciousness – in the black and white of news and TV screens – as, to Elizabethan audiences – were the personal and political conflicts and tragedies of Essex, Bacon, Leicester and the Cecils.[6]

Lurking here is both recall and repudiation of the Mercury production. Sub-titled 'Death of a Dictator', Welles' adaptation did 'deliberately exploit the historical parallels' by giving Caesar's faction fascist costume and gesture; evoking the Nuremberg Rally with columns of light beamed upwards from the stage floor; echoing Mussolini's Rome and its citizens in those of Caesar, and casting as Caesar an actor (Joseph Holland) whose resemblance to Mussolini was striking. At least as significantly, Welles had also cut and rearranged the text into a conscious exploration of tormented liberal resistance, primarily in the person of Brutus, failing against the manipulations of ruthless power politics with its capacity to generate hysteria in the mob.

This was not the first time that the contemporary moment had led to a fresh perception of the political potency of this particular play. In 1808, during an earlier period of European upheaval, explaining why it had 'been thought adviseable for some years past, that this tragedy should not appear upon the stage', Mrs Inchbald, introducing her edition of the play, suggested that 'when the circumstances of certain periods make certain incidents of history most interesting, those are the very seasons to interdict their exhibition'.[7] Just as George III's madness had led to the banning of *King Lear* from the English stage, so, she makes clear, in the aftermath of the French Revolution, a perceived equivalence in this play meant that 'till the time of the world's repose, the lovers of drama will, probably, be compelled to accept of real conspiracies, assassinations, and the slaughter of war, in lieu of such spectacles ably counterfeited.'[8]

But it was not merely analogy with revolution and regicide in France that kept the play off the English stage throughout the Revolution and Revolutionary War. That suggestion of the ably-counterfeited being at least as inflammatory as real events, is one that has underlain much theatrical censorship. Mrs Inchbald is succinct. A ban is appropriate:

> when men's thoughts are deeply engaged on public events, when historical occurrences, of a similar kind, are only held proper for the contemplation of such minds as know how to distinguish, and to appreciate, the good and evil with which they abound. Such discriminating judges do not compose the whole audience of a playhouse.[9]

The danger is seen to lie with the stirred-up responses of the undiscriminating: stage representation of an insurgent Roman mob might be as dangerous as news of an excited Parisian populace storming the Bastille; the demagoguery of a stage Antony, as reports of a real Robespierre or Danton. The power of dramatic performance can crystallise imaginative response to the moment, but the salient moment can also quicken perceptions about the play. Recalling Dr Johnson's coolness to *Julius Caesar*, Mrs Inchbald concludes that had he 'lived in the present time, perhaps this very "adherence to the true story" would have excited that warmth and that interest' he had found lacking.[10]

Previous to this, in the English eighteenth century, the crowd scenes of Shakespeare's play, performed by the company comedians, had not seemed significant. Ancient Rome had been a source for contemporary dramatic tragedies, such as Addison's *Cato*, which centred on noble, self-denying heroes, torn between duty and personal feeling, and *Julius Caesar* was taken to be the tragedy of Brutus, driven to betray his friend for the good of the state. The blow struck by Brutus in the assassination scene made the first dramatic climax; the second, and the crucial turning point of the play, from Betterton's Restoration production onwards, came with the 4.3. quarrel between Brutus and Cassius. The late eighteenth-century British proscription of the play, therefore, marked a new recognition of forces within the unadapted text. Intriguingly, pre-revolutionary France had been ahead of England in perception of the vulgar and potentially inflammatory nature of Shakespeare's writing. Discussing *Julius Caesar*, Voltaire surmised that 'perhaps the French would not permit one to present on their stage a Chorus composed of artisans and plebeian Romans',[11] and Le Tourneur, dedicating his 1776 translation of the plays to Louis XVI, decried Shakespeare's 'penchant for introducing the rabble onto the stage in trivial scenes', which reflected 'the libertarian and republican tendencies of the English', so unlike Louis' own 'quiet and obedient people'.[12]

In the twentieth century Shakespeare's play had been tentatively politicised in a number of non-English language productions before Welles turned his attention to it. At the Odéon in Paris, in 1906, André Antoine had associated the play with more recent events when he injected realism into his production of *Jules César* by using methods of staging the crowd similar to those he had developed in staging the events of 1789 in the Goncourts' *La Patrie en Danger* (1889) and the Silesian uprising in Hauptmann's *The Weavers* (1893).[13] Two Eastern European versions of Shakespeare's play in the inter-war years had shadowed advancing dictatorship in their stage effects. Leon Schiller's 1928 expressionist version for the Polish Theatre in Warsaw kept its crowd on stage, using them as an abstract mass whose movements signified, for example, both the play's literal storm and a metaphoric storm brewing. The Czech National Theatre production in Prague in 1936, directed by Jiri Frejka, worked images of totalitarianism into its set. Taking the lead from Cassius' 'why man, he doth bestride the narrow world like a colossus', the designer, Frantisek Tröster, included massive pieces of statuary and a huge representation of Caesar's head. Following Caesar's murder, the statues split, so that the Cinna scene was played against Caesar's ruins. Although the disbanding of the company after the Munich Agreement of 1938 prevented further political signifying, the kind of force and danger commentators picked up in these productions could believably have led to the flight of the conspirators and the unplanned murder of Cinna, which each of these productions retained.[14]

The excitement Welles' production stimulated demonstrates something of Mrs Inchbald's sense of informing 'warmth'.[15] As well as making the stir Welles indubitably relished, his production brought the political alertness of Central Europe to English-language Shakespeare. Barry Jackson's introduction of modern dress Shakespeare with his 1925 Birmingham Repertory Company *Hamlet* had suggested a way of quickening audience attention that had soon been imitated on the American as well as the British stage. Welles' own 'voodoo *Macbeth*' for the Negro Theatre Unit of Federal Theatre, which set the play on Haiti in the early nineteenth century, drew huge and enthusiastic audiences when it played in Harlem and on tour in 1936. But until early 1937, the Roman plays had remained fixed in the costume and landscape of Ancient

Rome. Herbert Beerbohm Tree, indeed, had cited the play as self-evident proof of the need for precise historical locating when he ridiculed William Poel's Elizabethanism, demanding, 'How could they do *Julius Caesar* in this fashion? – the play would lose its reality – its direct appeal – the forum is the forum, a structure, just as Caesar is Caesar, a man;' and William Archer, while acknowledging that Elizabethan dress might work for *Twelfth Night,* declared that it would be 'ludicrous' for *Julius Caesar.*[16] Antoine's and the Eastern European inter-war productions were all toga versions. Welles' *Caesar* was not just another modern dress Shakespeare. Probably taking his cue from an unacknowledged production by the Delaware Federal Theatre which, shortly before his, was staged 'with fascist trappings',[17] he not only used costume as a suggestive signifier but pursued the analogy through many aspects of the production. Although all the language spoken was Shakespeare's, Welles cut and rearranged the text to make firmer links with pressing concerns of his own present.

Shakespeare's plebeians in *Julius Caesar* have only some one hundred lines between them, but in those is registered, in 1.1, native wit and individuality; in 3.2, manipulability and mercurial shifting which can alter the tide of history, and, in 3.3, the Cinna scene, a startling capacity for unbridled violence. Had Shakespeare been only concerned with heroes, the play could easily have begun, as it did in its eighteenth-century adaptation, with Marullus' attack on the foolhardiness of the plebeians, but Marullus' mouth-filling 'Wherefore rejoice? What conquest brings he home?'[18] is *preceded* by dialogue and a more direct human encounter. As first a carpenter, and then a cobbler are identified and exchange verbal sallies with the Tribunes, not only the faces but the consciousness of two of the 'worse than senseless things' are glimpsed by the audience. As so often in Shakespeare, such foregrounding enables a more complex perceiving.

The tenor of Welles' production, and his free approach to the ordering and cutting of speeches, was announced in his staging of the opening scene. First, with the curtainless stage darkened, Blitzstein's 'Fascist March' sounded. Then the lights came up on Caesar, his military entourage and a group of citizens, not in a conventional set but on a series of Appia-style graded platforms in front of a bare, dried-blood coloured stage wall. Caesar, in a line poached from Casca at 1.2.14 of the Folio text, spoke first, ordering 'Bid every noise be still.' In Welles' version, as in the Folio's second scene, the line heralded the soothsayer's 'Beware the Ides of March' (1.2.18), which was spoken out of the gloom at the back of the stage, but the sequence was fundamentally altered by the change of speaker and occasion. Only after the warning and the departure of the crowd with Caesar did an abbreviated version of the exchange between Marullus and the Carpenter and Cobbler take place, but the individuation of the Cobbler, now deprived of his best jokes, had been forfeited. It was important to Welles' scheme that the audience was not alerted to humour or to separate consciousnesses within the crowd.

We don't know how the Chamberlain's Men played the forum scene. We do know that, with a company of some dozen plus a few hired men, there cannot have been anything resembling the vast crowds that inhabited the late nineteenth/early twentieth-century stages. Given what is known about direct address, it is hard to imagine the orations in 1599 being delivered otherwise than out to the yard, with members of the stage crowd between orator and audience. This was precisely what Welles did with the scene in 1937, as production photographs show.[19] Antony stood, like the European dictators in countless contemporary news images, on a raised platform with flags and banners behind him, lit from below, and casting a menacing shadow on the wall behind. The stage crowd was placed immediately in front of him, between his rostrum and the audience, so that his words were addressed directly to the audience and the on-stage crowd, both of whom had to look up and up-stage to him, as he confidently outsmarted Brutus. Previous to this, even in the densely populated productions of the Meininger (1874), Beerbohm Tree (1897) and Antoine (1906), the scene was fully contained behind the fourth wall. The speeches of Brutus and Antony were directed entirely to the *on*-stage crowd; often, indeed, with the orator side-face to the audience.[20] Such an effect is necessarily pictorial. In his early essay, 'On Staging Shakespeare and on Shakespeare's Stage', Welles had expressed his passion for 'that peculiarly pure theatre' for which Shakespeare wrote.[21] Although elsewhere, unhappy with contemplative monologues, he recast them as dialogue, here he recreated the Elizabethan practice of direct audience address and, doing so, retrieved for his audience something of the experience, not just the picture, of oratory.

In the Mankiewicz film, in a different, and for the participants a more immediately and personally threatening cultural situation, togas are back and so is monumental staging. The sets clearly say 'Ancient Rome' but, at least as clearly, they say 'studio-built' (built, incidentally, for *Quo Vadis*), and a crowd of more than a thousand crams into the Forum.[22] Houseman and Mankiewicz insisted on using black and white film stock to distance the film from the current vogue for Roman epics (and perhaps to assert its cultural significance by associating it with David Lean's acclaimed Dickens' films?).[23] But not only set and costume, but also the invocation of classical authority through the scrolled quotation from Plutarch which frames the film, serve to pull it into the sphere of Hollywood's Ancient Rome and away from its political present.[24]

For much of the forum scene, the cinema audience's view of the crowd is from over the orator's shoulder and, although each is often seen in close-up, neither Marlon Brando as Antony, nor James Mason as Brutus, ever looks directly into the camera. Houseman claimed that cinema allowed a larger scale than was possible in the theatre but, also, greater intimacy, because of the use of close-up. The film cuts Antony's 'Now let it work! Mischief, thou art afoot, / Take thou what course thou wilt' (3.2.253–4), at the end of the forum scene, replacing it with a close-up on Brando's smile (see Figure 7.1). This, Jack Jorgens claims in his account of the film, 'says it all'.[25] I am not so sure. Words are more evidently denotative and, here, Brando's earnest face during his oration, his tone of voice, as well as camera angles and crowd response, have already shifted the bias of feeling to Antony. The smile has to work very

Figure 7.1   Marlon Brando as Antony in Mankiewicz' *Julius Caesar*

hard if it is to alert the cinema audience to machiavellian intentions behind his oratory. (Indeed, the credit on the currently available video version of the film, which reads 'and Brando, in a surprise casting, portrays defender of the Republic, Mark Antony', presses in quite the opposite direction.)[26]

The activity of Welles' crowd was much commented on in reviews, the fullest appreciation coming from John Mason Brown:

> In groupings that are of the fluid, stressful virtuoso sort one usually has to journey to Russia to see, Mr Welles proves himself a brilliant innovator in his deployment of his principals and the movement of his crowds...he keeps drumming the meaning of his play into our minds by the scuffling of his mobs when they prowl in the shadows, or by the herd-like thunder of their feet when they run as one threatening body.[27]

The effect described there is evidently of the theatre. In the film, the huge crowd rushes wildly away, to be seen in long-shot smashing and burning. John Gielgud, Cassius in the film, recalled the crowd 'filling the screen at one moment or receding at will to a respectful distance', to 'allow the characters to fill the foreground, dominating Rome and its unruly citizens with ease'.[28] But at whose will is the crowd receding and dominating? For all the claimed verisimilitude, the spectator of the film is constantly aware that while the manipulation is claimed as Antony's, in reality it belongs with the selecting and moving camera. This is made even more apparent when a quotation from Plutarch, announcing the flight of the conspirators, is superimposed on the scene of smashing and burning. In the theatre, not only does the audience's gaze seem freer but, since presentation not verisimilitude was what Welles' staging offered, the movement and the thunder of feet of his thoroughly rehearsed and carefully orchestrated crowd of sixteen evidently carried conviction as a representation of the action the oratory had fired. The paradox of theatre is that it allows intense emotional response to coexist with recognition and relish of highly achieved artifice, on the part of character and of actor; of playwright and of director. Its audience is made party to the multi-layered nature of theatre. Mason Brown acknowledged this when he concluded his account of Welles' crowd manipulation with the comment, 'it is pure theatre; vibrant, unashamed and enormously effective.'

Welles' script reveals that his leading actors, who previously had played the conspirators, doubled as the speaking members of the crowd.

The responses, divided among them, seemed wild but, as a brief extract demonstrates, were carefully patterned to echo, contrast and overlap each other:

> *Antony*
> I fear I wrong the honourable men,
> Whose daggers have stabbed Caesar; I do fear it.
> *Sherman*   *Willard*   *Reid*
> Honorable men! Murderers!   Honorable men.
> *Mowry*   *Schnabel*
> Traitors!   Villains!
> *Cotten*
> The testament, read us the testament.
> *Lloyd*
> Read us the will!   (*A chant starts*)[29]

In the film, in contrast with the variousness of these cries and interjections, the camera for no apparent reason focuses repeatedly on four people, including the Cobbler and Carpenter of the opening scene. These four so bear the responsibility of voicing the shifting responses of the crowd in what is a careful adherence to the lines assigned by the Folio to four speaking Plebeians. There is confusion of form here: a resistance of the play-text to the cinematic medium. The Folio distribution of speeches, written for presentational performance, sits awkwardly with the assumptions inherent in the cinema's literalising use of a vast, quasi-realistic crowd. This is not a limitation of the cinematic medium as such: the confusion resides in the particular translation in this film of theatre script into cinema. (That memorable crowd scenes, with an interplay of the individual and the mass, can be created on screen is apparent in films as diverse as Alan Parker's *Evita*, where a particular observer convincingly draws the camera's attention because he comments on as well as participates in the crowd activity, and as Eisenstein's *Battleship Potemkin*, where, in the memorable Odessa Steps sequence, various individuals are successively featured within the mêlée and cross-cutting among them extends images that realistically would last one minute into five.[30] In such sequences, the director and camera have engaged in what might be appreciated as cinematic, not theatrical, artifice.)

The mistaking of Cinna the poet for Cinna the conspirator is told by Plutarch in his 'Lives' both of Caesar and of Brutus. In each, he states tersely that, the mistake having been made, the crowd killed Cinna in the market-place.[31] Shakespeare's placing of the killing immediately after the forum scene, which had been preceded by the killing of Caesar, provides a distorted reflection of the earlier death. What Shakespeare also adds to Plutarch, although the scene is only thirty-five lines long, is a representation of the ferocity of the crowd and the grim humour of an exchange that answers the defence of error with a mad logic, expressed in the devastating five-line exchange:

> *Third plebeian*: Your name, sir, truly.
> *Cinna*: Truly, my name is Cinna.
> *First plebeian*: Tear him to pieces, he's a conspirator!
> *Cinna*: I am Cinna the poet! I am Cinna the poet!
> *Fourth plebeian*: Tear him for his bad verses, tear him for his bad verses!
>
> (*Julius Caesar*, 3.3.26–30)

The scene was central to Welles' production. Extended by the repetition of lines and some importation of crowd commentary from *Coriolanus*, it became a fierce indictment of the mindless violence of those spurred on by demagogues. A circle of light picked out Cinna and those immediately surrounding him, to whom he showed the sheaves of poems he carried in his pockets, while shadowy figures in the surrounding darkness and off-stage voices chanted 'Kill. Slay.' The circle advanced step by step on the slight, suggestedly-Jewish, figure of Norman Lloyd, and, backed by more presences emerging from the shadows, closed in on him. Still crying 'I'm Cinna the Poet. The Poet,' he became one of the disappeared.

Whereas Welles' version of the scene, only finally established in dress rehearsal, was acclaimed as revelatory throughout the press,[32] in the MGM film it was shot but not used. Mankiewicz' script included graphic detail of the seizure and killing of the poet:

> The crowd is after him. Cinna trips and falls. He is caught by the heels screaming, down into the center of the Forum. From above and about camera, more citizens rush down into the Forum.
> Cinna's body is blotted from view by the mob as it smothers him within it...
> ...Cinna's body sprawls almost alone on the floor of the Forum.[33]

The sequence was not included in the final cut of the film. Instead, the camera moves from Brando's smile that 'says it all' to the mass activity of the milling citizens. The superimposition on the crowd scene of

Plutarch's mediating words further contains and curtails any horror that might reside in the images of mass hysteria, turning them literally into background before the film cuts to the proscription scene.

In Welles' version, the play became a warning against incipient total-itarianism, but also addressed a liberalism that resists but makes wrong decisions, allows the moment or force of an action to evaporate, is blind to the viciousness of power, and, putting faith in appeasement, as Brutus did in yielding the forum to Antony, lets slip the dogs of war. Reviewers commented on the quietness of Welles' own performance as Brutus – now far removed from the eighteenth-century self-denying hero – Stark Young in *The New Republic* thought him 'the prototype of a bewildered liberal', While Heywood Broun described him as 'the man who insists on fighting fire with a bucket brigade'.[34] Such a production threw out challenges: locally, to the Federal Theatre administrators who had bent before threats and withdrawn support for *The Cradle Will Rock*;[35] more widely, and most apparently, to democratic forces inert before the rise of European fascism, but also to subsequent theatre practitioners. When Bridges Adams had directed *Coriolanus* at Stratford-upon-Avon in 1933, only months after Hitler's seizure of power, he had consciously rejected any association of Shakespearean production with modern politics. Claiming to be the 'custodian of *the eternal values*', he declared it 'shock-ingly improper' if a theatre director 'turns his stage into a platform and takes sides in the temporal issues that divide us'.[36] Welles' *Caesar* had the effect of challenging mainstream English-language Shakespeare production, precisely by turning his stage into a platform for temporal issues. His staging was soon echoed in a production at the Festival Theatre, Cambridge, by Terence Gray in May 1938, and another by Henry Cass at the Embassy, London, in 1939, while in July 1938 one of the earliest BBC television Shakespeare productions put Caesar's faction into Italian military dress. The pursuit of the kind of equivalence Welles identified in his production has become common in subsequent staging of Shakespeare.

And this is what I want to consider in relation to Mankiewicz' film and Houseman's statement about it with which I began. I was intrigued to find the film described as 'a vigorous political thriller' in which contemporary audiences saw 'dilemmas (the rise of fascism, democracy threatened by rival forms of authoritarianism) reflected'.[37] My own repeated viewing does not lead me to see such dilemmas. What I see is an earnest attempt to put a revered stage play faithfully on film, with a bold mix of English classical actors, led by Gielgud, reprising his 1950 Stratford role of Cassius, and American movie stars, including, famously, Brando, his name just made as Stanley Kowalski in *A Streetcar Named Desire*.[38] Some of the speeches, including Brando's Antony in the forum scene and Gielgud's Cassius persuading Brutus, are compelling, but essentially they are star turns – it is the *actor*'s expressiveness that demands admiration, his command of the lines and the emotion. If there was such seeing as Houseman claims among 1950s audiences, perhaps it was because of the past association of Houseman, or of the play itself, with Welles. But, if so, the view was oddly retrospective and confused. Houseman's evocation of 'the Brenner Pass...Munich...the Pact' not only over-generalises, it distracts from the film's own immediate present. Had the Cinna scene been retained, it might have evoked the contemporary persecution of artists under totalitarian regimes; possibly, and more dangerously, it might have reminded audiences of hysteria and artistic persecution closer to home. What is striking when one sees the film now, is how little sense of the political climate of 1953 is evident in the film – except, of course, by decisive omission.

For these were the days of the House Un-American Activities Committee and Joseph McCarthy's investigations into communist infiltration of the American entertainment industry. Following the indictment of the 'Hollywood Ten' and the 1951–52 Congressional Hearings, when Hollywood had cravenly established a blacklist which denied employment to proscribed actors and directors (unless surreptitiously, under assumed names and without proper contracts), many, including Houseman, whose left-wing affiliations were recorded in FBI files, kept their heads down. Some left the country, among them Bertolt Brecht, Joseph Losey and Orson Welles, all three former associates of Houseman who, in Los Angeles in 1947, had produced Brecht's *Galileo* which had been directed, in close collaboration with the author, by Losey. Others, directors, actors and writers – Elia Kazan, Ronald Reagan, Budd Schulberg and John Dos Passos, among them – went before HUAC and named former colleagues as communists. Houseman's recurrence to an earlier politics; the film's return to togas and studio reproduction of Ancient Rome; the failure to use the Cinna scene (and the omission of the dark humour from the original scripting of it), all suggest an avoidance of issues that might have challenged the present moment.

Such avoidance is the more marked because historical analogy, a means already familiar in repressive European states, had simultaneously begun to be utilised by a few socially-committed artists, even in America, and was quickly picked up by audiences. In 1953, Arthur Miller, having had a script addressing corruption in the Brooklyn longshoremen's union rejected as 'anti-American' by Columbia Pictures because of his refusal to identify the gangsters as communists, had returned to the theatre to write *The Crucible*, his anti-McCarthy parable about witch-hunts and communal hysteria.[39] The previous year, *High Noon*, whose writer Carl Foreman was subsequently proscribed, had presented a hero, standing alone against bullying criminality, shaming and ashamed of the timidity of the townsfolk.[40]

No recontextualisation of Shakespeare, however seemingly depoliticised, is devoid of ideological implications. In 1950s Hollywood a Shakespeare play 'done straight', including notable Shakespearean actors and answering audience expectations of costume, set and verse speaking, could provide a gratifying sense of respectability for the studio and, indeed, for Houseman. The acclamation that had greeted Laurence Olivier's films of *Henry V* and *Hamlet* would be welcome to any studio and had, moreover, shown that Shakespeare could win Oscars and need not even lose money.[41] Only Hollywood's fourth 'full-scale studio feature-length Shakespeare' since the beginning of cinema,[42] the MGM *Julius Caesar* had its own claims to make – principally, perhaps, that Hollywood was open to the products of high culture and could handle them responsibly.

Indubitably, certain textual details of Shakespeare's play are registered freshly in Mankiewicz' film. Jealousy and suspicion are encapsulated in the camera's tracking down from the conspiring Brutus and Cassius onto Caesar's triumph and then back up, with Caesar's glance to them at their high window, before his 'Let me have men about me that are fat' (1.2.192). The co-existence of power with infirmity is neatly emphasised in Caesar's drawing over of Antony, between his ringing declaration 'for always I am Caesar', and 'come on my right hand, for this ear is deaf' (1.2.212–13). And the essentially wordless sequence of the rising storm, in which the screen darkens and leaves swirl around a deserted Roman square before the conspirators emerge from the shadows, captures something of the thrill of contemporary *film noir* and gives a glimpse of what might have been. But, for the most part, as Jack Jorgens admits in his largely sympathetic account of Mankiewicz' film, 'in seeking restraint and distancing effect, Mankiewicz often succeeded only in making scenes bland and visually dull'.[43] Indeed, Houseman's 1953 discussion of the film in *Sight and Sound* is followed on the next page of the journal by images from Carol Reed's *The Man Between*.[44] These are transfixing where those illustrating Houseman's *Julius Caesar* article are not. Reed's film, which is concerned with the smuggling of refugees from the east to the west in Cold War Berlin, is no match for his 1949 *The Third Man* and is now largely forgotten,[45] but the stills retain an immediacy that is the more startling because Mankiewicz' Brutus, James Mason, figures also as Reed's smuggler in *The Man Between*.

This matter of the stills raises a curious point in relation to discussion of the 1953 film and the 1937 stage production. Whereas every play performance involves a live – and potentially dangerous – interchange with the audience that makes it constantly subject to modification and change, a film is finished at the point of reception. The audience will respond but their response does nothing to alter the fixed form of the work. The fixity means that, while theatrical performance is ephemeral, a film can be viewed subsequent to its first run. What does change is the viewing situation, as the film is transposed to the small screen, in study or living room, or seen in the cinema in an ageing print, perhaps as part of an 'Historic Shakespeare' season or in a retrospective of one of its stars. Changed, too, is the audience, and its cultural moment.

A stage production cannot be retrieved even this far. It can only be aimed at from the traces it leaves. Because of the impact this particular production made, however, the traces are unusually strong, with a remarkable amount of surrounding material surviving. The archive to which we do have access includes production photographs, the designer's stage plans, Welles' adapted script, contemporary commentary and reviews, and subsequent recollections by those who planned, performed in or witnessed the production. And, of course, Welles' own films give the flavour of his imagination and working styles. None of this enables recreation of the performance, even were that desirable. What it does allow is a powerful sense of the production's achievement as a theatrical event, sharp insight into the cultural climate of the time, and realisation of the evident salience of the production within its historical and political moment. It also contributes to the debate about how performance archives might be used, since the very quantity of what does survive here challenges the tendency, in more sketchily memorialised productions, to make assumptions on the basis of a single production photograph or eyewitness' account.

It is tantalising, although perhaps unsurprising, to learn that Welles, who regularly reworked the Shakespeare projects that interested him and had already adapted *Julius Caesar* for record and radio, had proposed a modern-dress screen version of the play in November 1949. In 1953, living away from Hollywood and its witch-hunts, he had gained King Farouk's agreement to finance his film, but abandoned the plan when he heard of the MGM project. The script seems not to have survived but Welles' plan had been, by his own account, to shoot the work not in a studio but as if it were a documentary. (Houseman, now suspicious of

Welles' tendency to claim imaginative ascendancy in any project, returned the offered shooting script with lawyers' seals guaranteeing it unopened.)[46] I cannot suppose that Welles would have attempted to reproduce the 1937 *Caesar* on film, any more than he repeated his 1936 Federal Theatre production of *Macbeth* in his 1948 film. Twelve years on, Haiti and voodoo had given way to Scotland and Celtic crosses and to different kinds of experimentation with visual images and with the text.[47] Although evidently rooted in the earlier experience, each of Welles' productions offered a new engagement with medium and moment, a different remaking.

Now, when it is as common as not for directors to seek out equivalencies, audiences are familiar with the practice and there is rarely such an impact, unless – as the authorities feared in the aftermath of the French Revolution – contemporary circumstances strike a previously unacknowledged chord in the text. The initially gripping analogy quickly comes to seem too easy. The identification of Caesar's faction with fascism has become something of a cliché since Welles' production. Indeed, it was already on the way to being so in a Hammersmith revival of 1949, with Donald Wolfit as Brutus. Responses to the political gesture, and probably to the play too, become confirmatory with re-iteration, rather than, as they were initially, challenging or revelatory. (Setting the battle scenes of the history plays in the First World War has become a comparable cliché.) Although Trevor Nunn's 1972 blackshirt production for the RSC was hailed for 'speaking directly to us now',[48] to put Shakespeare into fascist costume in 1972 or, indeed, in 2001, as Edward Hall did in his production for the RSC, is a completely different kind of historicising from doing so in 1937. The immediacy of the particular image evaporates with the changed political circumstance. Indeed, Michael Croft's 1960 production for the Youth Theatre, in which Teddy Boys killed an effeminate Cinna with flick-knives, seems closer to the spirit of Welles' production than Nunn's version.

John Ripley, after a vividly detailed account of Welles' production, concludes that it 'must remain a matter of regret' that Welles 'lavished his genius on essentially a perversion of the play',[49] but this is to misconceive the nature of Welles' activity and to regret the reality that is theatrical adaptation. As with all his Shakespeare projects, Welles' *Caesar* emerged from a deep engagement with the Shakespeare text but, as the alteration to the title signalled, it was an emergence or, in more conventional critical terms, an adaptation and a recontextualising. The juxtaposition of the stage production with the film suggests that, besides the difference in the medium, the fundamental difference between them is the fact that in the stage production the fact that it was a remaking was recognised and embraced, whereas the film makes a self-deceiving claim to political and interpretative neutrality. The *New York Herald Tribune* reviewer claimed of the 1937 *Caesar*, with more enthusiasm than judgement, that 'never once does it seem to you that anything new has been written into Shakespeare's intent...you cannot escape the feeling that, with the clairvoyance of genius, he was predicting for us the cauldron of modern Europe.'[50] Arthur Colby Sprague was hostile to Welles' kind of adaptation and would recall his 1939 *Five Kings* (subsequently developed into the film *Chimes at Midnight*[51]) as one of the four worst Shakespeare productions he had seen in a long life of theatre-going. But he did identify the core of Welles' approach when he wrote:

> At least in such productions, we are under no misapprehension. The director is not inviting us to see a play of Shakespeare's. Rather he is exploring. What can be done, he seems to ask, in order to make a new play out of this antiquated material; a new scenario for these old characters, their lines not actually being rewritten but freely manipulated or left out? It is as if a problem were proposed, and we were to judge how well it had been solved.[52]

John Mason Brown, who relished the posing of the problem and its solution, interpreted the project positively. 'If the play ceases to be Shakespeare's tragedy,' he wrote of *Caesar*, 'it does become ours.'[53] Enthusiastic or hostile, such comments testify to the impact of the production on its own time and place.

Welles' method in relation to *Caesar*, as revealed in the archive, is self-evidently not the only valid way of reviving a classic text, and John Ripley is by no means the only commentator to advocate Shakespeare's text in Shakespeare's order.[54] I have wanted to draw attention to the intrinsic interest of the production as a piece of theatre, but also to its place as forerunner of the remaking of Shakespeare in different times and places that is so much a feature of present-day engagement with the plays, as demonstrated by the articles in this book. I have not here been arguing that subsequent revivals should attempt to retrieve or otherwise imitate Welles' version of the play, or even that they should find other, parallel, ways of recontextualising it. What I do suggest is that Welles' *Caesar* was a rare theatrical event, one commensurate in its impact on contemporary audiences with such other landmark productions as Granville Barker's or Peter Brook's *A Midsummer Night's Dream*, or Brook's *King Lear*, or Kozintsev's or Kurosawa's film versions of that play.[55]

The energy of the production, its theatrical liveliness, and the intensity and quality of its engagement with the Shakespeare text and with the cultural moment, are what offer the challenge to subsequent directors, audiences and critics of Shakespeare in performance. They are different in degree from those both apparent and concealed in the Mankiewicz film.

Notes and references

1. New York, 1937. John Ripley, in his detailed account of the production, says, 'a gimmick was needed to lend...contemporary excitement,' *Julius Caesar on Stage in England and America, 1599–1973* (Cambridge: CUP, 1980) 222. Michael Anderegg describes the production as 'opportunistic' in *Orson Welles, Shakespeare and Popular Culture* (New York: Columbia, 1999) 28.
2. *Julius Caesar*, MGM/John Houseman, 1953.
3. Federal Theatre's lock-out of the company to prevent performance of Blitzstein's piece is described in detail in John Houseman, *Run-through* (London: Allen Lane, 1972). A more sceptical account than Houseman's of the rupture with Federal Theatre over *The Cradle Will Rock* is given in Richard France, *The Theatre of Orson Welles* (London: Associated University Press, 1977) 100–1.
4. Particularly in *Run-through* and his other autobiographical account, *Unfinished Business* (London: Chatto, 1986).
5. Ripley 197. The word 'Anglophone' is needed too. André Antoine played a full text at the Paris Odéon in 1906, and the text played by the Meininger Company on its European tours, including that to London in 1881, seems to have used all the scenes, even if some were abbreviated.
6. Houseman, 'Filming *Julius Caesar*,' *Sight and Sound*, 23 (July–September 1953): 24–7.
7. 'Remarks,' *Julius Caesar*, in Mrs Inchbald, ed. *The British Theatre*. Printed Under Authority of the Managers from the Prompt Books, Volume 4 (London: Longman *et al.*, 1808) 3. Following the French Revolution, Russian companies, too, were forbidden to perform the play: a ban lifted only in 1897.
8. Inchbald, 'Remarks' 3.
9. Inchbald, 'Remarks' 3.
10. Inchbald, 'Remarks' 4.
11. Preface to *Brutus* (1731), repr. in *Shakespeare in Europe* ed. Oswald Lewinter, (Harmondsworth: Penguin, 1970) 29–41.
12. Le Tourneur's dedication is quoted in Matthew Ramsay, 'Revolutionary Politics and Revolutionary Culture,' *The French Revolution in Culture and Society*, ed. D. Troyansky, A. Cismaru and N. Andrews (Westport, Conn.: Greenwood, 1991) 60.
13. I discuss these productions and the relationship between them in some detail in Jean Chothia, *Directors in Perspective: André Antoine* (Cambridge: CUP, 1991) 67–79; 143–52.
14. These two productions are discussed in Dennis Kennedy, *Looking at Shakespeare* (Cambridge: CUP, 1993) 105–9.

15. This is indicated in the 157-performance run, which was remarkable for Shakespeare, and the enthusiastic reviews cited at notes 24, 29 and 46 below.
16. Letter to Viola Tree, 4.19.1912, quoted in Hesketh Pearson, *Herbert Beerbohm Tree* (London: Methuen, 1956; repr. Columbus Books, 1988) 160; William Archer, *The Theatrical World of 1895* (London: Scott, 1896) 219.
17. Anderegg notes that such a production happened and suggests that Welles may have heard of it, but there are no further details (27).
18. *Julius Caesar*, 1.1.32. Quotations from the play in this article are from the Oxford World's Classics edition, ed. Arthur Humphreys (Oxford: OUP, 1994).
19. See, e.g. Kennedy, 150; France, *Theatre of Orson Welles*, 113.
20. Illustrations in e.g. Speaight, Kennedy, Chothia.
21. 1934, reprinted in Orson Welles and Roger Hill, *The Mercury Shakespeare: Julius Caesar, Edited for Reading and Arranged for Staging* (New York: Harper, 1939) 22–8.
22. *Quo Vadis*, dir. Mervyn Le Roy, MGM/Zimbalist, 1951. Factual details from Houseman, *Unfinished Business*, 322–6.
23. Among Roman epics, besides *Quo Vadis*, c.f. *The Robe*, dir. Henry Koster, TCF/Frank Ross, 1953; for Lean's Dickens, see *Great Expectations*, dir. David Lean, Rank/Cineguild, 1946; *Oliver Twist*, dir. Lean, CFD/Cineguild, 1948.
24. As Kay Smith points out in her article in this collection, Mankiewicz would subsequently direct the notorious *Cleopatra*, TCF/Walter Wanger, 1963, and become involved in plans for a Shakespeare biopic.
25. Jack J. Jorgens, *Shakespeare on Film* (Bloomington: Indiana University Press, 1977) 100. Jorgens' chapter on the film offers a full critical appreciation and technical description of the film.
26. *Hollywood Treasures, the Fifties: Julius Caesar*, Warner Home Video, 2001.
27. *New York Post*, quoted in Houseman, *Unfinished Business* 160.
28. John Gielgud, *Stage Directions* (New York: Capricorn, 1966) 49.
29. *Orson Welles on Shakespeare: The WPA and Mercury Playscripts*, ed. Richard France (Westport: Greenwood, 1990) 146.
30. *Evita*, dir. Alan Parker, Entertainment/Cinergi, 1996. *Battleship Potemkin*, dir. Sergei Eisenstein, Goskino, 1925.
31. Plutarch, *The Lives of the Noble Grecians and Romans*, trans. Thomas North, (1579, repr. New York: Heritage Press, 1941): 'despatched him in the market-place,' 'Life of Caesar,' 1442; and 'slew him outright in the market place,' 'Life of Marcus Brutus,' 1867.
32. Press accounts in *Run-through*, 316–17, and France, *Theatre of Orson Welles*, 114. The rehearsals are described in *Unfinished Business*, 157–9.
33. Quoted in Jorgens 104.
34. Quoted in *Run-through* 318.
35. See note 3, above.
36. Interview in the *Birmingham Mail* (25.4.1933), quoted in Kennedy 126.
37. Houseman, *Sight and Sound* 26.
38. *A Streetcar Named Desire*, dir. Elia Kazan, Warner/Kazan, 1951.
39. 'The Crucible in History' in *Arthur Miller, Echoes Down the Corridor: Collected Essays*, ed. Steven R. Centola (London, 2000) 274–95, 282–3. *On the Waterfront*, wr. Schulberg, dir. Kazan, Columbia, 1954, addressing the same material as Miller's script, showed marked sympathy for the man, played by Brando, who names names.

40. *High Noon*, dir. Fred Zinneman, Stanley Kramer, 1952. According to Pauline Kael it was 'the Western form used for a sneak civics lesson,' *5001 Nights at the Movies* (London: Hutchinson, 1982) 250.
41. *Henry V*, dir. Olivier, Rank/Two Cities/Olivier, 1944, for which a special Oscar was awarded to Olivier; *Hamlet*, dir. Olivier, Rank/Two Cities/Olivier, 1948, won Best Picture Oscar, and Best Actor for Olivier.
42. Kenneth S. Rothwell, *A History of Shakespeare on Screen* (Cambridge: CUP, 1999) 28.
43. Jorgens, 103.
44. *The Man Between*, dir. Carol Reed, British Lion/Reed, 1953.
45. *The Third Man*, dir. Carol Reed, which notably stars Orson Welles and his colleague from Mercury Theatre days, Joseph Cotton, British Lion/Reed: 1949.
46. Factual information here from 'Welles' Career: A Chronology,' 323–453 in *This is Orson Welles*, ed. Jonathan Rosenbaum: Orson Welles and Peter Bogdanovich (New York: Da Capo, 1998) 301–2, 433.
47. *Macbeth*, dir. Orson Welles, Republic/Mercury, 1948.
48. David Addenbrooke, *The Royal Shakespeare Company* (London: Kimber, 1974) 66.
49. Ripley, *Julius Caesar on Stage* 232.
50. Quoted in France, *Theatre of Orson Welles* 105.
51. *Chimes at Midnight*, dir. Orson Welles, Internacional Films Española/Alpine, 1966.
52. A. C. Sprague, *Shakespeare Players and Performances* (London: Black, 1984) 106, 214.
53. Quoted in France, *Theatre of Orson Welles* 103.
54. The claim advanced most fiercely by William Poel in his assault on Victorian adaptation, cf. Poel, *Shakespeare in the Theatre* (London: Sidgwick and Jackson, 1913) 155, 156–76.
55. Granville Barker's production of *A Midsummer Night's Dream* was staged at the Savoy Theatre, London, in 1914; Peter Brook's, for the Royal Shakespeare Company, at Stratford-upon-Avon in 1970; Brook's RSC *King Lear* was staged at Stratford in 1962; Grigori Kozintsev's film *King Lear* was made in 1970 (Kozintsev, 1971), Akira Kurosawa's *Ran* in 1985 (Herald Ace/Nippon Herald, 1985).

8
Will! or Shakespeare in Hollywood: Anthony Burgess's Cinematic Presentation of Shakespearean Biography

Kay H. Smith

In early 1968, Anthony Burgess flew to Hollywood to discuss what he hoped would be a film script for his first major motion picture. He was known in Hollywood for his fictional biography of Shakespeare, *Nothing Like the Sun*, and this project was to be an offshoot of that, a life of Shakespeare that would also be a musical. From its inception, the project had two titles, *Will!*, the title Burgess preferred, and *The Bawdy Bard*, the title preferred by everyone in Hollywood connected with the project. Because of his success with *Nothing Like the Sun*, Burgess says, 'it was considered that I could produce something sensual and violent enough to be called *The Bawdy Bard*.'[1]

The idea of a musical version of Shakespeare's life seemed more than acceptable in a 1960s Hollywood which was riding a wave of very successful British musicals, like *My Fair Lady* (1964) and *Camelot* (1967), and historical blockbusters like *Lawrence of Arabia* (1962) and *A Man for All Seasons* (1966).[2] Warner Brothers Seven Arts was eager to create a similar success with Burgess's Shakespeare. William Conrad, a successful actor turned producer, had conceived the project and was instrumental in involving Burgess. In *You've Had Your Time*, Burgess describes how he warmed to Conrad, who, he noted, was 'a true actor, in that he knew Shakespeare' (143), and they became friends. Burgess was amused but somewhat alarmed by Conrad's improvisation of a song for the movie that began 'To be or not to be in love with you / To spend my life hand in glove with you' (143). Besides bad lyrics, Conrad's plan for the film included, Burgess noted, 'outmoded Shakespeare lore' like the legend that Shakespeare left Stratford because he had been caught poaching deer on the land of Sir Thomas Lucy, or the legend that he had held horses outside the Curtain playhouse before becoming a playwright (144). But Burgess could not completely condemn such material since he had not hesitated to use legendary material himself in *Nothing Like the Sun*. About the film project Burgess says, 'If I was a scholar, I'd have been outraged. But I'm only a novelist, as much a show-biz man, I suppose, as any juggler, soft shoe-shuffler, or film-deity, and I was intrigued.'[3]

This essay proposes to examine the results of Burgess's intrigue – how it led him to write a lengthy screenplay on a topic of high interest to him; how this screenplay, which has not been examined in any detail until now, affects studies of Burgess as novelist and screenwriter. The essay reveals as well why, given its cultural context, the musical was never filmed. The fact that the screenplay is a musical also allows me to examine the problematics of transposing Shakespeare's life and character into musical drama, particularly given the generic and structural requirements for musicals of the 1960s. Burgess's experiences in Hollywood also reveal, sometimes amusingly, patterns of Shakespeare's appropriation by Hollywood and Hollywood's appropriation of Britishness as a cultural export product. Fitting into this volume's theme of recontextualisation, by setting Burgess's unpublished play, *Will!*, into the context of his works one can examine not only Burgess's fascination with Shakespearean biography but also how Burgess planned to change, add to, and comment on the dramatically revealing if fictive aspects of creative Shakespearean biography.

From its inception this project was destined to reveal interesting difficulties. The first to present itself was that Burgess the novelist had a serious prior restraint in deciding how to handle a screenplay narrative of Shakespeare's life: he had sold a theatrical option of *Nothing Like the Sun* to a New York producer and 'even to lift one of my own lines from novel to script would be rank plagiarism' (*YHYT* 142). Thus he had to come up with an entirely new treatment of Shakespeare's life, and legendary material he may have eschewed for *Nothing Like the Sun* became necessary for *Will!*.

While Burgess had many problems to solve in finding the proper alternative material, of equal difficulty were the structural problems that Hollywood imposed on the story. The most successful British musicals, like *My Fair Lady*, were long, some over three hours, and typically had an intermission that divided the story in the middle. Burgess saw Shakespeare's story as dividing into three parts: his life up to leaving Stratford; his early success in Elizabethan London including his involvement with the Dark Lady and the noble patron; finally, his great 'tragic period' under James I, culminating in his retirement to Stratford, a prosperous gentleman (*YHYT* 145). Burgess had concentrated on the first two parts in *Nothing Like the Sun*, implying, in that work, that there was a link between disease and genius that impelled Shakespeare into his tragic period, but he had skipped over this period to conclude with Shakespeare's dying monologue. Indeed he had admitted in an article on the composition of *Nothing Like the Sun* that there was little of dramatic potential in the Jacobean part of Shakespeare's life, where the work – the production of the great tragedies – dominates.[4] This time, for the film, he would have to find a way to divide the life in two and include the potentially less dramatic period of Shakespeare's life. Moreover, as Rick Altman points out in *The American Film Musical*, the musical as a genre 'progresses through a series of paired segments matching the male and female leads' rather than following the development of a single character.[5] Yet the biography of an artist demands a single track of character development to support and demonstrate artistic development. And, more significantly, segments matching male and female leads would be difficult to achieve in Shakespearean biography, particularly because, with the significance of both Anne Hathaway and the Dark Lady to Burgess's scheme, it would be impossible for Burgess to fulfil the expectations of the genre and create a single female lead with whom to pair Shakespeare. This inability to match generic expectation can cloud a musical's reception, as Ramona Wray demonstrates in this volume in her discussion of the box office failure of Kenneth Branagh's musical version of *Love's Labour's Lost*.

The other challenge presented in the creation of a successful Hollywood musical was motivation. Burgess has an amusing anecdote in *You've Had Your Time* about his encounter with the studio 'motivation man'. To Burgess, the film's plot was 'just about a Stratford lad making it in the big time and getting laid by a black bitch' (145), but the motivation man wanted a 'single theme you could write on the back of a four-cent postage stamp . . . He was very fierce about motivation: a movie was like a locomotive, running on predestinate rails to a depot on whose platform all the luggage of past action was deposited: everything had to tie up with everything else, even if historical truth was violated' (145). This was, Burgess says, 'probably sound, even Shakespearean' (145). Burgess and the 'motivation man' decided on guilt as the motivating factor, guilt about Will's adultery, guilt about the death of his son, Hamnet, guilt over abandoning his wife for success in London. Of course the problem was that guilt and the musical did not necessarily go together well.

From the beginning of the project, Burgess's approach to the material was both eager and ironic. After all, this was a major studio project. The headline on the *Times* (London) article about the project read 'Millions on a Musical about Shakespeare'.[6] A successful film would make Burgess's name as a marketable Hollywood scriptwriter, a valuable credential since he was also working on a script for a film production of his novel, *Enderby*, in 1968, and hoped to see other of his books become film projects (*YHYT* 185). But the musical nature of the film both fascinated and repelled Burgess, a man who was more often fascinated than repelled by music. He wrote about twenty songs, both music and lyrics, that were recorded with full orchestration by Warner Brothers, but he was nevertheless concerned that the story was damaged by the songs, that Shakespeare's genius was diminished by the imposition of the standard lyrics of the 1960s musical, no matter how good the lyrics and music might be. 'Ghastly' is the word he used later to describe this mix, 'diminishing the theme and the characters' (*YHYT* 147). Burgess goes on to explain his dilemma:

> The truth was that only Shakespeare could write the lyrics and John Dowland the music. But, as the drama of the treatment developed, the irrelevance of the songs became all too clear. Plenty of singing in rural Stratford but not much occasion for it when Essex was executed or Will, if the Hays Office or the Catholic League of Decency allowed, handled his hard chancre. (147)

Yet a close examination of the lyrics in the screenplay manuscript reveals that Burgess wrote a combination of story and song that fits the needs of the musical format in a rather efficient way. There are group songs and set pieces, duets and love songs, conforming to what Rick Altman describes as the 'audio dissolve...Music appears on the diegetic track, diegetic noises are transformed into music' in what is 'the very heart of the style characteristic of the American musical'.[7] Undoubtedly, Burgess must have wondered how one could put bad lyrics like Conrad's 'to be or not to be in love with you' in the mouth of Shakespeare. But, as he notes, his larger problem was that his treatment of Shakespearean biography, with its narrative image dominated by guilt and its need to show Shakespeare's artistic development, went against the generic needs of the musical. Burgess feared not only the high standard of comparison to Shakespeare and Dowland as lyricist and composer, but also the growing irrelevance of the music to the plot and theme as they were developing.

The manuscript of *Will!* shows that Burgess tried to solve these problems by limiting them. The main characters, particularly Anne and Will, sing more at the beginning of the screenplay, but then much of the music becomes environmental and kinetic, as in the montage Burgess creates to celebrate Will's arrival in London, which he, taking historical licence, makes coincide with the defeat of the Spanish Armada in 1588 (64–9). In this sequence, Burgess combines a patriotic ditty with an aural montage based on London church bells. In the tradition of the musical's mixing of diegetic and extra-diegetic music, everyone sings: people on the street, people in shops, whores hanging out of windows, Will himself. The sequence is quite successful on its own terms and would have worked cinematically. Later in the screenplay, Burgess taps into the great riches of the Elizabethan period in order to solve the developing problem of material that was difficult to bring into line with the generic requirements of the musical. He sets Nashe's verses from 'A Litanie in Time of Plague' to music to accompany the closing of the theatres sequence in the screenplay. Cleverly, he sets to music not only several of Shakespeare's sonnets, but also a number of Shakespeare's own lyric compositions, from *Love's Labour's Lost*, *As You Like It* and *Much Ado about Nothing*. Thus by the end of the screenplay, the music sung by main characters has almost disappeared, but the film still contains ample music, mostly diegetic and lacking the full audio dissolve common to the musical: a good solution to a difficult problem. Nevertheless, as we shall see, Burgess remained uneasy about the music.

The project, still called by both names, *Will! Or the Bawdy Bard*, went forward rather quickly, in spite of the fact that this was a very difficult time in Burgess's life, with the death of his first wife and his remarriage to Liliana Macellari. The film was to be directed by Joseph L. Mankiewicz, who had directed *All about Eve* (1950), a film Burgess 'considered a masterpiece' (*YHYT* 186), as well as the acclaimed *Julius Caesar* (1953) with Marlon Brando and a film version of *Guys and Dolls* (1955). In spite of his experience with both Shakespeare and musicals, he was probably best known in the 1960s for the huge and expensive flop *Cleopatra* (1963), with Elizabeth Taylor and Richard Burton.[8] He needed a big successful movie and was hoping that *Will!* would be it (*YHYT* 185). Mankiewicz had already made some casting decisions – Maggie Smith as Anne, her husband Robert Stephens as Will, James Mason as Philip Henslowe, Peter Ustinov as Ben Jonson, Jessica Tandy as Queen Elizabeth. No decision was made about the Dark Lady, although Burgess somewhat facetiously suggested Diana Ross (*YHYT* 157). The plot began to take shape as a somewhat collaborative effort among Burgess, Mankiewicz and William Conrad.

Three manuscripts of Burgess's screenplay of *Will! Or the Bawdy Bard* exist, two in the Warner Brothers archive and one found in Burgess's papers at the Harry H. Ransom Research Center at the University of Texas. The manuscript from the Ransom Center represents most likely Burgess's first attempt at a full-length screenplay, having gained approval from Mankiewicz for his initial treatment of the material.[9] He later wrote more versions, but this is the one he chose to keep among his papers, apparently recopying it in 1984, and it is likely to be the most complete record of Burgess's work on this project. The manuscript is long, 219 pages, and includes all the lyrics that were later cut when Mankiewicz decided, to a mixture of disappointment and relief on Burgess's part, that the film was not, after all, to be a musical (*YHYT* 185). Although portions of the manuscript made an appearance in Burgess's later writing, particularly *Enderby's Dark Lady*, the manuscript itself has never been published; in fact it has never been carefully examined to determine both how it differs from Burgess's presentation on Shakespearean biography in *Nothing Like the Sun* and how it foreshadows Burgess's later writing about Shakespeare. Because of the obscurity of the text and the difficulty of obtaining it, as well as because of its later influence on Burgess's writing, I will use descriptive analysis to summarise the key points of Burgess's screenplay.

I want to describe three aspects of Burgess's screenplay of *Will!*: first, the way in which Burgess employs the necessary legendary material that he had left out of *Nothing Like the Sun*; second, the way in which Burgess puts Will into actions that have high cinematic as well as dramatic potential; third, the way in which he creates an entirely different relationship between Will and Anne Hathaway than the one found in *Nothing Like the Sun*, and thus an entirely different ending for the screenplay.

Since he could not use much of the actual story from *Nothing Like the Sun*, Burgess is much more reliant on Shakespearean legend in *Will!*. He makes extensive use of the old story that Will had been poaching from the lands of the local gentry, particularly Sir Thomas Lucy. Early in the screenplay, Sir Thomas Lucy threatens Will and warns him off his property (7). Later we see Will, Dick Field and Dick Quinney (historically authentic residents of Stratford) killing a deer on Sir Thomas's property and then giving it to a poor family. In fact, the poaching is linked to both an egalitarian theme – at one point Will says 'How can one man steal wild rabbits from another? God owns the wild rabbits' (9) – and to the major theme of frustrated gentility that runs through the screenplay: Will complains that 'Shakespeare is a better name than Lucy...He keeps his land: the Shakespeares lost theirs' (10). Later in the screenplay, when the Queen's Men come to Stratford, Dick Tarlton, the clown with whom Will has become acquainted, complains about the tavern fare and Will impetuously offers to get him venison (54). This time he is caught and jailed, to the disgrace of his family, particularly his wife Anne. He escapes and flees to London, but on his infrequent visits back to Stratford Sir Thomas Lucy is still after him. Eventually Will must ask Southampton and Essex to use their influence to mitigate Sir Thomas's wrath (125).

Surprisingly, Burgess stretches this dubious poaching material through the full length of his plot to create a climax that is both visually captivating and thematically appropriate. At the end of the story, Will, back in Stratford but depressed and unhappy, gets drunk with Ben Jonson and, ranting, wanders off in a snowstorm for one last shot at the Lucy deer. Lost in the woods, Will sees visions of his plays mingle with visions of his experiences, and we begin to understand why Burgess has hung on to the Lucy story for so long, as Will hallucinates images of the Dark Lady, named Lucy Negro – ironically a name that echoes Will's old enemy and promises both light (luce) and darkness (negro). But this Lucy whom he sees in the snowmist 'tears off her face to disclose a leprous horror' (217) as Will stumbles on to his death. It is clear from this summary of the poaching legend that Burgess is trying to reinvigorate this legendary material not by minimising it as one might expect, but by seeing imaginative links that can expand and become meaningful in terms of plot, theme and startling visual effect.

Burgess's Dark Lady in *Will!* is not the Dark Lady of *Nothing Like the Sun*, who is a Malay woman. While Burgess got the idea of a truly dark-skinned woman from G. B. Harrison, for *Nothing Like the Sun* he used his own experience of living in Malaysia to create a 'dark woman who came from the East – a woman like one of the Malays I had been hotly attracted to during my time as a colonial civil servant. I knew nothing about black women but plenty about brown.'[10] A dark-skinned woman playing the love interest of a white man in a 1968 movie was likely to be highly controversial, and this may explain why the part of the Dark Lady remained uncast for the duration of the project.

In *Will!* Burgess links this potentially controversial idea of the black mistress with one of the oldest pieces of legendary material about Shakespeare – the first Shakespeare Joke! In his diary, John Manningham of the Middle Temple has the following entry for 13 March 1601:

Upon a time when Burbage played Richard III, there was a citizen grew so far in liking with him, that before she went from the play she appointed him to come that night unto her by the name Richard the Third. Shakespeare, overhearing their conclusion, went before, was entertained and at his game ere Burbage came. Then, message being brought that Richard III was at the door, Shakespeare caused return to be made that William the Conqueror was before Richard the Third.[11]

While there are traces of this story in *Nothing Like the Sun*, in *Will!* Burgess uses the joke quite literally to create the circumstances of the meeting between Will and Lucy Negro, the Dark Lady of the screenplay. This is Burgess's most blatant use of legendary material and he takes a real risk in the screenplay of making the central love relation of the film faintly ridiculous by associating it with this old joke. Though he may have believed that it would work on screen, nevertheless it is likely that, later when Burgess came to satirise the work he had done on *Will!*, this kind of travesty of legendary material came to his mind.[12]

On the other hand, Burgess was quite capable of discarding old legends that were suggested for the screenplay and substituting something more dynamic. Burgess does not show Will holding horses at the playhouse door when he comes to London, as William Conrad had suggested. Instead, Burgess gives us several scenes of Will trying to break into authorship by selling his plays to that theatrical entrepreneur and brothel-keeper, Philip Henslowe. In the most effective of these sequences, Will accosts Henslowe and the player, Edward Alleyn, in one of Henslowe's brothels. Will begins to recount the plot of *Titus Andronicus*, filled with rape, mutilation, murder and cannibalism. As he does so, the whores and their clients begin to listen in rapt attention, putting aside their business with each other, and leaning over the balcony to see better. Then there is a sound edit and a visual overlap so that Alleyn's voice takes over the lines from *Titus* and we find ourselves watching the actual production in the Swan Theater (82–5). In small moments like this, Burgess demonstrates a necessary command of the visual medium in clever ways while avoiding piling on the legendary material.

In another visual sequence, Burgess faces the problem, more of a problem in the late 1960s than today, of showing too much violence, and again he proves to have a canny sense of how film 'works'. In this scene, Will, new to London, is attending his first execution – a hanging, drawing and quartering of Jesuit priests. Burgess shows the crowd lusting for blood and in the crowd Will spots a coach with a woman whom we shall come to know as Lucy Negro, his Dark Lady, whom the script directions describe as 'excited as by the prospect of sex' (79). Rather than show detail after detail in this gruesome execution scene, Burgess resorts to an old trick, a blind man who stands next to Will and asks excited questions. Members of the crowd cheer 'at what makes Will flinch' (80) and describe the scene to the blind man. Building up the morbid curiosity of the viewer, the camera finally cuts to the hangman who has just eviscerated one of the priests. Here are Burgess's directions from the script:

> The hangman grins, holding up the blood clotted pluck. The CAMERA pans down to the fire. The hangman throws the entrails on to it. There is a fine sputtering. Renewed cheers. (81)

Towards the end the scene, the camera returns to Will as he pushes out of the crowd, 'dashes to the camera and starts to vomit in it' (81). Burgess uses this 'blackout' of the camera as a cut to the next scene.

Scenes like this clearly indicate that Burgess had a keen visual, as well as a verbal, imagination and a visual vocabulary of editing techniques to go with the violence and squalor he was committed to putting on the screen. Often screenplays written primarily by novelists fail to take into account the needs of visual narration and tend to read like somewhat flat stage plays, but Burgess's screenplay is usually quite aware of and notes appropriate camera placement and movement, as well as other aspect of filmic vocabulary like editing, overlapping sound and montage. Burgess knows how to put Will into a variety of actions that literally show rather than tell the story.

I want to conclude this discussion of Burgess's screenplay with a look at the treatment of Anne Hathaway in *Will!*. In both *Nothing Like the Sun* and *Will!*, Burgess embraces the theory expounded by James Joyce in *Ulysses* that Shakespeare's wife, Anne, was unfaithful to him with his brother, Richard. Both *Nothing Like the Sun* and *Will!* revolve around the two poles of fair wife and dark mistress, both of whom ultimately betray the poet. Yet one of the key differences between these two works is in the handling of the fair wife. In *Nothing Like the Sun*, Anne is presented as lusty and sexually demanding. Will meets her on May Day, a traditional time for the sexual revels of the young, after being rejected by a dark girl who chooses to go off with a young miller's son instead of him. Getting blind drunk with rejected disappointment, Will simply wakes up, horribly hung over, in the arms of this unknown but experienced and somewhat older woman. There is no exposition, no acquaintance beforehand: this Anne Hathaway is like a lusty goddess of the woods, a Venus who simply (over)takes Will unawares.

In *Will!* more exposition accompanies the introduction of Anne Hathaway, who is presented much more demurely. Will meets her at his father's shop where she comes to bring a pair of gloves to be repaired. She is attractive and modest. While Will's father talks with her about her family, Will says to his brother Gilbert: 'that, Gilbert, is known as a woman handsome but past her first youth.' His father concedes that Anne is a 'sweet and pretty girl [who] . . . badly needs wedding', and warns his son to 'Keep away. Such women are dangerous' (12–15). Later, as in *Nothing Like the Sun*, when Will is rejected by his dark girl, he gets drunk and awakens in the arms of Anne Hathaway, but this is a very different Anne. The film script presents Anne in much more romantic cinematic terms, intercutting between the couple's lovemaking and the bringing in of the Maypole in a phallic montage that would have made Sir James Frazer proud. A postcoital Will and Anne are shown in long shot walking through the fields of rye, talking, laughing and holding hands (21–3).

There is much more going on in this alteration than simply meeting the visual and narrative needs of cinema. True, Burgess has added exposition appropriate to a more simplified and visual plot, and true, he has taken advantage of what film can do through visual juxtaposition. But in making Anne a modest though ageing virgin, Burgess abandons *Nothing Like the Sun*'s theme of the overlusty wife, a Venus who drives the young poet to disturbing bouts of sexual frenzy. In *Nothing Like the Sun*, Shakespeare is finally driven to leave Anne and Stratford because of his disgust at his wife's arousal at seeing an old woman beaten through the night streets below their bedroom window. In contrast, in the screenplay, Anne is much more straightlaced: Will, for instance, meets Anne for a second time just as she is leaving the Shottery church where she has gone to pray. Again, Burgess may have been impelled by issues of screen censorship to make these changes. It is hard to imagine a 1960s blockbuster musical like *My Fair Lady*, which is what *Will! Or the Bawdy Bard* was to be, pursuing a theme of sadomasochistic sex (though Burgess had certainly laid the groundwork for such a theme with the Dark Lady's arousal at the execution).

It would seem, however, that Burgess was less interested in the censors and more interested in a completely different conception of Anne Hathaway. In *Will!*, Anne Hathaway is a budding Puritan or Brownist whose cooling religiosity finally pushes her husband away. This conception of Anne is going to have long-term plot consequences in the screenplay. Unlike *Nothing Like the Sun*, in the screenplay Will never actually discovers his wife making love to his brother, but he has numerous ominous dreams presented in flash cuts that show what Will imagines is happening. His imagination indeed proves accurate when, near the end of the screenplay, his wife confesses her adultery before Will and her co-religionists. But Will understands that it is loneliness, not lust, that has pushed her towards adultery. Guilt, Will's guilt at what he has done to his family, is the dominant factor in the musical, just as the 'motivation man' had suggested. From the beginning of the musical until its end, Will can never be what Anne wants him to be, and this is made clear from a sequence of songs for Will and Anne that captures the conflict between his desire to seek his destiny and hers for quiet happiness at home. Will's song revolves around his self-identification with the constellation that forms Cassiopeia's Chair, which he sees as a huge W in the sky:

> My name in the sky
> Burning forever,
> Fame fixed by fate
> Never to die.
>
> (25)

Anne sees a different natural symbolism at work when she sings:

> Will o' the wisp,
> Do not desire
> To follow fame,
> That foolish fire.

Her song is loaded with homey imagery of baking bread, and crisp dawns:

> Better by far
> The fire at home –
> Smoke in the rafter
> Lamb's wool and laughter.
>
> (31)

These two songs are among the more successful lyrical pieces in the musical, and they point to a conflict quite different in form from the conflict of Will and Anne in *Nothing Like the Sun*. In fact, Burgess employs a frame story in *Will!* that emphasises the poet's guilt and frustration at his incompatibility with his wife. *Will!* starts with a scene of Shakespeare dying in his bed, the camera taking his point of view as he scans those around him. He sees Anne 'wrinkled as an applejohn, sour as a crab' (2) and hears her rattle the pennies in her pocket, waiting to put them on his eyes when he dies. Then his mind drifts away to that springtime when he had hoped to meet his dark-haired girl and met gingery Anne instead, and his story begins by going back to that time. At the end of the screenplay, after he has caught his last illness wandering and hallucinating in Sir Thomas Lucy's woods, the scene returns to his deathbed where Will's last words are 'my dear dear dear lord'. Anne says: 'I hope he was calling on God. I hope he has made his peace,' and Ben Jonson replies: 'Ah, woman, he has made more than you will ever understand.' The final words of the film are Anne's: 'It could have been so different. He could have made something with his life' (218). This frustrating and ironic ending is very different from the ending of *Nothing Like the Sun* with its emphasis on the muse, the Dark Lady whose final gift was disease, and the goddess whose final gift is death. Because of the emphasis in the screenplay on guilt, rather than on inspiration as in *Nothing Like the Sun*, Anne Hathaway plays a much larger role in Will's life and in his psyche, and the Dark Lady, his lover and ultimately his muse in *Nothing Like the Sun*, a much smaller one.

In examining *Will!* in detail, it is difficult not to speculate on Burgess's feeling about his material. Not being able to use *Nothing Like the Sun* because of rights restrictions must have been galling to Burgess, who nevertheless sneaked a good bit of useful dialogue from *Nothing Like the Sun* into the screenplay. Just as the characters are named differently in the two works, 'WS' being the interior man of *Nothing Like the Sun* and 'Will' being the exterior man of the screenplay, Burgess's approach to language is quite different in the two works. Burgess had serious doubts and concerns about how to bring the language necessary for film up to the higher literary standard of *Nothing Like the Sun* because he tended to scorn the language of the typical Hollywood film script. In an interview he says:

> Film people are very conservative about dialogue: they honestly believe that the immediate grasp of lexical meaning is more important than the impact of rhythm and emotionally charged sound. It's regarded as cleverer to pretend that the people of the past would have spoken like us if they had been lucky enough to know how to do so, delighted with the opportunity to view themselves and their times from our angle.[13]

In an article in the *Times* (London) in 1968, while Burgess was working on the screenplay, he comments further on problems in handling the speech in *Will!*:

> While I was in Hollywood I recorded some Elizabethan dialogue to show how like American it is, but the response I got was that it

sounded like Irish. It would certainly be a mistake to have Shakespeare spouting today's English.[14]

Of course, in one form or another, 'today's English' is an inevitable necessity in any contemporary film, whether it is historically-based or not. Besides accuracy in language, Burgess was also concerned with accuracy in setting. He feared that the director Mankiewicz would make a film that was full of pseudo-Renaissance settings just as *Camelot* was full of pseudo-Medieval settings (*YHYT* 186). This worry was justified by Mankiewicz's previous work on *Julius Caesar* – Jean Chothia points to the director's decision at the height of McCarthyism to put its cast back in togas, deflecting the political emphasis that Orson Welles had created by putting his cast into fascist uniforms.[15] Another film scholar has described the 'austerity look' of the Mankiewicz *Julius Caesar* sets.[16] While Burgess might not have wanted political statements embodied in costume and setting, he did want squalor, the kind of squalor that would have characterised the London of Shakespeare's day. '[Mankiewicz] would build Elizabethan London and, I feared, make it too clean. What I wanted was dirt, and plenty of it: greasy farthingales and black halfmoons on the fingernails of the struggling Bard' (*YHYT* 186). Thus, in *Will!*, Burgess emphasises the nastier realities of Elizabethan life. At one point Burgess instructs the camera to follow an open sewer on a London street, tracking 'dead cats and fish heads' (68). There are plenty of heads on pikes and chained criminals floating in the Thames's changing tides.

Burgess's doubts about the screenplay and the project in general were re-enforced by his growing sense that the film would never be made. In fact, in 1969, he contracted to write 'a brief biography of Shakespeare which should be sumptuously illustrated' so that he would not waste the research he had done for the film (*YHYT* 109). This is his 'coffee-table' book, called simply *Shakespeare*, which was published in 1970. Yet, even full of doubts, he was still working on the screenplay. As he says, 'Desperately trying to finish the script, I yet knew that it was not going to reach the screen' (*YHYT* 190). His premonition proved correct: Warner Brothers was being sold and even though studio executives supported the project, 'all existing enterprises were scrapped when the new regime started', as Burgess explained in an interview.[17] Burgess had bad luck with this project, just as he had bad luck with the *Enderby* film script that he was writing simultaneously with the *Will!* film script: in that case, the producer, John Bryant, who was committed to the project, dropped dead at the Cannes Film Festival (*YHYT* 185). Thus neither *Will!* nor *Enderby* were ever to make it to the screen.

One cannot help but be curious whether either one, but *Will!* in particular, would have been a success had it been made. After all, we have recently seen overwhelming interest in the life of Shakespeare in the 1998 success of the pseudo-biographical film, *Shakespeare in Love*.[18] Would *Will!* have been as successful as *Shakespeare in Love*? There are considerable and significant differences between the two. *Shakespeare in Love* privileges the part over the whole, emphasising an episode rather than thematising a life. This makes *Shakespeare in Love* more tightly organised and more seemingly complex within narrower bounds than *Will!*. In contrast, *Will!* consists of lots of small 'lies' – a complex compilation of fact and fiction often derived from reading the life into the work or accepting legendary material. *Shakespeare in Love*, on the other hand, depends upon one big 'lie', namely that Shakespeare wrote *Romeo and Juliet* based on a love affair of his own with a prominent noblewoman. Both history and source study refute the false if delightful premise of *Shakespeare in Love* with ridiculous ease, while the more historicised approach of *Will!* might have had greater appeal to a knowledgeable audience. Overall, we must remember that films are highly collaborative and note that *Will!*, like *Shakespeare in Love*, would have had an excellent cast, an experienced director, and, of course, a talented scriptwriter. While we can admire Geoffrey Rush's portrayal of Henslowe in *Shakespeare in Love*, we can still regret the loss of opportunity to have seen a quite different interpretation by James Mason, the Henslowe of *Will!*.

Overall, it is likely that *Will!* would not have done well at the box office, through no real fault of its own, but rather because of a seismic shift in tastes that was occurring while Burgess was working on *Will!*. The late 1960s saw the advent of the counterculture not only as a social phenomenon but also in films. *Easy Rider* and *Midnight Cowboy* both appeared in 1969.[19] While on a lecture tour of Australia and New Zealand, Burgess saw both films. He said they 'showed me the way the contemporary cinema was going and how old-hat and prissy *Will!* would have been' (*YHYT* 217). Ironically, it was on this same trip that Burgess found out that his novel, *A Clockwork Orange*, was definitely going to be filmed and that 'Stanley Kubrick was sending urgent cables about the need to see me in London on some matter of the script' (*YHYT* 217). The now old-fashioned *Will!* was being dropped, but Burgess was soon to find himself involved with the making of a film, *A Clockwork Orange*, that would define one element of the counterculture of the early 1970s.[20]

However, if one examines carefully what Burgess created in *Will!*, one notices aspects of the film that would have made it far less old-fashioned than the hopelessly outdated *Camelot* for instance. Burgess's insistence on the violent and the squalid is one of the more contemporary aspects of the screenplay, as is the idea, in the racially charged atmosphere of 1968, the year that Martin Luther King was killed, of a love affair between England's greatest poet and a black woman. The Dark Lady problem could have made the film more interesting and controversial, particularly if the Dark Lady had been played by Burgess's choice, Diana Ross.

When Warner Brothers abandoned the notion of making a film of *Will!* in 1969, Burgess may have been relieved. Over time, as I have noted, he began to see the many drawbacks of the project, particularly the 'ghastly' idea of a musical. Yet Burgess never really abandoned his screenplay, though he readily abandoned the idea of actually seeing it on screen. In fact, it was characteristic of Burgess as an author never to abandon anything that might be usefully linked with some future work. Many critics, Harold Bloom included, see links between Burgess's last Enderby novel, *Enderby's Dark Lady* and *Nothing Like the Sun*.[21] These novels seem similar to critics because the screenplay of *Will!* was never made public, even though Burgess quotes from it in his autobiography. In fact, *Enderby's Dark Lady* is an amalgam of *Enderby* and the screenplay of *Will!*. Though abandoned as a film project, much of the material of *Will!*, from the songs to the plot to the Diana Ross-like Dark Lady, makes a final appearance in *Enderby's Dark Lady*.

In *Enderby's Dark Lady*, Burgess is essentially bringing together and recycling a number of Shakespeare pieces he had written over the years, as well as using the experience and circumstances of writing them for the plot of the novel. Burgess wrote the short story 'Will and Testament', which begins *Enderby's Dark Lady*, in 1976. He read it for the first time at the Folger Shakespeare Library for a celebration of Shakespeare and the American Bicentennial, the very occasion that Enderby is called upon to commemorate at the satirically-named Peter Brook Theater in Indiana in *Enderby's Dark Lady* (*YHYT* 336). The short story that ends the novel, fittingly called 'Muse', was first published in *The Hudson Review* in 1968, the same year Burgess was working on *Will!*. The material in between the two short stories, in which Enderby is called to Indiana to write a musical of Shakespeare's life, is an imaginative reworking of Burgess's experiences in writing the abortive screenplay of *Will!*. In *Enderby's Dark Lady*, Burgess is both recycling the faintly ridiculous experiences he had in Hollywood and reconciling himself to the failure of his *Will!* to make it to the screen. Astonishingly similar to the way in which *Shakespeare in Love* turns to Shakespeare's own *Romeo and Juliet* to fill out the plot of the love affair between Will and Lady Viola, Burgess's novel turns to the plot and, interestingly, to the lyrics of *Will!* to create a love affair between the poet Enderby and the actress, April Elgar, who plays the Dark Lady in Enderby's production. Burgess never really gave up on *Will!*; he just repositioned it within *Enderby's Dark Lady*. Fortunately this recontextualised *Will!* still exists, though now embedded in a novel; unfortunately, for us and for Burgess, we will never have the pleasure of seeing *Will!* on screen.

Notes and references

1. Anthony Burgess, *You've Had Your Time* (New York: Grove Press, 1990) 142. All subsequent citations of this work will be included in the body of the text. If the context does not make the source of the citation sufficiently clear, this work will be abbreviated *YHYT* in the parenthetical documentation.
2. *My Fair Lady*, dir. George Cukor, perf. Audrey Hepburn, Rex Harrison, Stanley Holloway, Warner Brothers, 1964; *Camelot*, dir. Joshua Logan, perf. Richard Harris, Vanessa Redgrave, Franco Nero, David Hemmings, Warner Brothers, 1967; *Lawrence of Arabia*, dir. David Lean, perf. Peter O'Toole, Alec Guinness, Anthony Quinn, Omar Sharif, Horizon Pictures, 1962; *A Man for All Seasons*, dir. Fred Zinnemann, perf. Paul Scofield, Wendy Hiller, Leo McKern, Robert Shaw, Orson Welles, Columbia Pictures, 1966.
3. Anthony Burgess, 'To Be or Not to Be in Love with You,' *Show: The Magazine of Film and the Arts* 1.1 (1970): 76.
4. Anthony Burgess, 'Genesis and Headache,' *Afterwords: Novelists on Their Novels*, ed. Thomas McCormack (New York: Harper, 1968) 31.
5. Rick Altman, *The American Film Musical* (Bloomington, Indiana: Indiana University Press, 1987) 28.
6. Ernest Betts, 'Millions on a Musical About Shakespeare,' *Times* (London) 24 August 1968, 18.
7. Altman, 63.
8. *All About Eve*, dir. Joseph L. Mankiewicz, perf. Bette Davis, Anne Baxter, George Sanders, Celeste Holm, Marilyn Monroe, Twentieth Century Fox, 1950; *Julius Caesar*, dir. Joseph L. Mankiewicz, perf. Marlon Brando, James Mason, John Gielgud, Greer Garson, Deborah Kerr, MGM, 1963; *Guys and Dolls*, dir. Joseph L. Mankiewicz, perf. Marlon Brando, Jean Simmons, Frank Sinatra, MGM, 1955; *Cleopatra*, dir. Joseph L. Mankiewicz, perf. Elizabeth Taylor, Richard Burton, Twentieth Century Fox, 1963.
9. Anthony Burgess, *Will! Or the Bawdy Bard*, ts. Anthony Burgess Papers, Harry H. Ransom Research Center, University of Texas. Quoted with the permission of the Estate of Anthony Burgess. All subsequent citations of this work will be included in the body of the text. If the context does not make the source of the citation significantly clear, this work will be abbreviated *Will!* in the parenthetical documentation.
10. Burgess, 'Genesis and Headache,' 30.
11. John Manningham, *Diary*, Quoted in: Anthony Burgess, *Shakespeare* (New York: Knopf, 1970) 184–5.
12. See *Enderby's Dark Lady* (New York: McGraw Hill, 1984).

13. Quoted in John Cullinan, 'The Art of Fiction XLVIII: Anthony Burgess,' *Paris Review* 14. 56 (Spring 1973): 119–63.
14. Quoted in Betts, 18.
15. See Jean Chothia's *'Julius Caesar* in Interesting Times' in this volume.
16. Bernard F. Dick, *Joseph L. Mankiewicz* (Boston: Twain Publishers, 1983) 134.
17. Quoted in Cullinan, 133.
18. *Shakespeare in Love*, dir. John Madden, perf. Gwyneth Paltrow, Geoffrey Rush, Joseph Fiennes, Miramax, 1998.
19. *Easy Rider*, dir. Dennis Hopper, perf. Peter Fonda, Dennis Hopper, Columbia Pictures, 1969; *Midnight Cowboy*, dir. John Schlesinger, perf. Dustin Hoffman, John Voight, Sylvia Miles, United Artists, 1969.
20. *A Clockwork Orange*, dir. Stanley Kubrick, perf. Malcolm McDowell, Patrick Magee, Warner Brothers, 1971.
21. Harold Bloom, 'Introduction,' *Anthony Burgess*, ed. Harold Bloom (New York: Chelsea House, 1987) 5. See also Tom Stumpf, 'The Dependent Mind,' *Anthony Burgess Newsletter* 3 (2000) <*http://buweb.univ-angers.fr/EXTRANET/Anthony BURGESS/NLdmind.htm*>

9
The Singing Shakespearean: Kenneth Branagh's *Love's Labour's Lost* and the Politics of Genre

Ramona Wray

In a discussion of Hollywood cinematic practice, John Ellis has argued for the central importance of a pronounced 'narrative image'. Such an 'image' works, he suggests, as cinema's anticipatory reply to the question, 'What is the film like?'[1] Kenneth Branagh's filmic Shakespeares have always successfully invested in a such an overarching topos or unique selling point – the gung-ho spirit of *Henry V*, the tipsy Tuscan setting of *Much Ado About Nothing*, the unabridged nature of *Hamlet*.[2] As Ellis notes, industry discourse plays a key part in the creation of such narrative images, particularly in the earliest stages of a film's circulation, when publicity, marketing, distribution and exhibition are all being mobilised in mutually reinforcing roles.

With *Love's Labour's Lost*, Branagh's narrative image found its animating logic in a generic transformation.[3] In what was by far the most radical interpretative gesture of his career, *Love's Labour's Lost* was mooted as reinventing one of Shakespeare's lesser-known plays as a Hollywood musical from the 1930s. Pre-release machinery reiterated the singularity of the metamorphosis time and time again.[4] Trailers, stills and foyer displays offered verbal and iconographic expressions of the generic imprint. Both 'Tears, Laughter, Love and Romance' and 'Let's Face the Music and Dance' were highlighted on posters, which, alongside imagery of the masqued ball and chintzy heterosexual intimacy, communicated a vibrant impression of the period musical. Credit sequences and titles provided support for the perspective, while prospective comment contributed to the forcefully generic coherence of what G. Lukow and S. Ricci describe as cinema's 'intertextual relay'.[5] Preview observations traded on upbeat soundbites and generally described Branagh's concept favourably.[6] In the newly diverse context of Shakespearean cinematic appropriation, the potential merging of the drama and a musical in one of the least known plays appeared viable. When Harvey Weinstein of Miramax and *Shakespeare in Love* fame came on board for the American rights, predictions of box office smashes, Academy Awards and widespread acclaim ensued.[7] Such was mogul confidence that *Love's Labour's Lost* was signalled as the first of a new Branagh/Shakespeare movie trilogy.

On release, however, *Love's Labour's Lost* proved not to be the success that had been predicted. Critical comment was divided between a minority that regarded it as a curiosity and a majority that branded it 'Branagh's nadir as a director', 'a thing of shreds and patches … a failure'.[8] The film, which had cost eight million, took less than £350,000 in the UK, making it, according to the *Daily Express* reviewer, 'one of the biggest box office flops of 2000'.[9] As a result, the futures of both *Macbeth* and *As You Like It*, the second and third elements of the trilogy, were placed briefly in doubt.

At an early stage in the publicity process, Branagh himself had professed an anxiety about exactly how his generic focus would be received: 'What we've done with *Love's Labour's Lost*,' he stated, 'might provoke hostile debate.'[10] Certainly, by any standards, his generic transformation was risky: in the latter half of the twentieth century, commercially successful film musicals have been the exception rather than the rule.[11] Moreover, Branagh's musical is purposefully sited in a reconstruction of a past chronology (the 1930s), consciously invoking vocabularies at some distance from the modern viewer. This sets it apart from, to take a Shakespearean instance, Robert Wise and Jerome Robbins' *West Side Story*, a musical which invents as contemporary and conterminous the content of the story and the conventions of the genre.[12] Instead, *Love's Labour's Lost* exemplifies a type rarely seen outside of parody, a style of film designated by Rick Altman as a 'genre film' as opposed to a 'film genre' – that is, a cinematic work 'self-consciously produced and consumed according to … a specific generic model'.[13] Interestingly, Altman's acknowledgement that consumption and production need to operate in harmonious simultaneity is indicative of the ways in which recent filmic theorisations of genre have moved away from an emphasis on common characteristics. Critics insist, rather, on what Steve Neale describes as the 'multi-dimensional aspects' of generic classification, constructing genre as 'a phenomenon that encompasses systems of expectation, categories, labels and names, discourses, texts and groups or corpuses of texts, and conventions'.[14] Such theorising helpfully highlights both the processes of labelling/naming and the importance of audience knowledge/expectation; it focuses, in addition, on the cultural and institutional contexts within which genre is understood. However, while recent discussions are sensitive to the shaping powers of an audience, they tend to presuppose that both production and consumption invariably exist in easy equipoise. Relations between the two, it is assumed, are often comfortably congruent.

One of my arguments here is that the failure of *Love's Labour's Lost* provides a useful test case for separating out these functions and positing their relative autonomy. That is, inside a 'genre film', historical distancing may mean that it becomes possible for similar generic codes to be read differently. Indeed, genre disaffection and alienation in and of themselves may be the instruments through which alternatively dialogic readings can be released. The first part of this essay stresses the culturally contingent nature of genre by examining the ways in which *Love's Labour's Lost* works, through its reception, to produce a version of itself far removed from the *auteur*'s original conception. It takes as an exemplary moment one of the earliest indications that *Love's Labour's Lost* was not going to fare well – a private preview viewing at which Branagh and his backers realised that spectators were laughing in all the wrong places.[15] In situating the failure of *Love's Labour's Lost* inside its musical investments, this paper goes on to argue that a resistance to *Love's Labour's Lost*'s generic invitations opens the door to a series of narrative destabilisations which illuminate, not only the potentialities and limitations of the *fin-de-siècle* musical, but also the tenuousness of the play's contemporary purchase. In particular, I argue that Branagh's peculiar management of perceived reading difficulties (his post-preview decision radically to restructure the film, splicing into the musical continuum inserts of pseudo-*Pathé* broadcasts), while partially successful in pre-empting an ironic reaction and recasting pastiche as nostalgia, creates a generic mismatch, an out-of-place utterance which the intertextual relay arguably exacerbated. The essay subsequently contemplates the role of generic incongruity in shaping the film's multilayered and intricately allusive nostalgia.

On one level, *Love's Labour's Lost*'s utilisation of nostalgia is conventionally postmodern. A potent impression of the 1930s is manufactured, as Fredric Jameson would have it, 'through stylistic connotation': the film places in centre-frame symbolic objects, such as radiograms, cocktails, cigarette-holders and suitcases.[16] Indeed, in *Love's Labour's Lost*, the 1930s are realised *as* the musical, an elegant example of what Fredric Jameson describes as the 'history of aesthetic styles' displacing 'real history'.[17] At a deeper level, however, the ideological work preformed by nostalgia is not univocal. Rather, absorption in retrospection is seen to generate sequences of filmic collisions, narrative anomalies and temporal disjunctions. Examined in detail in the second half of the essay, this confusion of signifiers has as its by-product a confrontation with the film's political unconscious and, in particular, its reification of an ethics of retreat.

Pertinent to the arguments above are both the national implications of genre and the film's temporal location in recent transformations in Shakespearean filmmaking. Theoretical discussion tends not to address the possibility that genre and nation are intimately interlinked. In the case of the Hollywood musical, however, which revels in a spectrum of late-capitalist material signifiers, this dimension is abundantly evident. Produced at the time when Hollywood was coming into its own as the twentieth century's major fantasy-producing institution and quintessentially American, the musicals of the 1930s, perhaps more than any other species of film, envisage the US as an ideal of wish-fulfilment.[18] In its distinctive enlistment of the musical form, *Love's Labour's Lost* unwittingly sets up a disjunction between genre and nation: its implicitly patriotic and nostalgically 'British' sensibility runs against the grain of its generic aspirations. 'British' in the same way that Branagh's *Henry V* is an archetypally 'British' confection, *Love's Labour's Lost* makes available, at the very historical juncture when the country's influence in the EU appears to be on the wane, an invented Europe inspired by, and even in thrall to, the British imperative.[19] The result is a competition between representational forms, which sets on edge the variety of intercultural indicators, such as contrasting English and American accents, in evidence elsewhere. Playing against itself, the film therefore unwittingly focuses attention on the difficulties of arriving at an authentic expression of the past while simultaneously crystallising debates about the accessibility of historical 'truth' and the temptations of fictional practice. For Branagh, such temptations have a particularly Shakespearean inflection. Throughout this paper, it is contended that his film works metacinematically to reflect on the *auteur*'s place in the shift from staid, televisual productions of Shakespeare to looser, more inventive and restless modalities of appropriation. *Love's Labour's Lost* is caught in a limbo between venerating the bard and the rejuvenation and manipulation of Shakespeare on the popular screen and in mass media more generally.[20]

Crucial for the essay as a whole is the furnishing of an alternative context for understanding *Love's Labour's Lost*. In presenting Shakespearean romance as a modality we understand only through the dictating frameworks of US popular culture, Branagh's musical owes less to the heyday

of Hollywood and more to the heyday of British television – the experimental dramas of Dennis Potter and, in particular, the musical serials
Pennies from Heaven, The Singing Detective and *Lipstick on Your Collar*.[21]
This paper posits a productive connection between Potter's deployment
of melody and Branagh's use of music in his recent filmic statement. The
juxtaposition of the two *auteurs*, who share comparable ambitions and
fortunes, suggests that the key to understanding the totality of *Love's
Labour's Lost* lies closer to home than the film's generic persuasion and
pre-war setting would seem to indicate.[22]

After the completion of *Love's Labour's Lost*, Branagh accompanied
Weinstein and other executives to a sneak preview. Branagh, confident
that his product would play well with cinema audiences, recalls antici-
pating 'a great evening'. In retrospect, he describes the experience as:

> Agony. The audience didn't know how to take the film – some were
> laughing along with it, but the film was being mocked too. They
> weren't laughing at us, they were laughing near us ... [I thought] here
> I am at Planet Turkey, a great woofing dog that will be barking its way
> into the world shortly ... [We knew] we were in deep trouble.[23]

At an immediate level, then, the preview experience highlighted a
catastrophic wedge between the audience's reactions and the *auteur's*
expectations. Audience bemusement, incongruous laughter and specta-
torly ridicule – all are indicative of the gulf separating intention and
interpretation.

Branagh's sense of a dialogic interchange between a point of generic
inspiration and an appropriation is forcefully communicated in *Love's
Labour's Lost*'s absorption of many of the features associated with the
musicals of the 1930s.[24] In dispensing with almost three-quarters of the
Shakespearean text, Branagh ensures that music registers as the dominant pull on audience attention. Conventional iconography includes
period dress, a combination of gaudy and sepia tones, and a series of
impossibly extravagant physical elevations. As in the traditional musical, the sets are few in number and familiar (library, quadrangle, riverside and garden). Choreography is mainly inspired by Hermes Pan's
routines in RKO Astaire–Rogers musicals, and most dance numbers are
captured in long takes, with full body shots. At many points, the music
functions as it would have done in its earlier Hollywood incarnation;

that is, it helps to pinpoint romantic connections (couples are formed through the choreographed visuals of Jerome Kern's 'I Won't Dance, Don't Ask Me'); to interrupt the narrative with vignettes and interludes (such as in the aquatic rendition of Irving Berlin's 'No Strings (I'm Fancy Free)' *à la* Busby Berkeley); and, most importantly, to propel forward the plot. In the main, songs are woven seamlessly into the film fabric, musical lyrics working as an apt correlative to the play's sixteenth-century rhetorical expression. Thus Berowne's condemnation of academic monasticism is converted into the George Gershwin and Desmond Carter number, 'I'd Rather Charleston'. And, when Berowne, contemplating Love's elemental power, concludes 'And when Love speaks, the voice of all the gods / Make heaven drowsy with the harmony,'[25] the film slips smoothly into a joint performance of Irving Berlin's 'Cheek to Cheek', with its celestial refrain, 'Heaven, I'm in heaven'. Tried-and-trusted musical markers seem to be firmly in place, yet, as Branagh's regretful reflection on the preview makes clear, his target audience proved incapable of appreciating the film's signifiers of generic familiarity.

The multiplicity of media reactions helps to situate the failure to assess *Love's Labour's Lost* on its own terms. Certainly, the dominant impression that one gleans from popular coverage is the extent to which comment parallels and elaborates the preview audience's bemusement. Many commentators register a lack of certainty about how to read the film: the alien associations of the adjective 'surreal' are frequently utilised to describe a cinematic mode divorced from popular conceptions.[26] It might be argued, then, that key features that obtained with a particular relevancy in the 1930s reverberate with very different associations at the present cultural juncture. In particular, the musical and the 'Golden Age' of Hollywood's cinematic productivity have become bound up with an alternative set of expectations, promoting a breakdown in the regime of verisimilitude (the systems of plausibility, motivation and belief governing the reception process).[27] Consequently, examining the film without an appropriate interpretative lens, critics are able to bypass an engagement with its models, judging *Love's Labour's Lost* literally and noting the visuals only in order to label them 'self-indulgent' and 'fatuous' (allegations with which Fred and Ginger, in their equally implausible scripts, never had to deal).[28] Moreover, there is evidence to suggest that acting and gestures modelled on the style of the 1930s, and the tendency to slip into song and dance, are viewed today with sentiments akin to shame. 'Embarrassing' recurs as a salient epithet in reviews, pointing to a particularly awkward filmic encounter.[29] Anthony Quinn describes the general effect as 'insufferable... so bad my *seat* almost got up to leave', and his sense of squirm is echoed in the many reviews which liken *Love's Labour's Lost* to an 'end-of-term-play' or 'a Footlights revue' suddenly subjected to a merciless camera.[30] Few reviews, even those which were more kindly disposed, could resist poking fun at the performers, which implies that a critical suspension of disbelief – a dissolving into the film's imaginative landscape – had only imperfectly taken place. In particular, Branagh's age and physical appearance were singled out for unflattering remarks, in such a way as to indicate a skewed target of comic involvement.[31] *Love's Labour's Lost* may have been designed as 'a homage to the classical Hollywood musicals', but the critical reception makes visible the fact that, in the context of a late capitalist, postmodern moment, the musical is experienced only through the perspective of a posthumous and ironic cynicism.[32]

Faced with such a breakdown in producer–audience relations, Branagh's solution was to furnish a missing interpretative framework, a 'signal that this was a fun film, madcap, silly, that it was all right to laugh with it rather than at it'.[33] Intriguingly, his provision of a template involved splicing the musical continuum with a specific and equally outmoded generic modality. Throughout the *second* version of the film appears a *mélange* of studio-created and historically authentic *Pathé* newsreels, the distinctively British instrument of *reportage* pioneered in the 1930s.[34] Through its use of outmoded expressions, chirpy enthusiasms and jingoistic encouragements, the *Cinétone* voice consciously reintroduces and maintains the ironic note earlier entertained by the preview audience, creating, in an effect reminiscent of some musicals from the 1930s, an internal audience for the play's unfolding events.[35] For example, taking its cue from the decision to avoid women, the newsreel voice observes:

> It's a tall order by golly but this able young monarch, one of Europe's most eligible Royal bachelors, seems determined to show the world there's more to life than guns and warfare. He's an idealist. But we wish him and his three chums the best... More news as the adventure unfolds, but for now we wish them bon voyage, and good luck![36]

Euphemisms, proverbial phrasing and the suggestion of solidarity are put to work here to dispel an audience's unfriendly mockery, to dissolve distance and to promote an indulgent attitude towards the musical's fictively particularised environment. Bolstering the procedure is the visual contrast between the heightened colour of the action sequences and the scratchy black and white of the newsreels. This can be seen to operate in a comparable fashion to early experiments with technicolour, increasing, in the words of Jane Feuer, 'the voluptuousness of those parts of a film which ... represent fantasy', effectively setting up two worlds, fostering a dual reality effect (a type of 'play within a play') and signalling that one *habitus* should not be taken as seriously as the next.[37]

As a material reminder of the war to come, the newsreel plays an additionally important role in the film's establishment of the 1930s as a privileged yet circumscribed moment, a 'stolen, magical, idyllic time which nevertheless', in Branagh's words, 'had a clock ticking'.[38] Susan Bennett has noted the way in which 'nostalgia performs as the representation' of the utopian face of the past, and Branagh's perspective on the decade reveals just such a romantically-filtered selectivity.[39] Musical numbers hinting at a troubled future and conjuring up a glorious immediacy (Jerome Kern's 'The Way You Look Tonight', which, while focusing on the present, has as its central theme the anticipation of 'some day' when the protagonists are 'low' and the 'world is cold') help to construct the decade as an idyll that has been tragically eclipsed. But it is in the newsreel that the point is most powerfully expressed. Via this metacommentary, *Love's Labour's Lost* endeavours to make generic alienation operate productively, to facilitate the emergence of a doubled narrative and to repackage pastiche in a nostalgic register. The partial success of this repackaging is reflected in reviews which, at the same time as they describe *Love's Labour's Lost* as flimsy fare, also register the film's 'feelgood' effects and promotion of emotional amelioration.[40] Nor is the film nostalgic for the 1930s alone. A broad nostalgia for 'Golden Age' Hollywood is played out through specially-commissioned background orchestral themes. A stereotypical use of Elizabethan love imagery (such as a full moon, weeping willows and the sight of the Princess and her attendants hunting in the park) borrows directly from twentieth-century reflective constructions of the Renaissance. Even Branagh himself can be inserted into a nostalgic trajectory. Not only does his performance as Berowne hark back to his rendition of a similar Shakespearean type, Benedict in *Much Ado About Nothing*; the ensemble numbers – such as Irving Berlin's 'There's no Business Like Show Business' – and general camaraderie evoke the spirit of *Peter's Friends* and *In the Bleak Midwinter*, with their 'the show must go on' philosophies.[41] If *Love's Labour's Lost* yearns for a fictive pre-war interlude, then it also reminisces about Branagh's own 'golden' arrival on the cinematic scene. In the same way that the film remoulds the 1930s as a quasi-miraculous interruption in a bleaker continuum, so does it implicitly reimagine the Renaissance (and even, one might argue, the earlier cinematic heights scaled by Branagh as a youthful entrant to the Shakespearean arena).

The nostalgia produced in the film, however, does not always follow a smooth passage. Important, in this connection, is Branagh's move away from the musical's defining identity as an original score and his decision to utilise, instead, melodies which, in the filmmaker's words, 'give Shakespeare a run for his money'.[42] Assuming for themselves a canonical position in the popular consciousness, such songs have networks of association outside of any incorporating narrative. In its unconscious mobilisation of the contextual resonances of these forms of music, Branagh's film mirrors the conscious strategies of Potter's musical serials. Steve Brie's important pilot study of the English reception of *Lipstick on Your Collar* suggests that, while nostalgia is a fundamental determinant in the ways in which viewers negotiate the relationship between period music and popular representation, its precise *modus operandi* is rarely straightforward. Viewers may appropriate a visual and aural 'periodness' for their own nostalgic pleasures and purposes. In particular, according to Brie, the resurrection of historically-freighted melodies can stimulate extradiegetic satisfaction, precipitating a 'drift off' into 'musically-induced fabricated imaginings, or into memory narratives underpinned by personal history', all or some of which may be far removed from the *auteur*'s preferred interpretative template.[43] Such arguments may help to situate the more positive reviews of *Love's Labour's Lost*. Notably, critics who were complimentary were likely to record having enjoyed the music in the same moment that they sidelined – even urged a disregard for – the story's importance, illuminating a splintering of points of aesthetic appreciation.[44] In responding to the songs, other critics conjured related temporal and contextual locations. For example, a number of reviews explicitly privileged Irving Berlin's 'Lets Face the Music and Dance', which featured prominently not only in Potter's *The Singing Detective* but also in a series of high-profile television commercials from the 1990s for the Allied Dunbar Insurance Company.[45] This suggests that, for an audience at the beginning of the twenty-first century, nostalgia is mediated through a consciousness of the cultural practices of more recent decades. If the *fin-de-siècle* musical is invariably a multivalent gathering of reflections, a representational vehicle carrying in its train a number of layered meanings and messages, its reception might assume a corresponding open-endedness.

While externally-inspired agents can disrupt the ways in which canonical tunes are translated, internally-created associations further shatter the film's nostalgic investments. Crucially, the very act of recasting pastiche as nostalgia in itself generates incongruity. The separatist procedure allowing for a nostalgic view of Navarre abundantly illustrates this double bind. When the opening informs the viewer about the European situation as well as the dramatic story, for example, two headlines – 'New Ideas in Navarre' and 'War Imminent' – are brought into a precisely-dated chronological juxtaposition. In a visual continuation of the headline disparity, medium shots of the male protagonists sharing a joke are interspersed with images of bomber-planes, while a comparative voiceover simultaneously parallels the action of retirement with a gathering European crisis:

> September 1939. Ominous clouds of war may be hovering over Europe but here in Navarre, the young King, seen here returning from military manoeuvres, has announced an audacious plan...He and his companions are to cast off their military uniforms, while world events still allow, and devote themselves to a rigorous three years of study. That's right, three years.[46]

The problem with this alternating between external and internal events is that it has the effect of making the protagonists' flight into romance seem self-indulgently irresponsible. As a result of the uncertain fit between global conflict and romantic retrenchment, folly is at least partially politicised. Indeed, inside the above paradigm, the retreat of the 'boys' comes close to conscientious objection (only the reference to recent military action, and the portentous suggestion that the situation is contingent ['while world events still allow'], mitigate against this perspective). The point is underlined via images that emphasise the class-bound, familial and locational obligations of the leading personalities. Much as he did in *Hamlet*, Branagh consistently reminds his viewer that, as members of royal and aristocratic families whose nations are on the brink of war, the drama's players have the potential to act in an internationally important fashion. The death of the King of France, for example, is realised both as a personal tragedy (a close-up shot of the Princess' tears) and as a national disaster with ramifications beyond the immediate familial context (newspaper headlines suggest that France will fall without its figurehead). In episodes such as these, the overwhelming impression is not so much of conscientious objectors as of willingly blindfolded national powers.

Throughout these sequences, the camera continues to keep characters at a distance. When the Princess learns of the retreat from a newspaper, for instance, the point-of-view shot scans the columns to remind us that the wider interpretative community is more preoccupied with the progress of England's most famous son (after Shakespeare, of course), Winston Churchill. The move is awkward, leaving one uncertain of a gaze which relegates Allied foreign policy in favour of a filmic grammar inspired by Hollywood. Once paralleled, moments of political withdrawal intersect, in turn, with the play's metatheatrical allusions. Comments such as Berowne's 'The scene begins to cloud' (5.2.717) and 'That's too long for a play' (5.2.867) inevitably reflect upon the escalating situation peripheral to the main plot while pointing up issues of political neglect.[47] Maintaining the two-world narrative, and retaining audience identification with the protagonists, becomes a delicate balancing-act, one that is destabilised by the very nostalgic sensibility necessary for its inception and survival.

Most unpredictably, perhaps, the common dominator of nostalgia underlining *Love's Labour's Lost* is further compromised by its oddly 'British' inflections. If the songs and sets evince a retrospective experience which is open to all, these parts of the film simultaneously mark nostalgia off as a strictly English prerogative. This is nowhere more evident than in the scenes which discover, rather in the manner of Laurence Olivier's *Henry V*, World War II as a nationally cohesive and exclusive enterprise.[48] In Branagh's filmic comedy, an accelerated montage flits between six wartime scenarios: the Princess and her waiting gentlewomen are pictured being led away to internment in France; his Spanish status notwithstanding, Armado languishes in a POW camp; the King executes heroics at the Front; his comrades have resumed their roles as fighter-pilots (presumably for the RAF); amidst air-raids Berowne attends to the wounded; and Nathaniel and Holofernia (mysteriously returned to 'Old Blighty') are seen 'Digging for Victory'. Common to the sequence as a whole is a registration of the film's personalities as glamorously resilient, courageously corporate and purposefully involved in a larger endeavour. But the wider field of activity is figured in highly local terms. With the exception of the quick glimpse of Boyet, who has been recuperated as a leading member of the French Resistance, all of the shots privilege a 'British' context and figure Shakespeare's Gallic protagonists as little more than the English on holiday: the film both collapses and re-sorts the war's messy global trajectory. VE Day is constructed as an accomplishment in which all types of people (old and young/male and female) play a part, yet the roles elaborated are manifestly unequal.

The fate of the French is to be passive victims; the achievement of the British is to win glory in domestic and international spheres.

At once, of course, this is a species of nostalgia that removes to the periphery the Continental and American consumer.[49] At a deeper level, the essentially British orientation of the newsreel comes into tension with the musical's all-American modality. Crucially, the shift from one landscape into another (from the play-script to the war-script) does not only constitute a surface component of the literal narrative. It inevitably becomes, in the context of the film, a generic choice. The move into the musical environment is necessarily symbolically freighted – at best, fool-hardy evasion, at worst, political cowardice. Rather than imagining the musical (and the decade that is elaborated through its signifiers) as polit-ically neutral, the ill-matching nature of *Love's Labour's Lost*'s dual modes of representation mounts a challenge to the film's nostalgically freighted dependencies. Constructing the musical as a distractive indul-gence, generic discontinuity suggests an oppositional analysis of the 1930s in terms of a self-serving political myopia and a policy of appease-ment. Certainly, the fact that the immersion in music has a costly consequence is made clear in the newsreel's closing montage which includes glimpses of fascist regalia. Here, more than at any other point, are stressed not only the human ramifications of a politics of distraction but the concomitant competition between British and American styles of self-representation.

While the newsreel appears critically at odds with its generic enclosure, however, it also enthusiastically contributes to the escapism the musical espouses, suggesting that unmediated authenticity is not freely available. 'Royals Camping!', a typical headline, is shown to take extended prece-dence over a vital update on French border disputes, which illustrates the kind of skewed priorities that the newsreel itself attacks elsewhere. In fact, by prioritising glimpses into the protagonists' private lives, the newsreel becomes a microcosm of the displacing fantasies animat-ing the film as a whole.[50] Further, the formal cast of the *Cinétone* voice means that its invitations to participate take on discernible political resonances. As Fredric Jameson argues, with the break-up of accent, the location of power has been occluded. Accent no longer necessarily indicates who is in control: norms of verbal utterance (in this case, 'Received Pronunciation') have been 'reduced to a neural and reified media speech...which itself then becomes but one more idiolect among many'.[51] To a contemporary audience, this genus of voice is greeted with suspicion, since the newsreel form is now popularly recognised as one incarnation of the 'propaganda film'.[52] In its older, national, speech-pattern, then, the newsreel both raises questions about author-ship and betrays its shaping role as a linguistic instrument of ideological coercion.

The fact that the *Pathé* newscaster's voice is Branagh's own works to implicate *Love's Labour's Lost* in just such a process. The director is iden-tified as controlling agent, the paradoxical effect of which is to ensnare him in unresolved reflections upon censorship and creativity. The unsettling effect is increased as the film progresses because it is Branagh as authoritative voice who impresses throughout. Berowne, whom Branagh plays, is the only character able to move among the film's generic and ideological polarities. Nowhere is his singular dexterity bet-ter exemplified than when the montage shows a visibly anxious Berowne listening to news of encroaching enemy troops; the revealing next cut is to the King and his colleagues speculating upon the 'ladies' larking about in pin curls. It is Berowne/Branagh alone who, as *auteur*, slips between the film's opposed environments and who possesses the extra-play knowledge that enables him to exercise so nuanced a mobil-ity. Presiding over the film world in the guise of newscaster, and flitting in and out of its layered environments, Branagh is kept continually at the screen's imaginative forefront, in such a way as to suggest a Shakespeare who must be mediated and an interpreter who must be privileged. At times, Branagh's role even extends to a simultaneously retrospective and prescient rehearsal of his career thus far. Even in this connection, however, the film reveals more than it might intend. A number like Irving Berlin's 'There's No Business Like Show Business', for instance, can clearly be seen to mediate Branagh's own pivotal role in the Shakespeare industry.[53] But it also comments on his increasingly marginal role within the cinematic revival of the dramatist for which he has, in large part, been responsible: viewed in the spotlight of the film's commercial failure, lines such as 'Even with a turkey that you know will fold/You may be stranded out in the cold' reflect unflatteringly on the uncertain purchase of Branagh's recent Shakespearean outings.[54]

The self-consciousness that clusters around Branagh as controller extends into the self-consciousness of the film's singing and dancing technique. Its amateurish nature simultaneously forms a bridge with, and moves on from, Potter's trademark lip-synching techniques (whereby characters step out of the dramatic action to burst into song, using not their own voices but miming to original recordings).[55] Branagh's decision to cast non-trained performers for roles that demanded classical perfor-mative skills rides roughshod over the most basic convention of the musical: even if a plot constructs a character as an amateur, he or she is expected to demonstrate superlative qualities of movement and voice.[56] Confusion over the split between the casting decision and the generic promise of the inter-textual relay was rehearsed in many pejoratively-phrased reviews.[57] In interview, Branagh stated that he was 'happy to...encourage...a certain rawness in the singing and dancing', since this illuminated the situation of 'ordinary people...striving to express romantic urges and finer feelings in *unaccustomed* ways'.[58] Performative *gaucherie* is here justified on the grounds of an elaboration of the characters' *naïveté*, although Branagh misses the key point that Potter's television series have reinforced; that is, the 'ways' in which the discourses of romantic love manifest themselves in the social imaginary are always '*accustomed*', always routinised. As Roland Barthes famously noted, 'the amorous phenomenon is an "episode" endowed with a beginning... and an end'.[59]

Obviously, the newspaper and the war are external scripts that impact upon the lovers' life choices, but, through its particular amalgamation of different generic forms, *Love's Labour's Lost*, like the marginalia of Barthes' *A Lover's Discourse*, reveals other scripts (such as its songs and, of course, the Shakespearean text itself) as equally powerful promptbooks for self-representation. It is precisely this idea that is visually and aurally encapsulated when the four male protagonists not only write comparable love letters but also articulate their sentimentally-synonymous situations through a single song, George Gershwin and Ira Gershwin's 'I've Got a Crush on You'. By making of the song a simultaneously choral and communal set-piece, the direction ensures that, rather than the stress falling on individuation, a similarity of experience is underlined. A related emphasis finds meaning in one of Branagh's favourite pieces of camerawork, in which sequences of flash-frame close-ups show either the 'girls' or the 'boys' registering identical emotional expressions (in the scene devoted to the lovers' first meeting, for example, desire is inscribed in a reiterated visual physiognomy across all eight sets of faces). The four trench-coated Bogarts who replace the solitary nightclub owner of Michael Curtiz's 1942 Hollywood fantasy send the same message.[60] Branagh's belief in the authenticity of music as a channel for vernacular feeling notwithstanding, one effect of *Love's Labour's Lost* is to *disindividuate* its participants, the sheer appropriative weight of the film robbing them of a felt articulacy.

At an intertextual level, a cultivated amateurishness of technique becomes one of the instruments whereby the film reaches out to connect itself with cinematic history. An implicit ambition in *Love's Labour's Lost* is to dissolve the myth of the 1930s into a twentieth-century paradigm, but this is prevented by the accumulation of filmic detail and development that has come between these two chronological polarities. In particular, the gradual disappearance of performative versatility in actors/ actresses, and its replacement by the more powerful virtues of celebrity, are unwittingly engaged with in *Love's Labour's Lost*'s casting arrangements. Alicia Silverstone (the Princess of France) may be the established US star required to satisfy the box-office; in terms of her musical abilities, however, even among other non-professionals, she is clearly the weakest link. 'More prom queen than princess, and never in command of her lines,' Silverstone functions as a constant reminder of the obliteration of singing and dancing as essential qualifications in the Hollywood of modernity.[61] As part of its replacement of 'reality' with the trappings of genre, *Love's Labour's Lost* also conjures a narrower filmic trajectory, which leads from the buoyant vitality of the musical to the bleaker and more dispassionate reflectivity of the wartime romance (in which lovers often part and passion does not always prevail).[62] Bolstering the idea that the 1930s constituted a privileged space, the shift from musical to romance constructs World War II in terms of its aesthetic ramifications. The film's iconography gradually incorporates familiar motifs from films of the 1940s (such as *Brief Encounter*), mapping a cinematic route from innocence to cynicism, and from security to uncertainty.[63] The movement culminates in a company performance of George Gershwin and Ira Gershwin's 'They Can't Take That Away From Me'. One genre yields to another as the song, with its 'we'll-always-have-Paris' sentiments, complements a leave-taking scene purposefully presented as a reworking of *Casablanca*'s celebrated ending.[64] On the one hand, the generic dissolution comments upon the multivalent dynamic of cinematic memory; on the other hand, it reinforces the notion that, in Bennett's words, 'Nostalgia might best be considered as the inflicted territory where claims for authenticity are staged.'[65] By filtering its romantic conceits through a mesh of accreted influences, *Love's Labour's Lost* inefficaciously searches for a grammar of celluloid sincerity that will simultaneously revitalise and respect the integrity of the Shakespearean original.

It seems particularly odd then that having inaugurated a development which should allow contemporary audiences to understand the play's ending (arguably, to modern viewers, the least palatable part), Branagh chooses not to pursue it, preferring instead to reinstate the happy conclusion denied both by the drama and his war-time cinema narrative models. The tactic makes sense, however, within the context of the *faux* newsreel narrative, which demands that the immersion in romantic fantasy, like the cinematic dominance of the musical, is only ever a phase. In a not wholly successful endeavour to restore an authentic masculinity, the play's twelve-month separation period is extended to World War II's six-year hiatus.[66] The final narrative resolution (which is engineered via the unions of the couples after their war engagements) attempts a reconciliation of the film's polarised values – material realities now blend with the world of imagination, with notions of spontaneity, impulse and pleasure. This is signalled at the level of the film's appearance: gradually, a wash of colour seeps in, a visual and ideological replacement for the similarly symbolically-loaded sequences of black and white. Once again, America is omitted in a montage of harmonising visuals that underscores the cultural preeminence of London and Paris. If the reintegrated cinematography represses the spirit of 'Old Sam', it simultaneously returns the film to its generic roots. The ending constitutes Branagh's reworking of the classical conclusion of the musical, although in that generic form, resolution is usually achieved through the union of a couple, the two halves of which represent contrasting dimensions of a dream/reality dichotomy.[67] But with Branagh, filmic opposites are merged in the experiences of couples joined through a shared bond of global conflict.

The film, however, cannot opt out of the implications of its chosen reorientation so easily. In the absence of a Shakespearean script, a final set of clichés stands in for a concluding narrative, as visions of the reunited couples are filtered through the staged reunion photographs of VE Day. Susan Stewart has argued that 'the narration of the photograph itself becomes an object of nostalgia'.[68] But, like all evocations of the past in this film, such retrospection does not go unchallenged. In that they come as the climax to a sequence of competing conventional iconographies, these moments have a jarring effect. The sense of friction is realised when one of the concluding shots shows a newspaper bearing the wrong date: 11 November was when World War I, not World War II, ended. It is a small and unconscious error. Yet it is a deeply Freudian mistake: by breaking down the boundaries between the wars, this parting chronological rupture introduces a notion of historical indeterminacy, which works against the rest of the film's multiple constructions of the 1930s in general – and the musical genre in particular – as specially demarcated arenas. The temporal breakdown stands as an overdetermined moment, robbing the decade of the distinctive identity *Love's Labour's Lost* works so hard to institute elsewhere. In executing this repressive function, it highlights the ways in which *Love's Labour's Lost* constitutes a summation of, and a response to, the world of the simulacrum, in which political memory is always mediated and in which instruments of mass representation jostle for privilege. Branagh's failed attempt to rework Shakespeare for a *fin-de-siècle* sensibility leaves his spectators in a cultural nowhere, adrift in a flood of discrete and disassociated generic frameworks. His filmic experiment emerges as a confused amalgam, a screen product hesitating between modes of inter-textual communication, layerings of nostalgic construction, and colli-sions of generic and national identification. Finally, the name of the newspaper (*The Globe*) in which the dating mistake appears alerts us to the correspondingly embattled locations of Branagh himself, as he strives to vindicate himself as domestic *auteur* and to fix his place in the precarious universe of the Shakespearean present.[69]

Notes and references

1. John Ellis, *Visible Fictions: Cinema: Television: Video* (London: Routledge, 1981) 30.
2. *Henry V*, dir. Kenneth Branagh, Renaissance Films, 1989; *Much Ado About Nothing*, dir. Kenneth Branagh, Samuel Goldwyn Company/Renaissance Films, 1993; *Hamlet*, dir. Kenneth Branagh, Castle Rock, 1996.
3. *Love's Labour's Lost*, dir. Kenneth Branagh, Pathé/Intermedia, 2000. Criticism has yet to engage with *Love's Labour's Lost*. The only items published thus far are Samuel Crowl's brief discussion in 'Flamboyant Realist: Kenneth Branagh,' *The Cambridge Companion to Shakespeare on Film*, ed. Russell Jackson (Cambridge: CUP, 2000) 237–8; and Laurie E. Osborne, 'Introduction,' *Colby Quarterly* 37 (2001): 10–11.
4. *'Love's Labour's Lost': Production Information* (London: Intermedia, 2000) *passim*.
5. G. Lukow and S. Ricci, 'The "Audience" Goes "Public": Inter-textuality, Genre and the Responsibilities of Film Literacy,' *On Film* 12 (1995): 29.
6. Preview comment described Branagh's concept as 'a brilliant...idea.' 'The story...is tailor-made for the songs of Cole Porter,' anticipated one critic, while others drew attention to the movie's 'pedigree' and its 'encompassing' of 'Kiss Me Kate and...That Shakespearean Rag.' See Demetrios Matheour, 'Film,' *Empire* 30 April 2000: 121; Tony Howard, 'They Can't Take That Away,' *Around the Globe* 13 (2000): 37; Edward Porter, 'Musical Dares,' *Sunday Times: Culture* 2 April 2000: 9.
7. *Shakespeare in Love*, dir. John Madden, Miramax/Universal, 1999.
8. Steve Grant, 'Video,' *Sunday Times: Culture* 27 August 2000: 27; Potter, 'Musical Dares,' 9.
9. 'Ken's Labour's Lost on the Bard,' *Daily Express* 30 January 2001: 39.
10. Sarah Gristwood, 'What is this thing called *Love's Labour's Lost?*,' *Guardian* 27 March 2000: 9.

11. This does not necessarily mean that the musical has resisted metamorphosis into other forms. For discussion of the evolution of the traditional musical into the 'rock musical' (films such as *Grease* [1978] and *Dirty Dancing* [1987] would be relevant examples), see Jane Feuer, *The Hollywood Musical* (Basingstoke: Macmillan – now Palgrave Macmillan, 1993) 130–8.

12. *West Side Story* , dir. Robert Wise and Jerome Robbins, United Artists, 1961.

13. In explicitly identifying *Love's Labour's Lost* with one particular genre, Intermedia, the production company, further worked against current fashions. As Altman notes, 'Though distributors and exhibitors during Hollywood's golden years rarely violated the generic contexts implied by the parent studio,' contemporary 'exhibition practices... regularly recast a film generically,' working hard 'to multiply the number of genres with which a film is implicitly identified.' Rick Altman, *Film/Genre* (London: British Film Institute, 1999) 144.

14. Steve Neale, *Genre and Hollywood* (London and New York: Routledge, 2000) 2, 17.

15. This incident is related in David James Smith, 'In the Company of Ken,' *Sunday Times: Magazine* 20 February 2000: 36–7.

16. Fredric Jameson, *Postmodernism, or, The Cultural Logic of Late Capitalism* (London and New York: Verso, 1991) 19.

17. Jameson, *Postmodernism* 20.

18. Although musicals were being produced in Britain in the 1930s, their form is less extravagantly distinctive. See Stephen C. Shafer, *British Popular Films 1929–1939: The Cinema of Reassurance* (London and New York: Routledge, 1997).

19. On the national inflections of Branagh's earlier work, see Graham Holderness, ' "What ish my nation?": Shakespeare and National Identities,' *Textual Practice* 5 (1991): 74–93.

20. On such transitions, see Lynda E. Boose and Richard Burt, ed., *Shakespeare, the Movie: Popularising the Plays on Film, TV and Video* (London and New York: Routledge, 1997); Richard Burt, *Unspeakable ShaXXXspeares: Queer Theory and American Kiddie Culture* (Basingstoke: Macmillan – now Palgrave Macmillan, 1998).

21. *Pennies from Heaven* (1978), *The Singing Detective* (1986) and *Lipstick on Your Collar* (1993) were television series originally produced by, and screened on, the BBC television channel.

22. At first glance, figures such as Potter and Branagh may appear unlikely bedfellows. However, a more leisurely look reveals situational and ideological connections. Both are the closest that Britain has had to an *auteur* in the last thirty years. Both have argued passionately for the democratising potential of their medium. Where Branagh rehearses the ideal that his films make Shakespeare available for everyone, Potter has imagined television creating 'a common culture' which bridges the gap 'between dons and coal-miners.' At the same time, these two popular interpreters have been put on the cultural rack, vilified on crosses erected by the British media. See the interview with Branagh featured on *The South Bank Show* (23 January 2000). See also Ramona Wray and Mark Thornton Burnett, 'From the Horse's Mouth: Branagh on the Bard' in Mark Thornton Burnett and Ramona Wray, ed., *Shakespeare, Film, Fin de Siècle* (Basingstoke: Macmillan – now Palgrave Macmillan, 2000) 165–78.

For Potter's views, see Dennis Potter, 'Cue Telecine – Put on the Kettle,' *New Society* 22 September 1966: 457.

23. Smith, 'In the Company' 36–7.
24. For a discussion of prototypical features, see Rick Altman, *The American Film Musical* (Bloomington: Indiana University Press, 1987) 28–58. Other overviews include Feuer, *The Hollywood Musical passim*; Neale, *Genre and Hollywood* 104–12.
25. William Shakespeare, *Love's Labour's Lost*, ed. John Kerrigan (Harmondsworth: Penguin, 1982), 4.3.320–1. All further references appear in the text.
26. See the radio and TV clips reproduced on *'Love's Labour's Lost': UK Broadcast Coverage*. This video compilation forms part of the Kenneth Branagh Archive, donated by the filmmaker to the Queen's University of Belfast (henceforth cited as K.B.A, Q.U.B.).
27. Neale discusses the concept of verisimilitude in *Film/Genre*, 31–9.
28. Allan Hunter, 'Film,' *Express* 31 March 2000 (K.B.A., Q.U.B.); Alexander Walker, 'Let's face the music and prance,' *London Evening Standard* 30 March 2000 (K.B.A., Q.U.B.).
29. Anthony Quinn, 'Film,' *Independent* 31 March 2000 (K.B.A., Q.U.B.); Nigel Andrews, 'Ken and Patricia's Labours wasted,' *Financial Times* 30 March 2000 (K.B.A., Q.U.B.).
30. Antonia Quirke, 'Why do Shakespeare at all if you're going to do it like this?,' *Independent on Sunday* 2 April 2000 (K.B.A., Q.U.B.); Walker, 'Let's face the music and prance,' n.p.
31. Adrianne Pielou, 'Natascha Faces the Music,' *You Magazine: Mail on Sunday* 2 April 2000 (K.B.A., Q.U.B.); Allan Hunter, 'Film,' *Express* 31 March 2000 (K.B.A., Q.U.B.).
32. *'Love's Labour's Lost': Production Information* 27.
33. Smith, 'In the Company' 37.
34. For an overview of the evolution of this peculiarly British form, see Rachael Low, *The History of British Film 1929–1939: Films of Comment and Persuasion of the 1930s* (London and New York: Routledge, 1997) 9–59.
35. On MGM's reliance on an internal narrative audience, see Feuer, *The Hollywood Musical*, 31–4. The device is clearly Shakespearean. For a discussion of this and other self-conscious devices in Shakespeare, see Robert Stam, *Reflexivity in Film and Literature: From Don Quixote to Jean-Luc Goddard* (New York: Columbia University Press, 1992) 3–5.
36. Kenneth Branagh, *'Love's Labour's Lost': A Musical Adapted from the Play by William Shakespeare: Screenplay* (K.B.A., Q.U.B.).
37. Feuer, *The Hollywood Musical* 67. In this sense, the *Cinétone* announcer occupies a position analogous to the chorus in Shakespearean drama. Of course, Branagh had previously appropriated the choric device to excellent effect in his film version of *Henry V*.
38. Burnett and Wray, 'From the Horse's Mouth' 174.
39. Susan Bennett, *Performing Nostalgia: Shifting Shakespeare and the Contemporary Past* (London and New York: Routledge, 1996) 5.
40. Alan Frank describes having 'felt 100 percent better for having seen it – both times,' despite his more reserved headline. See his 'Not too Bard at all, Ken,' *Daily Star* 31 March 2000 (K.B.A., Q.U.B.). Similarly, Adrianne Pielou describes an emotional transformation from dull and uninspired to

'exhilarated.' She left the film 'wishing there was a flight of steps [she] could dance to.' See her 'Natascha Faces the Music,' n. p.

41. *Peter's Friends*, dir. Kenneth Branagh, Samuel Goldwyn Company/Renaissance Films, 1992; *In the Bleak Midwinter*, dir. Kenneth Branagh, Castle Rock, 1995.

42. *<http://www.pathe.co.uk/LLL/docs/cont4.html>*.

43. Steve Brie, 'Yesterday Once More,' *The Passion of Dennis Potter: International Collected Essays*, ed. Vernon W. Gras and John R. Cook (New York: St. Martin's Press – now Palgrave Macmillan, 2000) 210.

44. See, for example, Gerald Aaron, 'And the bard plays on,' *Jewish Chronicle* 31 March 2000 (K.B.A., Q.U.B.); James Cameron-Wilson, 'Love's Labour's Lost,' *Film Review* March 2000 (K.B.A., Q.U.B.); Sarah Gristwood, 'Classical Gas,' *Nine to Five* 27 March 2000 (K.B.A., Q.U.B.); Caroline Westbrook, 'Love's Labour's Lost,' *Empire* April 2000 (K.B.A., Q.U.B.).

45. See, for example, 'Love's Labour's Lost,' *Total Film* March 2000 (K.B.A., Q.U.B.); David Jays, 'Love's Labour's Lost,' *Sight and Sound* April 2000 (K.B.A., Q.U.B.); Barry Norman, 'Ken's labour of love,' *Radio Times* 8 April 2000 (K.B.A., Q.U.B); Angus Wolfe Murray, 'Ken's dancing queens,' *Edinburgh Evening News* 30 March 2000 (K.B.A., Q.U.B).

46. Branagh, *Screenplay* 1 (K.B.A., Q.U.B.).

47. Branagh, *Screenplay* 54, 58 (K.B.A., Q.U.B.).

48. *Henry V*, dir. Laurence Olivier, Two Cities Films, 1944.

49. Films such as Roberto Benigni's *Life Is Beautiful* (Miramax, 1997) demonstrate that trading upon received ideas about American intervention and liberation is a necessary ingredient in the achievement of commercial success.

50. It might not be accidental, therefore, that, as Branagh was planning *Love's Labour's Lost*, he was rehearsing a starring role in Woody Allen's *Celebrity* (Miramax, 1998), a film which addresses the late twentieth-century fascination with the famous.

51. Jameson, *Postmodernism* 17.

52. See, for instance, Sumiko Higashi, 'Melodrama, Realism and Race: World War II Newsreels and Propaganda Film,' *Cinema Journal* 37.3 (1998): 38–61.

53. Interestingly, in moments such as these, Branagh is close to that other major Hollywood genre of the 1930s, the biopic. For a discussion of the musical biopic, see Feuer, *The Hollywood Musical*, 96–102.

54. Branagh, *Screenplay* 53 (K.B.A., Q.U.B.).

55. This technique has been most recently utilised to general acclaim in the American television series, *Ally McBeal*. Here the songs offer interiorised perspectives on characters' situations and motivations. The best discussion of Potter's utilisation of this technique can be found in Glen Creeber, *Dennis Potter Between Two Worlds: A Critical Reassessment* (Basingstoke: Macmillan – now Palgrave Macmillian, 1998) 134–44.

56. *'Love's Labour's Lost': Production Information*, 20. The exception to the generally only average and occasionally awful singing and dancing is Adrian Lester's superlative performance. Since Lester is black, this lends an interesting edge to Courtney Lehmann's article on Branagh popularism coming unstuck on multinational grounds. See her *'Much Ado About Nothing?* Shakespeare, Branagh and the "National-Popular" in the Age of Multinational Capital,' *Textual Practice* 12 (1998): 1–22.

57. *Love's Labour's Lost,* wrote one critic, is 'full of folks who can't sing or dance [in roles for which they are] unsuitable and obviously untrained.' See Grant, 'Video' 27. 'The dancing...is unadventurous and noticeably slap dash,' noted another, 'no match for the shows of regimented agility...of Hollywood's golden-age musicals' (Porter, 'Musical Dares' 9). Critics such as Christopher Tookey, 'left wondering why real singer-dancers were not called in to do the job properly,' were presumably reacting to the way in which an amateurishness of technique calls attention to the fictionality of the screen action and the implausibility of the film's personalities. See Christopher Tookey, 'Bard is beyond our Ken,' *Daily Mail* 31 March 2000: 52.

58. *'Love's Labour's Lost': Production Information* 20.

59. Roland Barthes, *A Lover's Discourse: Fragments* (Harmondsworth: Penguin, 1977) 193.

60. *Casablanca,* dir. Michael Curtiz, Warner Brothers, 1942.

61. Porter, 'Musical Dares' 9.

62. A similar trajectory is traced in Colin Shindler, *Hollywood in Crisis: Cinema and American Society 1929–1939* (London and New York: Routledge, 1996).

63. *Brief Encounter,* dir. David Lean, Pinewood Films, 1945.

64. The idea of a final bow for the musical is captured in the rendition of the penultimate song (Irving Berlin's 'There's No Business Like Show Business'), which involves the entire company and is presented as a generic finale. It is also notable that, after the ending proper (the VE photographs), the film tracks backwards to replay 'There's No Business Like Show Business,' reinforcing the notion of this song as the 'proper' finale.

65. Bennett, *Performing Nostalgia* 7.

66. In this connection, there are stylish linguistic correspondences – Rosaline's requirement that Berowne should 'Visit the speechless sick' (5.2.840) to 'jest a twelvemonth in an hospital' (5.2.860) is translated into a sequence that, deploying both authentic footage and purposefully-created montage, shows Berowne working in a military hospital with the potent symbol of the Red Cross emblazoned on his sleeve.

67. On this point, see Feuer, *The Hollywood Musical* 71–3.

68. Susan Stewart, *On Longing: Narratives of the Miniature, the Gigantic, the Souvenir, the Collection* (Durham and London: Duke University Press, 1993) 138.

69. My thanks to Pascale Aebischer, Mark Burnett, Ewan Fernie, Aaron Kelly, Clare McManus and Sharon O'Dair for their generous help with earlier drafts of this essay.

10

Romeo and Juliet: the Rock and Roll Years

Robert Shaughnessy

> Romeo loved Juliet
> Juliet she felt the same
> When he put his arms around her
> He said Julie Baby you're my flame
> Thou giveth fever
> When we kisseth
> Fever with thy flaming youth
> Fever
> I'm afire
> Fever yea I burn forsooth

The lines form the second verse of a song which is generally regarded as one of the great modern songs, first recorded by Peggy Lee in 1958,[1] and subsequently covered more times, and by a wider range of recording artists than it is sensible to contemplate, ranging from Elvis Presley in 1960 to Madonna in 1992. It also contains what is probably one of the best-known Shakespearean allusions in popular music. Both in its form and subject-matter, 'Fever' is simple to the point of the elemental in its appeal. Stripped of instrumental accompaniment apart from percussion, finger-snapping and double-bass employing a simple blues rhythm, played at a moderate but intense tempo, the lyric is structured around the repeated, urgent one-word refrain ('fever'), giving vocal and musical shape to a sexual desire which seems barely containable within the song itself. It is a desire which is raging, consuming, anarchic and mutually annihilating, and which promises to undermine the foundations and dissolve the boundaries of identity itself ('When you put your arms around me / I get a fever that's hard to bear'). It is also, as the primitivist arrangement of Peggy Lee's rendition insists, a universal and elemental force which confounds and transcends time and space, and whose apotheosis is rapturous self-immolation ('what a lovely way to burn').

Although 'Fever' starts simply as a red-hot love song, its progression is from the personal to the mythical and universal, emblematically represented by two romantic narratives guaranteed instant recognition: Captain Smith and Pocahontas (who 'had a very mad affair'), and Shakespeare's lovers. The Shakespearean citation is at one level merely one of countless examples of how the figures of Romeo and Juliet have become deeply embedded within the western cultural imagination as what Jonathan Bate calls its 'archetypal myth of youthful passion';[2] a myth currently represented pre-eminently within popular culture by Baz Luhrmann's cult Bard flick *William Shakespeare's Romeo + Juliet*.[3] It is also, as the allusion to Captain Smith and Pocahontas confirms, an invocation of that passion acted out in defiance of parental authority and across a cultural or ethnic divide. Within the lyrical scheme, the anarchy of desire manifests itself through the witty juxtaposition of contrasting verbal registers: Juliet becomes 'Julie Baby'; Romeo's mode of address a comically anachronistic *bricolage* of jazz slang, quotation ('flaming youth' being derived, inappropriately enough, from the violent confrontation between the Prince of Denmark and his mother in *Hamlet*: 'To flaming youth let virtue be as wax / And melt in her own fire' [3.4. 84–5][4]), and a burlesqued Shakespearean idiom ('Fever yea I burn forsooth'). The conjuncture simultaneously affirms the popular myth, extrapolating the feverish desire which is the subject of the song as a universal truth, and mockingly subverts its high-cultural associations, as the ardent verbiage of courtly love is undercut by the spontaneous and irresistible demands of the body and artifice surrenders to nature.

In its use of archetypal material which is derived from an ostensibly Shakespearean source, but which (either at the point of production or consumption) is not necessarily informed by 'real' knowledge of its narrative, its characters, or their significance, 'Fever' is a relatively sophisticated example of Shakespeare put to use within popular song.[5] The distinctive quality of 'Fever', as an instance of playfully literate popular song lyric-writing, lies in its hybrid character, which marks it as a version of what Mikhail Bakhtin terms 'double-voiced discourse',[6] whereby a verbal register drawn from a high-cultural idiom is placed in comic, possibly critical juxtaposition with the vernacular, the stock phrases and speech patterns of everyday life, or, as here, with a particular subcultural argot. But lyrical ingenuity alone does not explain the nature of its success in its own time, nor why it has remained a standard for so long. 'Fever', which remained in the British charts for eleven weeks, reaching number five, was an odd, atypical hit for the 1958 singles market, which was showing the increasing dominance of the newly emergent form of rock and roll (an epoch whose inauguration was marked by the number one success of Bill Haley's 'Rock around the Clock' two years earlier). Peggy Lee had an established background in blues and swing; as a variety of pleased but puzzled contemporaries observed, the 'musicianly' values observed by this record seemed at odds with what many commentators regarded as the banality, commercialism, stupidity, and even outright immorality, of rock. Writing in *Melody Maker*, Steve Race articulated the representative view of a popular music press that had yet to switch its allegiance from blues and bebop to pop, by describing 'Fever' as a 'great record' that had enjoyed a chart success usually afforded to 'baying vocal groups and splay-legged caveboys', and concluding that it offered hope for a music-buying public 'deafened and depraved by the rock'.[7] This alarmist view of rock and roll (echoed across the cultural spectrum, often in more extreme terms) was not that of Lee herself, who accounted for the song's appeal by stressing its affiliation to the emergent musical form, pointing out that it was in fact appropriated from an existing 'real bang-away rock 'n' roll version of "Fever" ... stripped ... to the bass line and rebuilt'.[8] In short, and despite Race's rather perverse implicit insistence upon the purity of jazz, it is a musical *hybrid*, in the sense that it engages in crossover, exchange and dialogue between diverse (and here, supposedly antagonistic) cultural and musical idioms.

The musical form and style of the song, and the reconciliation that it offers between blues and pop, is precisely attuned to its lyrical content. Race suggests that 'the final key' to the success of 'Fever' lies here, with its inference that 'the great lovers of history not only felt the sting of teenage passion ... but spoke of it in the teenage vernacular'; mimicking Lee's double-voiced tactics, he suggests that 'a rose by any other name would still be a gas'. This was particularly timely. If the period of 'Fever''s release was a transitional point in the development of post-war popular music, it coincided with – indeed, is structurally related to – a major cultural shift in European and American culture, which was reflected in an equally significant shift in the critical and cultural understanding of Shakespeare's play. The connection that Steve Race, and Lee herself, make between Romeo and Juliet and 'teenage passion, teenage vernacular' is itself symptomatic of that change, which stems from a radically new conception of the nature of adolescent experience, and of the cultural position and social significance of youth. In the 1950s,

Romeo and Juliet became teenagers. In the remainder of this paper I will develop some of the implications of this shift with reference to a range of Shakespearean cultural materials aimed at (and shaped by) the youth cultures that it ushered into being: *West Side Story*, Zeffirelli's 1960s stage and screen versions of the play, and their subsequent musical afterlife, as well as the scholarly and popular editions of the same period.

Each night I defy you stars up above

Although it seems like an easy and obvious victory for realist common sense, the deployment of Romeo's and (more often) Juliet's youth as an index of verisimilitude has now become so thoroughly naturalised that we may need reminding that, during the 1950s, the period in which it first became a key issue, 'youth' was an unstable and contested category. As the authors of one of the landmark studies of post-war youth subcultures point out, 'youth' was

> one of the most striking and visible manifestations of social change in the period. 'Youth' provided the focus for official reports, pieces of legislation, official interventions. It was signified as a social problem by the moral guardians of the society – something 'we ought to do something about'. Above all, Youth played an important role as a cornerstone in the construction of understandings, interpretations and quasi-explanations *about* the period.[9]

Youth was therefore 'a powerful but *concealed* metaphor for social change'.[10] To ascribe Romeo and Juliet identities as teenagers (or to align teenagers with Romeo and Juliet) is an anachronistic manoeuvre which obscures the fact that the 'teenager' is him- or herself an invention new to the post-war period, a new class of consumer, but also a potential criminal, sexual and religious deviant, positioned at (and produced by) the intersection of an array of discourses of gender and sexuality, racial difference and class mobility. Modern western culture defines the teenage state on the one hand in relation to a biologically-driven process of maturation, and on the other to a provisional and performative identity, riven by desires which are at once heartbreakingly profound and comically transient, and assembled from an array of hedonistic allegiances to fashion, cinematic mythology, narcotics, and, above all, to the pop music in which those loyalties are celebrated. The smoothness with which critical, theatrical, cinematic or colloquial discourse conflates the youth of Romeo and Juliet with their identity and status as (young) lovers, as adolescents, or as teenagers, as if these terms were natural and transhistorical givens, tends to conceal the potential contradictions between terms which already have their own rich and intricate histories. The teenager as a post-war phenomenon is no more historically bounded than the concept of adolescence, as it has emerged and subsequently mutated from Victorian medical sexology; while 'youth' is a term which, deployed within the context of talk about Shakespeare, can seem simultaneously archaic and contemporary.[11]

If the 1950s discourse of the teenager registered this indeterminacy in a wide variety of cultural spheres, it manifested itself in Shakespearean scholarship, pedagogy and performance in some curious ways. One symptomatic text is the New Cambridge Shakespeare edition, published in 1955, and edited by John Dover Wilson and G. I. Duthie. The Cambridge *Romeo and Juliet* marks a shift of emphasis for a series that had been running since 1921, being dedicated to the editors' 'former students at McGill and Edinburgh Universities'. As one of the final volumes in a series that was nearing the end of its period of scholarly ascendancy (soon to be eclipsed by the first volumes of the new Arden), the edition seems to be directly aimed at this constituency. On one level, is characterised by a remarkably sentimental view of the play's protagonists, who are simply 'two wonderful young people who love each other',[12] as well as by the directness with which it addresses a youthful contemporary readership. Gazing benignly (one imagines) across the calm of the quadrangle, Wilson (then in his seventies[13]) felt happy to write that 'there is not a line in the play that leaves a bad taste in the mouth of one who knows and understands anything about the mind of the Elizabethan Age, or even of the modern undergraduate' (xxxvii). If the invocation of an Elizabethan *mentalité* as a strategy of negotiation between past and present recalls Tillyardian historicist tactics, the appeal to the sensibility of contemporary youth is more unexpected: historical difference is both acknowledged and abolished in the space of a sentence. But while this question of difference appears to be resolvable on the literal grounds of taste, it returns elsewhere in a less settled form. In another passage (easily envisaged as an aside coined to solicit a laugh in an undergraduate lecture theatre) Wilson (or Duthie) comments on Juliet's 'Was ever book containing such vile matter / So fairly bound?' (3.2.83–4): 'when a girl in our own age is troubled by the thought that the boy she adores, though delightful to all appearance, may be at root wicked she does not usually express her heart-sick feelings like this...She speaks more directly, more spontaneously' (xxxiv–v). What starts out as a jocular attempt to connect the play's

Petrarchan idiom with the world of teen romance ends up as a rather lame *non sequitur*, as if its author were suddenly stumped, either by the implications of opening up such a dialogue between high and low culture and everyday life, or by the prospect of what such directness and spontaneity might actually entail. However indulgent an account of the young the Cambridge edition might seem to offer, it is tempered a certain restraint – Romeo and Juliet are 'very fine young people, certainly: but both of them are lacking, at certain points, in mature poise and balance' (xxx) – but also by the unseen powers which ensure that youth's radical exuberance is contained, and ultimately curtailed: 'the stars, or Fate, or Destiny, or Fortune, or whatever other specific name may be applied to the cosmic force with which we are concerned, brings the lovers together, gives them supreme happiness and self-fulfillment for a short time, and then casts them down to destruction' (xvii). Although youth is laid to waste by the existing social order, the final result is that 'society is redeemed through suffering and loss' (xxv). If the deterministic ideology of tragedy reflexively inscribed in this account was (despite its continuing longevity within Shakespearean criticism) starting to show its age by the mid-1950s, its emphatic reiteration here may well be a reaction to the cultural shifts that were beginning to make possible an alternative reading of the play as a tragedy rooted in social rather than cosmic contradictions, in which conflicts, not only between young and old but amongst the young themselves, reflect tensions which were less easily reconcilable than the traditional belief in catharsis permits.

Had Wilson and Duthie been listening to the popular music culture of the 1950s, they might have recognised the grounds upon which such a reading might take shape, notably in the post-war period's best-known *Romeo and Juliet* derivative, *West Side Story* (1957). As with 'Fever', hybridity is once again the key, in terms of genre, narrative organisation, musical form and relation to Shakespeare, but also with regard to the musical's politics. Originally entitled *East Side Story*, Leonard Bernstein (together with playwright Arthur Laurents) had initially planned the musical in the late 1940s as 'a modern musical version of *Romeo and Juliet*...about a Jewish boy's star-crossed romance with an Italian Catholic girl set against the clashing street gangs on New York's lower East Side.'[14] By the mid-1950s, this scheme had lost its topicality, so that the project was reconceived as 'the love story of a native-born boy of Polish descent and a newly arrived Puerto Rican girl' relocated to the upper West Side.[15] As Peter Conrad has demonstrated in a suggestive analysis, the subsequent success of the musical stemmed from its capacity to tap into the anxieties of post-war bourgeois America. As an

'American tragedy' which concentrates 'less on Romeo and Juliet than on the discontents that environ them', *West Side Story* presents a liberal plea for ethnic tolerance, diagnoses the malaise of a culture 'emotionally disturbed and psychologically sick', and allegorises the Cold War, 'align[ing] the gulf in New York between privilege on the East Side and poverty on the West Side with the tension between Western capitalism and the communism of the Eastern bloc'.[16] Conrad traces the means through which *West Side Story* assimilates a tradition of operatic adaptation that had been most recently represented by Prokofiev's *Romeo and Juliet*; but one can also detect attempts in the musical to engage with the language, style and musical idiom of the emergent youth cultures of its time. In the arias, duets and other set pieces Bernstein's debt to his classical mentors is acknowledged and elaborated, but it is in the choral routines that the incorporation of elements drawn from the popular musical avant-garde (jazz, blues, bebop) join with the resources of dialogue and characterisation to provide a notation for deviancy. In 'Jet Song' dissonant jazz riffing backs a territorial self-definition conveyed through a snarling, faintly ludicrous macho posturing that culminates in a volley of ersatz expletives (motherlovin', buggin'); 'Cool' picks up the argot of jive and the cadences of bebop to recommend the acquisition of black style as a tactic of self-discipline, a means of regulating and re-directing the aggression and paranoia that are endemic to the urban environment.

Here *West Side Story*'s exclusive whiteness (symptomatised by the fact that Maria is initially seen amongst the wedding dresses of a bridal-dress shop) is both evasive and, with regard to its ethical and musical project, oddly contradictory. As the title indicates, the matter of urban location is central to the scheme: the careful placement of the story within the streets of the upper West Side succeeds in keeping it territorially and racially distinct from Harlem, a few blocks further north. In reality, however, what the newly suburbanised white New York middle classes feared at the turn of the 1960s was not the rumble but the race riot. The coupling of Tony and Maria is mild enough compared to the prospect of the inter-racial pairings that really alarmed conservative America. What we see in *West Side Story* is an attempt to negotiate these possibilities at a discreet distance. When Robert Wise came to film the musical at the beginning of the 1960s,[17] he found himself drawn into the kind of quasi-sociological mapping and surveillance that characterised mainstream culture's relation to youth during the period, as he and scriptwriter Ernest Lehman 'roamed the West Side, talked to delinquents pointed out to them by New York City detectives, investigated the social and psychological conditions that produced gang warfare, went so far as to study the speech patterns of young toughs'.[18] Indeed, following the title sequence, the film establishes its credentials by means of the perspective of surveillance: a long tracking shot of Manhattan soundtracked by the ominous rumble of urban jungle drums which encrypt an implicitly threatening and disruptive blackness within the heart of the white urban experience. Notwithstanding this commitment to social realism, the youth of *West Side Story* sang and danced to the incorporating rhythms of the Broadway musical rather than in any of the more threatening musical languages generally associated with juvenile delinquency (and often regarded as its source); thus *West Side Story*'s account of youth culture proceeded by means of orchestral instrumentation and arrangements, and the operatic conventions of overture, recitative, chorus aria and duet. Within such an idiom, traces of black musical culture of the twentieth-century Americas are detectable only in the guise of a deeply wary hybridisation of the classical and the contemporary vernacular.

Transforming Romeo and Juliet into Tony and Maria, Prince Escalus into Officer Krupke, Chorus into a chorus line of Jets and Sharks, Verona walls into mesh fences, the balcony into the fire escape, Bernstein definitively repositioned *Romeo and Juliet* within the contemporary urban world. More than this: by moving the tragedy across the Atlantic, down the social scale, into the arena of racial conflict, and onto the terrain of mass culture, Bernstein plotted the co-ordinates of the emerging youth culture that, together with *West Side Story* itself, would provide the key terms (although these were often unacknowledged) of reference for subsequent stage and screen versions of the play. Not that this was evident in academic criticism that followed, or in the scholarly and pedagogic materials that emerged in its wake and that were clearly destined for the student market. If the New Shakespeare series carries the weight of the élite educational tradition within which it originated, a rather different student readership might be envisaged for the Signet Shakespeare *Romeo and Juliet* which appeared in 1963. Edited by Joseph Bryant, this was an early entry in a series geared towards the consumption of Shakespeare in a rapidly expanding secondary and tertiary education market; it was still in mass circulation three decades later. The verdict of the compilers of the guide *Which Shakespeare?* is that the edition 'shows signs of its 1960s context' in that it proposes that 'the lovers were let down by the older generation and that Romeo ought to have listened to Mercutio, of whose sexual cynicism [Bryant] thoroughly approves'.[19] Actually, it is an edition more divided in its sympathies than this suggests. Bryant affirms that blame lies less with the lovers than with 'all those whose thoughtlessness denied them the time they so desperately needed', but nonetheless concludes that Elizabethan audiences 'knew by training what to think of young lovers who deceived their parents'.[20] Importantly, Bryant counters what he regards as the simplistic, youth-oriented view of the play by emphatically differentiating Shakespeare's work from the popular cultures that encourage misreading, as manifested in 'other, very different things – second-rate farces, dramatic and non-dramatic, hack work generally, certain comic strips, even – in which the same conventions have been used'.[21] T. J. B. Spencer, editor of the 1967 Penguin edition, addresses the student and lay readership in equally stern terms: 'most discussions of *Romeo and Juliet*, and most stage productions, give a simplified view of the play'; and this is the fault of popular tradition: 'because it is one of the most familiar of Shakespeare's plays – not only in itself but also in operatic and film versions – it is known with preconceptions'.[22] If the idea of attempting to erase cultural history to arrive at the correct reading of the play seems a questionable educational philosophy in principle and an arduous undertaking in practice, this is exactly the point. In the changing educational circumstances of the 1960s, and in the context of a school and university system where, as Allon White puts it, 'the social reproduction of seriousness is a key process',[23] it enabled the stratification of simple and sophisticated, naïve and mature responses to the play.

If the play's vulnerability in the theatre to contamination by the traces of the popular compromises its status (at least in Spencer's terms), academic discussion of *Romeo and Juliet* since the 1960s has nonetheless taken place in the context of a general recognition of performance's capacity to contribute to critical debate. In the case of the Signet *Romeo and Juliet*, this is marked by the inclusion amongst the supporting critical materials of John Russell Brown's account of Zeffirelli's 1960 production at the Old Vic.[24] As an intervention which negotiated the relationship between youth and adult culture, the popular and the serious, in ways which were further elaborated in the film version discussed in the next section, it is worth briefly pausing over this as another production of the play whose interpretive emphasis and general *mise-en-scène* yield unintended subcultural affiliations. John Stride (Romeo) and Judi Dench (Juliet) were both in their mid-twenties; Stride at least 'looked more convincingly in his teens than other actors of the part who have been equally young in fact'.[25] The youth of Verona were 'immediately recognizable as unaffected teenagers'; Alec McCowan's Mercutio was 'a beatnik, a John Osborne invention; a man who didn't want to grow up',[26] and Benvolio 'Cliff to Mercutio's Jimmy Porter'.[27] But the key to the production lay in the relationship between these quintessentially English and American character referents and the Italianate emphasis which Zeffirelli regarded as central to both the play and his approach. Seeking 'a combination of Italian feelings applied to a masterpiece of the classical English theatre', Zeffirelli identified Italian-ness with passionate lyricism, freedom of emotion, action and expression, spontaneity and youth. Invoking an image of Mediterranean culture which English audiences would learn to love through youth-oriented films such as *Summer Holiday* (1962),[28] Zeffirelli relieved the drabness of the autumnal London in which the production opened with a world of sunlight, bells and dust, wherein 'against blue skies, huge walls appeared soft ochre', which opened with mist filling the stage while 'boys lay about in the heat of an Italian summer's morning' and 'a tenor sang quietly to a guitar'.[29] But for young Britain in the early 1960s, Italy provided more than the iconography of hot-blooded passion, romance and adventure: in the espresso bar, the Vespa motor scooter, and the immaculately tailored suit, Italian style provided the materials for the formation of a youth subculture (most clearly exemplified by Mod) that attempted self-definition without importing its terms of reference from the United States. If, as Levenson concludes her discussion of the production, Zeffirelli's *Romeo and Juliet*, which continued to tour at home and abroad for several years, 'touched a chord in the responsive audiences who made it one of the Old Vic's biggest successes after World War II',[30] its association with a youth culture which was itself in an excited state of flux may go part of the way towards explaining its appeal. And if Zeffirelli's treatment was 'post-*West Side Story*' (as Levenson has it[31]), it was in the sense that it attempted to reclaim the play for European, rather than American, youth.

Here's goodly gear

Released in one of the watershed years in the history of post-war youth culture (1968), Zeffirelli's film of *Romeo and Juliet* has been widely acknowledged as both an unashamed piece of populist Shakespearean cinema and a determined pitch at a youthful audience.[32] As Jack Jorgens summarises, it is 'a "youth movie" of the 1960s which glorifies the young and caricatures the old, a Renaissance *Graduate*'.[33] My aim here is to develop this perspective by focusing upon the ways in which the film is repeatedly invaded by a generic vocabulary which implicates it even more firmly within pop (counter)culture than has previously been recognised. The film begins with an aerial shot of Verona and Laurence

Olivier's quietly somber intonation of the Chorus. Overlaid is the title (William Shakespeare's *Romeo and Juliet*) set in cod-medieval graphics that also invoke the Tolkienesque album-cover artwork of acid rock. No sooner is the picture-postcard Italianate setting established than we home in on the spectacle of a pair of bulging codpieces, belonging to Sampson and Gregory, clad in flamboyantly psychedelic red and yellow doublet and hose: fair Verona takes on the characteristics of the Haight-Ashbury and Carnaby Street. With the uncontrolled cackling and wild stares of the well and truly stoned, Capulet's men tumble into a scrap with a group of Montagues whose dark-hued sartorial conservatism identifies them more closely with the world of the straights. The behaviour of these youths (who display the fey butchness of contemporaries like the Rolling Stones' Brian Jones) is characterised by abrupt and arbitrary mood swings, from languor to manic *bonhomie* to murderous rage, a kind of reefer madness which suggests every possible fear of the drug-fuelled activities of the counter-culture. Meanwhile, as the film was on release, students were tearing up the paving stones in Paris, being gassed and shot by state troopers in universities in California, rioting in Grosvener Square; as Jorgens remarks, the youth in this film are 'children of the feud, just as a generation of Americans were children of Vietnam'.[34] When the scene is afforded a reprise as tragedy with the death of Mercutio the same sartorial scheme prevails – but Romeo and Tybalt are now in shirtsleeves, as if replaying the duel from Olivier's *Hamlet*, relocated to the streets and reframed by shaky *vérité* camerawork, forcing youth to helplessly play out a tragedy scripted by its parents.

Our first glimpse of Romeo, however, reveals a figure who is both a gentler kind of hippie (carrying not a sword but a flower, signifying his desire to make love rather than war) and a remnant from an earlier era, with an aura of innocence reminiscent of the young Cliff Richard; throughout the film he is drawn into violence only reluctantly.[35] Even the duel with Paris was omitted from the final act; the scene was filmed but later dropped, as Zeffirelli subsequently rationalised: 'We had to cut the killing of Paris, which I shot. You don't want that. I mean young people wanted us to have the romantic meeting between the dead girl – who was not dead – and Romeo who had threatened to kill himself. If he was a murderer – "Ugly boy, ugly boy!" It wouldn't have worked.'[36] This Romeo was certainly no 'ugly boy': in contrast to the cosmic pageboy crops sported by the rest of the film's youth, he has a neat Beatles-style moptop. Hair, appropriately enough, is a crucial signifier throughout the film. Romeo's clean-cut aspect becomes increasingly dishevelled as the love tragedy gathers pace and he is drawn into the violent world his initial appearance seems to resist. Olivia Hussey's Juliet, similarly, is styled within the household of the Capulets as an embryonic hippie chick, whose status is conveyed through the disposition of her hair, as its extravagantly dark length is confined in tresses and sensible Juliet cap. Her first meeting with Lady Capulet presents them as a slightly asymmetrical doubling of youth and age. Both wear long red frocks. The mother's hair is arranged as a beehive and completely encased within a huge black cap, affording her a more than passing resemblance to the elongated cranium of Dan Dare's adversary, The Mekon. Her bust and neck are completely enclosed within a choking jewel-encrusted bodice, while the sight of Juliet's tresses hints at the rebellion to follow. When Juliet literally lets her hair down later in the film, it is unsurprisingly at the moment of soft-core sexual abandon in the balcony scene. Nonetheless, this is only the first stage in the journey towards their full sexual encounter, for she is dressed and still wearing a hair band. At her next appearance she has embraced the counter-cultural dream of an alternative society of rustic simplicity, dispensing with her mother's wardrobe for a peasant-like, 'ethnic' simplicity of cut and colour, plain natural fabrics (which now mirror those of the Nurse), while her hair flows down her back, seemingly having lengthened and darkened. Although both Romeo and Juliet comb their hair neatly and dress up for their marriage ceremony, this only foreshadows an increasing dishevelment, first as Romeo is muddied and bloodied in the fatal fight with Tybalt, and then as Juliet receives the news of her cousin's death with hair now completely loose in a long white smock (in the next scene, even Lady Capulet appears with hair down and flowing freely, although when she next appears it is firmly back under control). The climactic moment, of course, is the bedroom scene, where the naked Romeo and Juliet awake to the sound of the lark, and where Juliet's hair provides a useful screen for the body parts which the film is not permitted to disclose. As Douglas Lanier notes, nudity in Shakespearean production is usually an insistent and confrontational tactic, an 'assertion of physical presence' that implies a movement 'from bookishness to embodiment'.[37] Although Romeo and Juliet's nudity here is evidently realistically motivated by the dramatic situation, it is also an almost subliminal gesture towards the counter-culture within which the naked body functions as a primary symbol of freedom from repression and inhibition, its exposure a celebration of youth, naturalness and free sexuality. Throughout the scenes that follow, Juliet's hair remains unbound (although sleekly coiffured for her apparent reconciliation with her parents over the match with Paris). When borne, seemingly dead, to the tomb of the Capulets, it has been neatly bundled back into a cap which she slips off as she regains consciousness; and at the end of the film, when Romeo and Juliet are finally laid to rest, it is a measure of the extent of her victory that her hair is left loose.

Our Tune

If flyaway hair is one of the film's more volatile signifiers of youth, Nino Rota's musical score is the component which is central to its efforts to enforce narrative, visual and aural cohesion, and to secure empathy with its youthful protagonists. Its core is the Love Theme which, subject to a range of variations, underscores each of the major romantic and/or tragic moments. Rota's carefully symmetrical Love Theme is highly derivative, being based upon on modulations from A minor to E major via consecutive fifth intervals; the crucial phrase (divested of the off-key elements of its source) is virtual kissing cousins with one of *West Side Story*'s best-known leitmotifs. It is this second-hand, already-heard quality which accounts for the Theme's effectiveness both within the film and beyond. It is first heard during the scene of the masked ball as accompaniment to Juliet's exit from the dance floor while Romeo watches. After a couple of bars, the instrumental leads into the song 'What is a Youth?', delivered as a vocal interlude by a Donovan-style folk singer to Capulet's assembled guests, which forms a frame for the first meeting of Romeo and Juliet. It is also another instance of discursive rupturing, for although the sequence is ostensibly located within the pro-filmic space, it does not quite fit within the narrative's prevailing realism. The stance of the singer, his direct address to camera, the encircling audience (as if for an early modern episode of *Ready Steady Go!*), and the simultaneously diegetic/extra-diegetic status of the song, draw upon the conventions of the musical and, more particularly, the emergent codes of pop music television and film. Despite (or perhaps because of) this momentary loosening of the realist vocabulary, the visual and musical effect of the sequence is firstly to depict youth and age temporarily united in attendance to the song, and secondly to transform the arena of the lovers' meeting (an antechamber on the edge of the social space of the household) into a place where Verona's laws of time and space do not fully apply. Here the wistful phrasing of the Theme is paired with a question-and-answer lyrical scheme (in part a pastiche of songs from *Twelfth Night*, *The Merchant of Venice* and elsewhere) which emphasises the dual nature of youth (it is 'ice and fire') and its transience ('the rose will fade'). The tryst between Juliet and Romeo, for which the Theme provides a running commentary (reaching a crescendo, according to the conventions of screen romance, with the first kiss), is thus placed as an illustrative interlude in the instrumental bridge between the penultimate and final verses. The dialogue between the lovers occupies the slot which, in a pop song, would be filled by a guitar solo; the lovers themselves become accessories in an early music video. As the Theme recurs throughout the narrative, increasingly ominous and poignant, it is as if it is as much remembered as heard. The orchestral arrangement underpins the balcony, bedroom and tomb scenes, and for the parting of the lovers a pizzicato harp helps to construct Juliet as an angel; during the marriage ceremony it is carried – barely audibly – by church organ and choir. Each recurrence takes the doomed optimism of the first meeting further into the world of tragedy.

But the reverberations of the Love Theme extend beyond the film itself. Issued as a single from the soundtrack album that accompanied the film's release, the 'Love Theme from *Romeo and Juliet*', as arranged and performed by Henry Mancini and his orchestra, reached number one in the American Billboard chart in 1969. It was also published as sheet music, and within a year there appeared two new arrangements for solo piano and two for concert band, as well as individual arrangements for solo organ, elementary orchestra, dance band and (rather alarmingly) military band. Sheet music including the vocal part from the film was published under the title 'What is a Youth?'; finally, a revised version with new lyrics was released as a single as 'A Time for Us (Love Theme from *Romeo and Juliet*)'. With its verse-chorus-middle-eight structure, this variant confirmed the Love Theme's adherence to the classic pop song format. It also reiterated the link with *West Side Story*'s 'Somewhere' ('There's a place for us . . .'), reorienting its utopian yearning for erotic and social transformation away from location and towards temporality: 'A time for us, some day there'll be a new world / A world of shining hope for you and me.' This also modified the sentiment of the film ballad, substituting for the former's resigned submission to transience a more optimistic embrace of transcendence. Although this version failed to repeat the immediate success of Mancini's instrumental (reaching only number ninety-six on the Billboard chart), it has subsequently been covered many times (it features, for example, on the *16 Most Requested Songs* of Ray Conniff and Johnny Mathis).

The instrumental has become an even more familiar component of popular culture's romantic soundtrack. Perhaps its most well-known manifestation within British culture was as part of the radio feature from which the title of this section is derived, a popular and long-running item on the morning show fronted by Simon Bates on BBC Radio 1 during the early 1980s. In this instance, the Theme supplied the background to, and punctuation of, Bates's readings of (apparently) true stories of love and loss contributed by listeners. As the tales of ordinary love lives unfolded through Bates's pointedly sombre, strangely formalised delivery, the presence of the Theme tended to abstract character and narrative from the realms of the familiar, repositioning them within a timeless and universal romantic music-drama enacted somewhere between high culture and everyday life. Sometimes the stories would end happily, often not; the key generic characteristic being the role of chance, luck or bad timing in the progress of love; the end of the item was the playing of the 'special' song that epitomised the relationship. As this would always be a song already known and liked by the millions tuned in to the show, the feature was in effect taking the suspended opposition between intimate experience and the public sphere that is inherent in the on-air dedication into a new realm of extremity, as the ownership of 'our tune' extended out through the airwaves in a momentary fantasy of national communal intimacy. It is tempting to regard the entire exercise as evidence of the warped tastes, maudlin sentimentality and voyeuristic tendencies endemic within popular culture, but this is, in a sense, to miss the point. At the level of content, the feature did not offer quite the endorsement of normative sexual and familial values that one might have expected from public service broadcasting during the Thatcherite 1980s: the stories told of jealousy and betrayal, of bitterly divided loyalties, and of same-sex relationships, and were presented non-judgementally. Moreover, the presence of the Theme itself, as an anomaly within the pop-music flow of daytime Radio 1, was not without significance. Although many listeners may have missed the Shakespearean connection, the incursion of what sounded like a musical idiom from another cultural space momentarily resisted the hierarchical stratification of musical forms according to the dictates of taste, education and class. Whether its audiences recognised it or not, the hidden logic of Our Tune's appropriation of Rota's Theme in order to define a shared emotional landscape was to temporarily reposition everyday existence within the realms of the timeless and the sublime. It is a species of the activity which Michel de Certeau characterised as reading-as-poaching, in which the lay consumer of culture 'invents in texts something very different from what they "intended" (...detaches them from their (lost or accessory) position...combines their fragments and creates something un-known in the space organized by their capacity for allowing an indefinite plurality of meanings'.[38] In this instance, significance resided in the hybrid incongruity of the musical and cultural registers in play. Maybe even the merest hint of Shakespeare in the 1980s pop world of Shakatak and Shakin' Stevens was enough to indicate a displaced, indirect and unfocused desire to dissolve the cultural hierarchies which, striving to keep them separate, reflect and perpetuate the conditions of discrimination and inequality which, for all too many, continue to act as the real source of tragedy in life or in love. What Our Tune taught was that time and narrative could lend perspective and understanding, and that music, above all, could reconcile and heal.

One is tempted to read this as a deeply traditional Shakespearean sentiment, but we have, it appears, strayed a long way from what might officially be designated as Shakespeare here (far further even than the relatively reverential Peggy Lee). At best, the Shakespearean dimension of Our Tune is located at several removes; its 'Shakespeare' little more than a ghostly echo which marks it as distant kin to what Barbara Hodgdon in this volume refers to as the works' 'reincarnations'; it is an example that Michael Bristol and Kathleen McLuskie have recently described as 'a fundamental transformation of cultural experience, a kind of postmodern life after death for the great works of literature' as they adjust to 'other, more restless habits of cultural consumption created by typically late modern institutions such as tourism, theme parks, and the shopping mall' (and, one may add, popular music).[39] To those who would see all this as yet more evidence of the 'dumbing down' of Shakespeare, Shakespeare studies and cultural analysis, it might be as well to take that epithet at its word, and to read the products of popular culture amidst the cross-cultural borrowing and reinvention that has been mapped in another context by Dennis Kennedy in response to the question of 'what is it that endures when [Shakespeare] is deprived of his tongue?'[40] At the very least, a consideration of the transmission, translation and transformation of the works' dramatis personae, narratives and iconography into the zones of contemporary culture but in which, paradoxically, Shakespeare is alien and speechless, and in which he has neither authority nor affect, promises to reposition the more avowedly and visibly responsible reworkings of the canon within theatrical, screen and critical performance. Shakespeare may be left without words but, possibly without knowing where they came from, we continue to hum the tunes.

Notes and references

1. 'Fever' was issued as a single on Capitol records in 1958 and subsequently included on the compilation album *Bewitching Lee! Peggy Lee Sings Her Greatest Hits* (Capitol Records, 1962).

2. Jonathan Bate, *The Genius of Shakespeare* (London: Picador, 1997) 278.

3. Since Luhrmann's emphatic appropriation of the play for *fin-de-siècle* youth culture has already received its due share of critical attention, I shall only allude to it in passing here. For particularly acute readings of the film and its spin-offs, see Barbara Hodgdon, 'William Shakespeare's *Romeo + Juliet*: Everything's Nice in America?' *Shakespeare Survey* 52 (1999): 88–98, and Courtney Lehmann, 'Strictly Shakespeare? Dead Letters, Ghostly Fathers, and the Cultural Pathology of Authorship in Baz Lurhmann's *William Shakespeare's Romeo + Juliet*,' *Shakespeare Quarterly* 52 (2001): 189–221.

4. Quoted from Philip Edwards, ed. *Hamlet, Prince of Denmark*, The New Cambridge Shakespeare (Cambridge: CUP, 1985).

5. For a (largely inconclusive) attempt to trace the logic of the Shakespearean allusion in pop, see Janell R. Duxbury, 'Shakespeare Meets the Backbeat: Literary Allusion in Rock Music,' *Popular Music and Society* 12 (1988): 19–23.

6. See Mikhail M. Bakhtin, *The Bakhtin Reader*, ed. Pam Morris (London: Edward Arnold, 1994) 103–12.

7. Steve Race, ' "Fever" by Peggy Lee: Sanity in the Top Twenty,' *Melody Maker* 25 October 1958, n.pag.

8. Don Bailer, 'Peggy Sets a Feverish Pace,' *New York Mirror* 20 August 1958, n.pag.

9. John Clarke, Stuart Hall, Tony Jefferson and Brian Roberts, 'Subcultures, Cultures and Class,' *Resistance Through Rituals: Youth Subcultures in Post-war Britain*, ed. Stuart Hall and Tony Jefferson (London: Hutchinson, 1976) 9.

10. Clarke *et al.* 9.

11. For a discussion of Romeo and Juliet's 'youth' in the context of late Victorian culture, see Robert Shaughnessy, *The Shakespeare Effect: A History of Twentieth-Century Performance* (Basingstoke: Palgrave – now Palgrave Macmillan, 2002).

12. John Dover Wilson and G. I. Duthie, ed. *Romeo and Juliet*, The New Shakespeare (Cambridge: CUP, 1955) xvi.

13. It may, of course, have been the more youthful Duthie, who had just turned forty when the edition was published, who wrote this; the co-editorial credit offers no sure way of telling.

14. Stanley Green, *Broadway Musicals: Show by Show* (London: Faber and Faber, 1985) 175.

15. Green 175.

16. Peter Conrad, *To Be Continued: Four Stories and their Survival* (Oxford: Clarendon Press, 1995) 89–92.

17. *West Side Story*, dir. Robert Wise, United Artists, 1962.

18. *West Side Story* Soundtrack Recording, sleeve note.

19. Ann Thompson, Thomas L. Berger, A. R. Braunmuller, Philip Edwards and Lois Potter, *Which Shakespeare? A User's Guide to Editions* (Milton Keynes: Open University Press, 1992) 154.

20. Joseph Bryant, ed. *Romeo and Juliet*, The Signet Shakespeare (New York: New American Library, 1964) xxxviii, xxiv.

21. Bryant xxvii.

22. T. J. B. Spencer, ed. *Romeo and Juliet*, The New Penguin Shakespeare (Harmondsworth: Penguin, 1967) 7.

23. Allon White, *Carnival, Hysteria and Writing: Collected Essays and Autobiography* (Oxford: Clarendon Press, 1993) 131. This remark is quoted by

Simon Shepherd and Peter Womack in the course of an analysis of the reciprocal dynamics of the treatment of Renaissance drama within the theatre and the academy. In the post-war period in particular, they continue, 'the theatre has absorbed...the priorities of education. However pleasurable it is, a revival of a Renaissance play always carries...the sign of *seriousness*' (Simon Shepherd and Peter Womack, *English Drama: A Cultural History* (Oxford: Blackwell, 1996) 120).

24. John Russell Brown, 'S. Franco Zeffirelli's *Romeo and Juliet*,' *Shakespeare Survey* 15 (1962): 147–55. Rpt. in Bryant 199–213.
25. Brown 200.
26. Brown 200.
27. Jill L. Levenson, *Shakespeare in Performance: Romeo and Juliet* (Manchester: Manchester University Press, 1987) 97–8.
28. *Summer Holiday*, dir. Kenneth Harper, Associated British Pictures, 1962.
29. Levenson 100–2.
30. Levenson 104.
31. Levenson 103.
32. *Romeo and Juliet*, dir. Franco Zeffirelli, Paramount, 1968.
33. Jack J. Jorgens, *Shakespeare on Film* (Bloomington: Indiana University Press, 1977) 86.
34. Jorgens 87.
35. Romeo's flower-child associations have been noted before, of course; most recently by Deborah Cartmell, 'Franco Zeffirelli and Shakespeare,' *The Cambridge Companion to Shakespeare on Film*, ed. Russell Jackson (Cambridge: CUP, 2000) 212–21.
36. Franco Zeffirelli, 'Filming Shakespeare,' *Staging Shakespeare: Seminars on Production Problems*, ed. Glenn Loney (New York: Garland, 1990) 245.
37. Douglas Lanier, 'Drowning the Book: *Prospero's Books* and the Textual Shakespeare,' *Shakespeare on Film: Contemporary Critical Essays*, ed. Robert Shaughnessy (Basingstoke: Macmillan – now Palgrave Macmillan, 1998) 187.
38. Michel de Certeau, *The Practice of Everyday Life*, trans. Steven Rendall (Berkeley: University of California Press, 1984) 169.
39. Michael Bristol and Kathleen McLuskie, 'Introduction,' *Shakespeare and Modern Theatre: The Performance of Modernity* (New York and London: Routledge, 2001) 10.
40. Dennis Kennedy, 'Introduction: Shakespeare without his language,' *Foreign Shakespeare: Contemporary Performance* (Cambridge: CUP, 1993) 17.

11
Re-Incarnations

Barbara Hodgdon

For Peggy Phelan

I have been seeing a lot of Hamlet lately, and the suddenness of my current obsession with him has caught me somewhat unawares, for aside from eulogising Mel Gibson's ass some years ago in print,[1] Hamlet and I have not had a particularly close relationship. A confession. When attending to the play in the theatre – though not to *most* films – I sink into its prolixity: held captive by Hamlet's theatre of delay, revenge and family romance, I grow resty, turn into a detached, even resistant spectator – yet I always hope that something will actually *happen* to surprise me. How is it, then, that drama's Mistress Overdone,[2] promiscuously eager to snuggle up to any 'concept' – Shakespeare's exercise in waking dead ghosts – has returned to haunt me?[3]

First, a fable of origins. I began thinking about the idea of reincarnations as a potentially productive metaphor for the sorts of Shakespearean repetition compulsions at work in late twentieth- and early twenty-first century performative culture – and that led me to Michael Almereyda's stunning film of *Hamlet*, where reincarnation functions in much the same way as astronauts reentering the atmosphere, bringing back auras from a strange world. How might Almereyda's film initiate a conversation that might explore how 'Shakespeare' and 'the Shakespearean' emerge from such cultural performances, about how such performances get reconstituted or refunctioned when it is 'Shakespeareans' who are doing the looking?[4]

But other Hamlets kept stalking me, leaving spectral leftovers. Flying home from London after seeing Simon Russell Beale's Hamlet, I read a Dalziel and Pascoe police procedural, its chapters prefaced with epigraphs from *A Tale of Two Cities*: 'I am going to see his ghost. It will be his *ghost* – not him!' 'I have sometimes sat alone...listening, until I have made the echoes out to be the echoes of all the footsteps that are coming by and by into our lives.' 'For as I draw closer and closer to the end, I travel in the circle, nearer and nearer to the beginning.'[5] Sounding uncannily like Hamlet, these phrases also resonated with Russell Beale's performance which, for the first time ever, bound me to *Hamlet* in the theatre.[6]

Months later, I went to New York to see Adrian Lester play Hamlet. But before the evening performance, and while keeping the horizon of my thought full of *Hamlet*, I saw another show, a warm-up, a diverting appetizer – Theatre de Complicite's *Mnemonic*.[7] Interweaving the story of Virgil (his name surely no accident) with those of his lover's disappearance and of the 1991 discovery of a 5,000-year-old iceman in an Alpine glacier, this performance sutured living to dead bodies, revealing how, as memories collide and converge, past generations live on in our very blood and bone and descend from us. As I began to write, this baffling yet compelling theatre piece, chaining memory to time and to origins, also haunted me – and became lashed to *Hamlet*, which articulates the remembering, repeating and working through that not only shadows psychoanalysis but also describes what it is to make theatre. And then I remembered that before psychoanalysis had a hand in memory, there were other ways to understand memory – ideas based on the temporal priority of brain development. Neurologists tell us that we remember things in our bodies long before we have words, narratives or plots like *Hamlet*'s and that before the neo-cortex there was the cortex. And I wondered if before *Hamlet* there is mnemonics.[8]

These events, then, shape my thinking about these performances – *Hamlet* in three parallel universes. My strategy is to read Hamletically, which is to say, provisionally, through Hamlet's own paradoxical premise: that meaning can be read off another's body, all the while maintaining that his own body has 'that within which passes show', speaks a language of actorly, if not theatrical failure, hints at the limits of performance. But then another spectral figure, Peggy Phelan, appeared, reminding me that performance is predicated on its own disappearance and that my desire to preserve its elusive life, whether as critical or archival work, is basically conservative.[9] Although her words give me pause, I still want to imagine that, as in *Mnemonic*, something substantial can be made from fragments, from ghosted traces, and that, through a kind of talking cure (another sort of reincarnation), I can work towards a form that enacts the affective force of these performance events. Like Hamlet, I write from loss; like him, too, I write to remember.

When he first appears as Hamlet, Russell Beale also is writing. Kneeling behind a large trunk – his father's coffin? – he is absorbed in making notes in a small journal, an action that not only suggests his bookishness but also sets him apart from, even refuses to acknowledge, the state occasion taking place behind him. In this single self-alienating moment, he appeared to resist the whole shape of the play in which he finds himself and, by presenting himself as more 'authentic' than the other performers, to redeem Hamlet's famous 'seeming'. Isolated, he appeared already bounded in a nutshell, that contracted vision of inner space to which he will later refer as a place of dreams and recollections. Some sense of the stage as just such an arena had already been established by John Caird's *mise-en-scène*. A dozen or more trunks placed in a circle allude to its life as a touring production, extending the trope of the travelling players outward to frame the performance as well as to embrace the (Stanislavskian) journey of its central character. Even more aptly, the set's high panelled walls, candled chandeliers and single central crucifix suspended in the flies defined a ritualised space, a darkened mausoleum-like surround with niches in which, as the performance began, the actors appeared, their heads and torsos haloed by back-lighting. Emerging like so many revenants in a phantasmatical dumb show, they came forward, formed a line and turned upstage, exiting left and right – as though to acknowledge that staging *Hamlet* is always an exercise in reincarnation, a surrogate performance taking place in a memory space on which modernity presents 'period revivals' from the Shakespearean canon.[10] Re-membering *Hamlet* as ritual return, this prologue also intensifies the proximity of theatre to other experiences, whether those of religious ritual (ever-present here in the recurrent *Te deums*) or those of the psychoanalytic encounter, its secular equivalent.

As a stage role, Hamlet can be considered a set of actions that holds open a place in memory, waiting to be re-fleshed by an actor who steps into it, bodies forth its complex suitings (or mismatches) of word and action into new patterns.[11] Commemorating and validating that cultural memory, a photograph of Russell Beale's face mirrored (upside down) by a skull appears on the poster and programme cover – a classic *memento mori*, emblematic of being and not being. Premised on the expressive face, the codes it cultivates also replicate critical narratives of interiority (the eyes have it) so that something like a theatrical unconscious leaks into the image. Yet in Russell Beale's case, the body which accompanies that face is entirely at odds with the 'ideal' Hamlet-body – lean, conventionally handsome, coded by blackness and melancholic self-absorption. Because I had read the piece from a Worcestershire paper titled 'Tubby or Not Tubby: Fat is the Question' – perhaps the cruellest line ever written of so accomplished an actor – more than anything else, I wanted his performance to disprove that headline.[12] Curiously enough, however, body was *precisely* the question, for this Hamlet-body was that of an adolescent male, a boyish man as yet unsure of himself, one who finds theatre addictive because it veils the self in an other: often, he seemed like the youngest person on the stage.

But that is not the point I wish to pursue. Rather, what I find intriguing is how the London press lifted Hamlet free of Russell Beale's body entirely. Insisting that his performance lay elsewhere – in the head and heart – they wrote strings of descriptors: intellectual, charming, witty, aching regret, thinking, feeling, reserved not flaunting emotion, telling sorrow, anti-romantic, 'a perfect Hamlet for the age of irony'.[13] Perhaps one way to account for this phenomenon is as atonement for their Worcestershire colleague, but these critics also can be seen as imbricating themselves in the dramaturgy of transference, speaking of how seeing and hearing Russell Beale's Hamlet triggered memories that forgot the performer himself and entered each spectator's associative field. As Herbert Blau writes, 'It's as if the performance remembers the prospect also familiar to psychoanalysis: that the text in the presence of the Other always speaks more than it knows.'[14] Or, as one (American) critic put it: '[Russell Beale's] Hamlet grows in front of our eyes, and we grow with him.'[15]

Although Hamlet claims that what lies 'within' cannot appear, his speech *is* revelatory, his most ostentatious form of showing. Here, Russell Beale's performance worked to re-inflect Hamlet's words, making them *re*-markable. It was like listening to a highly intelligent reading in which the auditor's experience occurs through the actor's process of passing on his own recovered physical relation to the text – a form of what Bruce Wiltshire calls 'standing in', a process that floods out to include the spectator, who stands in for the character as well as for 'himself' as a member of an offstage community.[16] I find these ideas – 'passing on' and 'standing in' – especially generative, for both align productively with Joseph Grigely's notion of performance as a site of passage for the text.[17] Yet I also want to travel away from the idea that 'Shakespeare's text' was exclusively what Russell Beale's performance was being made *from*. For in those initial moments, when my connection to 'Hamlet' became even more immediate because, like him, I also was taking notes, any distance between performer and audience disappeared in what became a dialogic exchange that touched on the very nature of memory as a psychic process in which we are audience to ourselves.

During 'To be or not to be', for instance, rather than marking the surface of the speech with physical signs of his own emotional investment,

Russell Beale, by keeping his body still, invited spectators' moment-to-moment attention to how he was producing the words and responding to himself doing so – what one critic called 'invisible acting'.[18] Marked off from character, the language seemed, suddenly, to belong not just to 'Hamlet' but to every *body*, turning spectators into silent secret sharers who might supplement, defer to or/and displace Hamlet's associations with their own. Though some claimed that the speech was 'about' suicide, the process of transference being enacted overwhelmed any thoughts of what it *meant*. For, as Derrida writes, since speech is already structured by difference and distance as much as writing (or text) is, to mean is automatically *not to be*.[19] And at least for me, Russell Beale's 'To be or not to be' was 'about' *being there*. Ultimately, perhaps reading performance Hamletically is to read as one's own analyst in his theatre of memory, for it is by experiencing grief through another's performance, and then through his own mimicry, that Hamlet can transform the repetitive force of trauma, overcome it and generate recovery. One telling sign of that recurred, a fragmentary resonance. Calling attention to his 'too too solid flesh', Russell Beale held his hands away from his body, his fingers spread, viewing them with disgust, wishing them away. Hours later, as he is dying, he again stretches out his hands, looks at them in amazement. Resembling the habit of a reader who returns to a previous page to check a point, the gesture goes far beyond simply helping either text or playwright to make a point.[20] For in that moment of repetition and remembrance, his Hamlet balances on the precarious edge between being and not being: it is just such performative remainders that count.

Of these three *Hamlet*s, this performance most instantiates *Hamlet* as it wants to be something other than theatre – that is, as it approaches 'real life'. Perhaps it is best understood as what Roland Barthes calls a text of pleasure[21] – in this case a performance text – precisely because it so amply fulfils both specular and auditory desires, so willingly aligns itself with modernity's realist or naturalistic modes. British theatrical Shakespeare at its best, it is also the most acutely tuned to its status as 'revival', the most invested in memorialising 'textual Shakespeare'. Even its closural moves forcefully signalled that this was simply one of a long chain of performances, an even longer chain of *Hamlet*s. For after the Ghost came forward through an opening in the set's back wall, all the bodies rose to take up their initial positions on the trunks and, after Horatio bid Hamlet good night, the actors returned to the niches from which they had emerged as the evening began, the light slowly fading on their faces as they waited to be re-awakened by that most memorable of all opening lines, 'Who's there?'

Are these words, as Herbert Blau claims, a challenge from Shakespeare's text to the performer?[22] Peter Brook had used them that way in *Qui est là?*, his workshop meditation on playing *Hamlet*.[23] But even before Horatio spoke them in Brook's current *Tragedy of Hamlet*, it was obvious that the 'thing' which was about to appear would meta-theme 'theatre' as 'performance' – or performance art. The playing field – a square orange padded carpet on which stacks of cushions and several stools formed blocks of colour, light and shade, all framed by a black surround – turned Brook's famous empty space, the site Blau marks as resembling consciousness itself,[24] into a Rothko painting. And whereas Caird's RNT staging *plays* on the notion of touring, Brook's comes prepackaged to tour, baggage claims not required. Here, too, the idea of *Hamlet* as ritual return reappears, though with a difference, for while Caird's staging occurs within a memory space layered with religious allusions, Brook, envisioning the play as secular ritual or myth, uses *Hamlet* as a projective site on which to articulate the haunted mnemonics of grief and loss. Scored for an intercultural cast who double and redouble roles, his staging is the antithesis of Robert Lepage's *Midsummer Night's Dream*, which provoked London critics into colonialist mode,[25] for despite incorporating 'others', Brook's minimalist, modernist *Tragedy* remains indisputably western. A chamber play or string octet, its movements resonate with a variety of performative styles; but above all, it is *Hamlet* as redesigned for and developed around its central performer, Adrian Lester.

Entering upstage left to sit on a pile of cushions off the playing space, Lester glances quickly at the audience, then looks down – still an actor, not yet 'Hamlet'. Tense, alert, Scott Handy's Horatio steps onto the carpet; bells ring, spreading out the silence as he searches the house before addressing the Ghost, who moves slowly down an aisle and onto the carpet, passing Horatio without responding to his urgent 'Speak!' to sit upstage right opposite Lester: he who will play both father and step-father facing he who will play the son, two 'dead spirits', walking shadows who are not yet 'characters'. Reassuring himself, Horatio evokes the gracious time which protects mortals against dead men walking, and leaves. As Lester steps onto the orange carpet, it is Hamlet in mourning who now appears: tears fill his eyes, running down his cheeks as, speaking of his 'sullied flesh', he lets the words invade his body, tell it what to do, asking whether he *must* remember. Peggy Phelan writes: 'Just as linguists have argued that syntax is "hard-wired" into the brain, which allows infants to discern specific sounds as language bits, it may well be that the syntax of loss, one of the central repetitions of subjectivity, is hard-wired into the psyche.'[26] In Lester's performance, that syntax of loss surfaces in physical display, body choreography.

What surprises is not just *how* things happen but *when* they happen.[27] Smoothing out initial narrative moves and jostling this first soliloquy out of place so that everything serves both central tropes and the central performer – who is almost continuously onstage – this opening shakes *Hamlet* out of its scenic metaphors, robbing it immediately of one means through which 'Shakespeare's text' re-circulates and re-affirms traditional values, opens up the possibility of interrogating canonical authority. As an act of resistance, dismantling and redesigning the logos enables spectators to see or to *re*-see what has been covered over by cultural–ontological habits of mind and to experience an entirely different way of *being* in Shakespeare's (theatrical) world.[28] To say this, of course, is simply to echo what Brook himself has said repeatedly: 'It is only when we forget Shakespeare that we can begin to find him.'[29] Yet (even after all these years), Brook's ideas about 'finding' Shakespeare clearly also depend on reincarnating a (somewhat gentled) Artaud: 'Instead of relying on texts regarded as definitive and sacred we must...put an end to the subjugation of theatre to the text, and rediscover the notion of a kind of unique language halfway between gesture and thought.'[30] The result: a Barthes-ean text of bliss[31] – canonically unsettled, filled with (habitable) aporias; *Hamlet*'s early modernity haunted by a modernist mnemonics that accommodates only what suits it, nourishes recollection by sharpening and isolating stimuli, rooted in the concrete – spaces, bodies, gestures, objects, images.[32] Less as more.

Reading less as loss, mainstream as well as (some) academic reviewers undertook salvage ethnographies, listing missing persons, speeches and scenes – a process which almost inevitably works to replace performance with text. The *New York Times*'s Ben Brantley, for instance, characterised his experience as 'like speed-reading something I already knew. I always got the sense but not necessarily the sensibility'; finding Lester's performance 'enchanting but seldom emotionally gripping', he advised going to see Russell Beale's Hamlet for the latter.[33] There is always, of course, a (non-Brechtian) dream of Shakespeare's text that exceeds any possible enactment; but the main reason, I think, that this fantasy remains so magically prevalent, especially among literary critics accustomed to doing all sorts of (unnatural) things with texts, is that those critics imagine theatrical performance as a site of stability, a place where text-y Shakespeare lives out the formalist truths of unity and coherence their poststructuralist philosophies have disavowed. Another fable. Despite arguing for a critical practice that will *un*-mark 'Shakespeare' as text in order to *re*-mark performance as the more crucial term, and also despite Brook's mantra to forget Shakespeare, once I had returned home after seeing this *Hamlet*, I immediately attempted to reconstruct something like the playing text. Doing so, as it turned out, proved that memory operates in oddly absolute ways: for precisely because Brook had 'pruned away the inessential',[34] the more I was able to recall what *happened* in *Hamlet* and in Lester's performance.

That performance is perhaps best theorised as a poetics of material perception or as a dialectic – not just speaking 'Shakespeare' but talking back to him, recreating the links between word and flesh as process rather than acting out its results.[35] Witty and light, Lester's performance wrote 'Hamlet' onto his body, physically annotating the words, which appeared constantly in movement. In the hands of another actor, this process of driving thought towards the body would be called illustrating or demonstrating – what the Stanislavskian actor is warned to avoid in his search for a deeper emotional 'truth'. Here, however, it is precisely this manner of suiting word to action, so that the idea or metaphor arises from the body and is driven back into it – something similar to Artaud's notion of the body parts sending one another echoes[36] – through which Lester's performance conveys feeling. Sitting close to actor and playing space as I did at the second of the two performances I saw, I could *feel* the movement between body parts, experience it transferring to my own body, as though Lester were extending an invitation, if not to physically replicate his performance, at least to share – voluntarily or involuntarily? – Hamlet's experience of remembering, repeating and working through a painful emotional past.

Yet it was not Artaud's Balinese dancers who were haunting me. Instead, watching Lester best my own memories – or expectations – of what I had imagined I might see, I felt a strange kinesthetic empathy with him. Given the differences between us – race, gender, age, dancing ability – this was most unlikely, but nonetheless, desiring to partner something, if not exactly 'him' or Hamlet, I dreamed of Fred Astaire and Ginger Rogers, wondered where – or who – 'my' Horatio was. One body remembering another self? Psychoanalysis, after all, is the performance of body memory; tapping out the words, Lester was dancing through Hamlet's mourning.[37] And I wondered whether what I had experienced was a kind of transference, a double movement through which my own memories of loss (a father, a mother, the threatened loss of a son) seemed to move from my body to his through a dream of dancing. Speaking of how dancing *consciously* performs the body's discovery of its temporal and spatial dimensions, Peggy Phelan writes that dance and psychoanalysis capture two different ways of framing bodies as they gesture towards and away from the formlessness of their own flesh; choreography and psychoanalysis, she remarks, would do well to join in a conversation about the body's time.[38] *Hamlet*, then, as marking the body's time, rehearsing its loss?

At least to some extent, emphasising grief and mourning blocks out the trappings of revenge tragedy; after all, the two mark opposite impulses: revenge directs retribution towards the other, mourning inflicts it on the self.[39] Perhaps that latter impulse also accounts for why Lester's Hamlet repeatedly tries to leave the playing space: the only thing which brings him back, as Beckett says, is the dialogue.[40] Such moves sort with Hamlet's doubleness, caught between being and seeming: does he seek a world where 'seeming' is *not* the question, a place beyond the actions that a man might play? Or is this simply a desire for the restful 'land of the dead' off the playing carpet, inhabited by ghosts – or actorly shadows? Consistently, when he returns, it is to be weary, distanced, self-ironic; vacillating between being there and not being there, it is as though he is always working towards the soliloquy that is entirely extraneous to the narrative – the one which is Hamlet's signature as well as that of the play.

If most *Hamlet*s turn on the question of whether 'this thing' will appear, here that question became, would 'To be or not to be' *ever* appear? When it does – in the place of 'How all occasions do inform against me' – it is not just re-functioned but freshly re-motivated. So positioned, it does indeed inform against Hamlet, for it is bracketed by two appearances of Ophelia, one a dumb show, the other her mad scene, played as a soliloquy made up of fragmented phrases from her speeches and accompanied by the onstage musician who, just this once, enters the playing space. After Claudius confronts him, demanding where he has hidden Polonius' body and banishing him to England, the stage empties except for Hamlet. Turning to go, he sees Ophelia passing upstage of the playing carpet: they glance at one another, her silent figure reminding him of the effects of his rash action, both aware of the impossibility of closing the gap between them – and then she is gone. Her trajectory, finally, is *not* to be. Still standing, Hamlet now faces the audience, takes his pulse, gouges his arm with his nails: proof that he lives or self-punishment? Then he kneels: pausing after 'to die' he breathes out an 'o', his eyes closed; they open as the ideas of sleep and dream, which bring a slow smile before, rubbing one hand against the other, he writes off the thought. 'There's the respect that makes calamity of so long life' gets swept aside; recalling 'the pangs of despised love', he looks off towards where Ophelia had disappeared. Again trying out self-erasure 'with a bare bodkin', he raises a hand to worry his head, 'puzzl[ing] it out' until, on 'conscience doth make cowards of us all', both arms go limp, 'los[ing] the name of action'. Spotting Rosencrantz and Guildenstern approach, he looks down at his wrist, slashes it across with one hand and, quickly kissing the imaginary wound, comes to his feet: 'O from this time forth, / My thoughts be bloody or be nothing worth.'

Like Hamlet's other soliloquies, this one becomes a confession – that is, a mnemonic performance, that most intensely self-reflective act of memory as it is re-performed in the now.[41] Here, too, this seductively labryinthine speech, twisting towards an answer that never comes, becomes a turning point at which, having confronted and rejected suicide with a kiss, Hamlet appears poised for action. Yet if the borrowed coda from 'How all occasions' transforms inaction to resolve, it is also the case that the indecision usually associated with 'To be or not to be' has undergone a sea change to make of this *Hamlet*'s closing moves something rich – but not altogether strange. For, as in Caird's staging, after Hamlet's death the dead rise slowly to their feet. But whereas Caird's ending, despite gesturing towards repetition, is covertly stabilising, this *Hamlet*, travelling backwards, begins again. Unlike its opening, where actors were called up to life from outside the playing space, all now inhabit it. Standing amidst them, Horatio speaks – 'But look, the morn in russet mantle clad / Walks o'er the dew of yon high eastern hill. / Break we our watch up' – marking the end of playing – and of spectating, closing off this event. But then, addressing a point halfway between playing space and audience, he asks, 'Who's there?' – again summoning up a phantasmatical body he cannot yet see or touch. If this question has an answer, I do not think it is Old Hamlet's Ghost that he anticipates, though it might be that of Hamlet himself. But however read – and Brook, ever adept at mystification, remains silent on this point – turning back to repeat itself constitutes this staging's most metatheatrical gesture. Metatheatrical, but also meta-thematic – or, perhaps more appropriately, mnemonic: reminiscent of Eliot's *Four Quartets*, that quintessentially modernist saga celebrating memory, loss and desire: 'And the end of all our exploring / Will be to arrive where we started / And know the place for the first time.'[42] Knowing the place, of course, is not the same as knowing what will happen next: travelling on its edge, *Hamlet* here appears to have reached a point of perfect equipoise, ready to look at itself in yet another mirror, about to become something other than it was – call it a reincarnation – a 'what if' story that is and is not the same.

If Caird's and Brook's stagings articulate ambivalent responses to modernity along a spectrum from hesitation to fascination, Michael Almereyda's independent film takes *Hamlet* into urban paranoia, towards the high anxiety of postmodernism.[43] Set in New York, the film's most significant stylistic features are tied to the appetite for a world transformed into images of itself, a world of radiant, ephemeral surfaces. Even a random selection of frame stills reveals Denmark's prison as re-membered through Debord's society of the spectacle, where simulacra rule.[44] Brushing in allusions to *Hamlet*'s opening, Almereyda establishes that locale with a low-angle shot of Manhattan's canyon of skyscrapers at deep twilight, against which several intertitles (a convention borrowed from epics or history films) set out the plot's initial moves; as a plane flies over, the camera pans to the Denmark Corporation's circular logo on a Panasonic billboard, then lowers to frame the glass and steel façade of Hotel Elsinore and its doorman, the lone sentry on these ramparts. The ensuing sequence, in which Hamlet constructs himself, proposes 'character' through the image-repertoire of video – a more intimate, personal form of memory-making than cinema, hand-held, ever-ready. Appearing in close-up on a monitor, Hawke's Hamlet speaks 'I have of late, wherefore I know not, lost all my mirth'; interrupted by pauses as he drinks or sighs, or by a ringing phone, the speech continues as voice-over for a rapid flow of images – a silhouetted man, the skeleton of a horse, a Renaissance prince's head sketched by Leonardo, a stealth-bomber, a target's cross-hairs, an explosion, the slithering tongue of a cartoon 'animal' – each illustrating or riffing off his words – a refiguring that recalls Lester's performance. But rather than fusing language to body, this sequence not only drives metaphor into image, divorcing it from the body to alienate and fragment Hamlet's thought, but also introduces a trope of fragmentation which recurs throughout. In a shift from black-and-white video to colour film stock, the camera then frames Hamlet, his own gaze masked by sunglasses, at his computerised editing deck, looking at the sequence; turning away, he lies down, and the screen goes to video snow before a cut to the title HAMLET, white against a brilliant red ground.

Disenchanted, secularised, this prologue juxtaposes the eerie nocturnal glow of urban architecture to Hamlet as a double man: object as well as subject, absent as well as present, as though to articulate the apparent disappearance, or displacement, of the unconscious into a primal scene of virtual technology. That disjuncture or doubleness also registers in two publicity images for the film: the poster, where Hawke's Hamlet, his head angled into a pose that resonates with the image of

Malcolm McDowell for Kubrick's *Clockwork Orange*, stares out from a digitised background of video snow – or fuzzy stock quotations – that seem about to penetrate one side of his head; and a press packet photo, a seemingly uncomposed Kodak moment cut from royal family life, in which, against a looming cityscape, he appears off-centre, the model of self-conscious disaffection, his knitted Andean ski-cap giving him a grunge image that tips him towards homeless outcast, marking him as a rebel without class, a deliberate irritant to his mother and his suit-smooth stepfather.

In Almereyda's film, remembering, repeating and working through becomes tied to the mnemonics of computerised video and, in turn, to a double auteur-ship in which Hamlet as filmmaker replicates Almereyda. Scanning images of his father and mother into his computer editing deck, he attempts to reconstruct his ruptured family by reproducing and reinscribing bygone patterns that define and dominate his thought, deconstructing the very notion of self. And, just as this constellation of family, desire and the phantasmatic precisely tropes the nexus lying at the core of the television apparatus itself,[45] the idea of reincarnation takes on special force for, like Hawke's Hamlet, Sam Shepard's Ghost, appearing first on a closed-circuit TV monitor and then vanishing into a Pepsi One machine before coming to life, is a double man, virtual as well as real. Although Hamlet can control and manipulate the past as image, representation cannot contain the Ghost's sudden, surprising physicality – made all the more startling because Hamlet and the spectator see the Ghost simultaneously, one of the few times the film invites such specular identification. Once the Ghost enters Hamlet's apartment – where a video image of burning oilfields alludes to purgatory's fires – he becomes a threatening presence who backs his son around the room as, working him up to vengeance, he insists on remembrance with an impassioned embrace; his equally sudden disappearance sets time and the image further out of joint in a quickened image chain: Denmark Corporation's logo whirling out of focus; crowds in jerky slow motion on the streets; video snow. Aptly, too, in this film that constantly tropes repetition ('To be or not to be' heard first as fragments, recurs), the scene has a later reincarnation, for as Claudius more coolly incites Laertes to revenge, similar movements within the frame make it a back-to-back copy of the earlier father–son encounter, even to seeing Claudius' ghostly reflection in the window. Such repetition not only bonds Hamlet to Laertes but makes the Ghost and Claudius 'seem' alike – an uncanniness that echoes in Brook's staging, where the two *are* the same, embodied by the same actor.

Filming Hamletically also involves foregrounding discontinuities of sound and image, a strategy that becomes especially obvious in Hamlet's soliloquies, most of which occur in partial voice-overs, as though to mark a discontinuity between voice and body separating 'that within' from surface show. Moreover, Hawke's laid-back verse-speaking often seems determined to jangle verbal rhythms out of tune, even to offend the ear. Yet in some sense that is precisely the point. Whereas it is always the case that the actor on film has less corporeal density than an actor in the theatre, whose performance depends in part on the resonance of being looked at, altered and stirred by the spectator's gaze,[46] Hawke is an immaterial man – all image. As such, his Hamlet indeed 'seems': despite frequent close-ups and extreme close-ups of his eyes which put him in the spectator's face, any 'deep' interiority associated with emotional realism goes missing. Although that is less the case with other performers, overall the film marks not just the waning of affect but of rich verbal communication in present-day culture, substituting for the memory of that heritage the ephemera of media culture, throwing up a phenomenal screen of currency exemplified by a series of product placements: Pepsi, Marlboros, Apple lap-tops, Seagrams, Gilbey's gin, Carlsberg (a Danish beer), Boss, Louis Vuitton, the Times Square electronic stock board.[47] In this intensely retinal, powerfully televisual world, saturated by empty images of late capitalism, relations between human beings are displaced into and conveyed by machines: communication is by telephone, answer-phone and speaker-phone, camera and cam-corder, video monitor, photograph, surveillance camera – sophisticated technologies of information and disinformation delivery, sources of paranoia in postmodern culture. So when the Ghost vanishes into a Pepsi machine, when Hamlet questions the meaning of existence walking through the 'Action' aisle of a Blockbuster video store displaying a poster for *Deep Impact*, surrounded by rentable commodities that remind him of what he is not, or when Shakespeare's verse is interrupted by the roar of a jet, a ringing phone or Eartha Kitt mewing at taxi passengers to fasten their seatbelts, it reads not just as a casual one-off but also, Almereyda himself writes, as 'a way to touch the core of Hamlet's anguish, to recognize the frailty of spiritual values in a material world, and to get a whiff of something rotten in Denmark on the threshold of our self-congratulatory new century'.[48]

Yet it is precisely that Baudrillardesque urban world, its seductive colour and noise, which binds willing spectators to the film, largely through *mise-en-scène* and a brilliant use of New York locations. The Guggenheim, the RCA building's fountain, Saint Gaudens's monumental sculpture of Nike leading General Sherman to civil-war victory, the swimming pool – all associated with Ophelia; the glass walls and floors of cold rooms – hard, slick surfaces to which nothing sticks and on which people appear to be ever slipping off, present to themselves and others only as ephemeral reflections; the neon-green bar, drowning voices in techno-rock; the Hopper-like diner where Hamlet composes verses to Ophelia; an all-night convenience store, its windows plastered with Hallowe'en cut-out witches and skeletons; the repeated images of the cityscape at twilight or dawn which, like Ozu's pillow shots, mark a pause, convey the sense of having been in this shot, this scene, before – the sense of time as repetition. This also is a world that aligns capitalist dynamics – in corporate America, equivalent to the state – with family dynamics, as in a gangster film like *The Godfather*, where family *is* business. Certainly the laundromat scene where, washing the blood from his clothes, Hamlet comes clean about where he hid Polonius' body glances specifically at the genre; elsewhere not only does the film blur distinctions between family space and office space so that the two appear contiguous, but the Denmark Corporation's circular logo seems an ideal image for the hegemony of commodity capital, continually marketing 'the family' even as it invades private space. Moreover, there's a conjuncture here between the engineered production of social relations and engineered desire inducement that interfaces not just with modes of seeing but with how the film constructs subjectivities.[49] Both Hamlet and Ophelia may resist being moulded into proper subjects of commodity capital, yet both are embedded in its logic and in its technologies of delivery and exchange: he as a would-be filmmaker, a surrogate Almereyda preoccupied with recapturing psychic loss in flickering digitised (or pixellated) surfaces; she as a photographer, producing still images, reminders of what has been forgotten – her own loss painfully obvious as she tosses them away, stand-ins for her flowers.

Not only does everything in their world seem to block their relationship but each also is urged to repress the psychic pain associated with loss. With even the human capacity for sensation and affect commodified, Hamlet works to suppress the losses that beat away at him by ordering the flood of images that bombard him. Yet despite his apparent desire to reconstruct himself and so to make some latent, nostalgic alliance with the Hamlet who is the liberal humanist subject, this seems irretrievable in the performative mode he has chosen: media, the cultural dominant of late capitalism.[50] For just as the film commodifies Hamlet's identity, so is memory commodified, its rites tied up with a random cannibalisation of other cinematic commodities, a multiplicity of signs and surfaces from which original signifieds have been erased. And just as Almereyda's film alludes to other *Hamlet*s – Hawke films himself with a gun in his mouth, *à la* Mel Gibson in *Lethal Weapon*; one of Ophelia's remembrances is a rubber duck, recalling the 1987 *Hamlet Goes Business*; Carter Burwell's electronic sound track is interspersed with music by Tchaikowsky, Lizst and Gade from other Shakespeare films – Hamlet's experimental videos raid cinema history, quilting images from filmed Shakespeare together with a barrage of others. In a 'first draft' of 'The Mousetrap', footage of James Dean in *East of Eden* (eat your heart out, Ethan Hawke) rubs against an image of John Gielgud's Hamlet, holding Yorick's skull, meta-theming a theatrical-cinematic citational past. This practice becomes most brilliantly self-reflexive when the titles for 'The Mousetrap – A Film by Hamlet' replicate those for the film itself, again connecting Almereyda and Hamlet as filmmakers. An archival assemblage, in part a witty response to Bazin's famous question, 'What is Cinema?', this pastiche, which might be subtitled 'Hamlet's Dream', turns memory into a pseudo-spectacle where home movies of a child's bedtime – a *Father Knows Best* family ritual – open onto Monty Pythonesque images of the poisoning, which yield to a collage of famous moments from silent cinema and then, as the child comes downstairs and peeks around a corner, to a primal scene: a Roman soldier kisses Cleopatra's hand; a perverse kiss clipped from the porn classic *Deep Throat*; a smirking king settling the crown on his head. Articulated through a weave of insides and outsides, memory exceeds the image-object in a repetition of psychic trauma that perfectly accommodates to the commodity logic that drives the film.

That impulse towards excess carries forward to mark the final moments of Hamlet's consciousness. Charging Horatio to tell his story, Hamlet imagines his last film – a blurry black-and-white video chain keyed by his gaze which functions in part as instant replay. Here, images of his father, Gertrude, his graveyard fight with Laertes and Claudius punching him in the laundromat are framed by close-ups of Ophelia as Hamlet touches her face and kisses her. And it is her presence that not only gives the sequence narrative continuity but also invades the next images. For in juxtaposing a shot of Hamlet's blood-covered body to a silhouetted image of Sherman's equestrian statue, its guiding 'angel' now seen against a nighttime sky punctuated by a vapour trail, the film connects the earlier moment of Ophelia's betrayal to Hamlet's death to figure her, in more than one sense, as Hamlet's 'final girl'.[51]

Working within a transhistorical arena of affective memory, neither Caird's theatre piece nor Brook's performance art engages with history;

forgetting Fortinbras, each closes by opening onto its own, or another (theatrical) succession. Given that the maxim 'Always historicise!' defines *materialist* history, it is fitting that Almereyda's capitalist legend does remember Fortinbras, for the rights of memory he holds are those of history. And it also is fitting that the film pushes Fortinbras into pure image – as a front-page photo on *USA Today* which Claudius tears through at his press conference, as headline news – 'Denmark thwarts Fortinbras' – and, on the plane to England (Hamlet travels first class), where his image on the front page of *Wired* and on a video newscast of a proposed corporate take-over prompts Hamlet's 'How all occasions do inform against me', spoken to a lavatory mirror. And it is Fortinbras' video image which presides over the film's finale, as another corporate mouthpiece, media pundit Robert MacNeil speaks his words – 'This quarry cries on havoc...O proud death, / That thou so many princes at a shot / So bloodily hast struck' – followed, by way of moralising commentary, with those of the Player King: 'Our wills and fates do so contrary run / That our devices still are overthrown; / Our thoughts are ours, their ends none of our own' – which then reappear on a video prompter.[52] Imprisoned as newsprint or video-text – the technologies of history in media culture – Fortinbras is always already mediated: part fact, part fiction, he is just another commodity. That he is not a 'real' commodity also marks this Fortinbras, and this film, as peculiarly American, suggesting as it does that the world's biggest conglomerate still sustains the fantasy of a brilliant young warrior-leader who, performing a kind of second coming, will take up the rites of memory. As the video prompter slowly scrolls down, making 'Shakespeare's text' disappear, the screen goes to black – a reminder of how cinema itself is perpetually about leaving,[53] not only insofar as it obeys its famous definition, 'death at 24 frames per second', but also insofar as it instantiates our own disappearances, bespeaks our loss.

Theatre, performance and cinema all respond to a psychic need to rehearse for loss, invite us to reassess our relations to grief and mourning. Among these is mourning for the lost performance. Certainly, as Lester's performance ended, I was in tears, desiring this brilliant 'thing' that had appeared to stay a while. One moment in particular does. It is the moment when Hamlet asks the Gravedigger to let him see Yorick's skull – placed atop a long bamboo staff: handing it over, the Gravedigger, ad libbing, says, 'Enjoy' – and Hamlet does. Turning the pole ever so slightly so that Yorick's head and body, as though responding to his questions, looks to Horatio, to the audience, and back to Hamlet, he's suddenly in a Charlie McCarthy world, inflected with a bit of Crab the dog: vaudeville and music hall crowding in as Yorick, Hamlet's opposite, double and mask, speaks for him. Carefully laying Yorick's 'body' down, Hamlet covers it with a purple cloth, shrouding the skull, now facing the audience, evoking John Donne's statue in St Paul's. Later, Horatio would topple over Hamlet's still kneeling dead body with a single touch so that, replacing Yorick's, it too lay at the carpet's edge. With a sudden shock of memory, those images fused, returning me to *Mnemonic*, where, at the close, the company disassembled and reassembled a chair – imagined as retaining the shape and aura of both father and lover – so that it 'became' the iceman's skeleton, the material echo of an upstage video projection of the iceman's figure beneath which, on a hospital gurney, an actor's nude body replicated the image. Layers of memory and experience, coming together, extending backwards into the past and forwards into the spectator's present in a seemingly endless circle, connecting the dead to the living through the body's time.

I want now to gather up some other ghostly fragments, the properties associated with each Hamlet: for Russell Beale, a little book of written memories; for Lester, Yorick's skull atop a bamboo pole, death's body as ventriloquist's prop; for Hawke, a camcorder and editing deck, technologies for constituting and reconstituting the subject through a stream of images. Together, these trace the passage of Shakespeare's text through different allegories of delivery, moving from the book to the dancing body to the ghost in the machine, each, like the performance from which it comes, expressing a particular performative force, the working of culture at a given moment in history. Writing of how the peculiar properties of germ cells counter the organic process of development towards natural death, Freud speaks of how, 'under favourable conditions, they begin to develop – that is, to repeat the performance to which they owe their existence';[54] these, he claims, are the true life drives. In the case of the organic entity called *Hamlet*, there is always a tension between fixing it as a theatrical corpse or growing it anew, reinhabiting its roles through the remembering, repeating and working through which is performance – memory's *alter ego* – playing with the dead.

Notes and references

1. See my 'The Critic, the Poor Player, Prince Hamlet, and the Lady in the Dark' in *Shakespeare Reread: The Text in New Contexts*, ed. Russ McDonald (Ithaca: Cornell University Press, 1994) 259–93.
2. The phrase is from Bert States, *Hamlet and the Concept of Character* (Baltimore: Johns Hopkins University Press, 1992) xxiv.

3. For a deep historical inquiry of *Hamlet*'s ghosts and hauntings, see Stephen Greenblatt, *Hamlet in Purgatory* (Princeton: Princeton University Press, 2001).

4. See my '10 Things I Hate About (Performed) Shakespeare,' keynote address for symposium on performance, University of California, Berkeley, February 2001.

5. Reginald Hill, *Recalled to Life* (New York: Delacorte Press, 1992).

6. On the National Theatre production with Russell Beale, see Jonathan Croall, *Hamlet Observed: The National Theatre at Work* (London: Royal National Theatre Publications, 2001).

7. *Mnemonic*, devised by Theatre de Complicite (London: Methuen, 1999). On the staging, see Helen Freshwater, 'The Ethics of Indeterminacy: Theatre de Complicite's "Mnemonic,"' *New Theatre Quarterly* 17.3 (August 2001): 212–18.

8. For this 'spool', I am indebted to an e-mail conversation with Peggy Phelan, 14 June 2001.

9. See Peggy Phelan, *Mourning Sex: Performing Public Memories* (London and New York: Routledge, 1997) 3. See also Joseph Roach, *Cities of the Dead: Circum-Atlantic Performance* (New York: Columbia University Press, 1997) 3–4.

10. See Joseph Roach, 'History, Memory, Necrophilia,' *The Ends of Performance*, ed. Peggy Phelan and Jill Lane (New York: New York University Press, 1998) 27.

11. See Roach, 'History, Memory, Necrophilia' 26.

12. See Georgina Brown's review, *Mail on Sunday* 9 October 2000, in which she refers to the Worcestershire review.

13. These descriptors occur *passim* in reviews of Russell Beale's performance. See *Theatre Record* 20.18 (3 October 2000): 1113–18.

14. Herbert Blau, *Take Up the Bodies* (Urbana: University of Illinois Press, 1982) 66.

15. Ben Brantley, 'The Prince in Us All,' *New York Times* 1 June 2001: B1, B5.

16. See Bruce Wiltshire, *Role Playing and Identity: The Limits of Theatre as Metaphor* (Bloomington: Indiana University Press, 1982) 42–43. See also David Cole, *Acting as Reading: The Place of the Reading Process in the Actor's Work* (Ann Arbor: University of Michigan Press, 1992) 211–12.

17. See Joseph Grigely, *Textualterity: Art, Theory, and Textual Criticism* (Ann Arbor: University of Michigan Press, 1995) 118.

18. Brantley, *New York Times* 27 April 2001: B1, 22.

19. See Jacques Derrida, *Of Grammatology*, trans. Gayatri Chakravorty Spivak (Baltimore: Johns Hopkins University Press, 1976) 142–4, 158, 246.

20. See 'The Question of Criteria for Judging Acting,' in *Brecht on Theatre*, ed. and trans. John Willett (New York: Hil and Wang, 1964) 56.

21. See Roland Barthes, 'From Work to Text,' *Image/Music/Text*, trans. Stephen Heath (New York: Hill and Wang, 1977) 155–64.

22. Blau, *Take Up the Bodies* 40.

23. On Brook's 1995 *Qui est là?*, see Andy Lavender, *Hamlet in Pieces* (London: Nick Hern Books, 1995) 47–92.

24. See Herbert Blau, *Take Up the Bodies* 7.

25. See my 'Looking for Mr. Shakespeare After "The Revolution": Robert Lepage's Intercultural *Dream* Machine', *The Shakespeare Trade: Performances and Appropriations* (Philadelphia: University of Pennsylvania Press, 1998) 171–90.

26. See Phelan, *Mourning Sex* 5.

27. Although I was conscious of textual absences as well as rearrangements while watching the performance, rather than remarking on those here, I want to stay close to the theatrical experience and to avoid privileging the idea that Shakespearean performance is (always already) a text of loss.

28. See Denis Salter, 'Outside Shakespeare/Inside Québec: Paula De Vescocelos's Metonymic Performance Text,' *Le Making of de Macbeth*, in *The Performance Text*, ed. Domenico Pietropaolo (Toronto: LEGAS, 1999) 152–77.

29. Peter Brook, *Forget Shakespeare*, Barbican Centre, London, Shakespeare Festival programme, 1994.

30. Antonin Artaud, 'The Theatre of Cruelty (First Manifesto),' in *Antonin Artaud, Selected Writings*, ed. Susan Sontag (New York: Farrar, Straus and Giroux, 1976) 242–3.

31. See Barthes, 'From Work to Text.'

32. See Pierre Nora, 'Between Memory and History: *Les Lieux de Mémoire*', *Representations* 26 (Spring 1989): 18, 19, 24, 45.

33. Brantley, 'The Prince in Us All.'

34. Peter Brook, 'Director's Note,' BAM programme, 2001.

35. See Sergei Eisenstein, 'Montage 1937,' in *Selected Works*, ed. Michael Glenny and Richard Taylor, trans. Michael Glenny (London: BFI Publishing, 1991) 136.

36. Artaud, 'On the Balinese Theatre,' in *Artaud* 217.

37. See Phelan, *Mourning Sex* 52, 69.

38. See Phelan, *Mourning Sex* 5.

39. See Stephen Greenblatt, *Hamlet in Purgatory* (Princeton: Princeton University Press, 2001) 207.

40. Beckett cited in Herbert Blau, *The Audience* (Baltimore: Johns Hopkins University Press, 1990) 87.

41. See Richard Terdiman, 'The Mnemonics of Musset's *Confession*,' *Representations* 26 (Spring 1989): 26–27.

42. T. S. Eliot, 'Little Gidding,' in *The Complete Poems and Plays, 1909–1950* (New York: Harcourt, Brace & World, 1962) 145.

43. For the filmscript, see *William Shakespeare's Hamlet, A Screenplay Adaptation by Michael Almereyda* (London: Faber and Faber, 2000).

44. See Guy Debord, *The Society of the Spectacle* [1970] (Exeter; Rebel Press, 1987); see also Jean Baudrillard, *Simulacra and Simulations*, trans. Paul Foss, Paul Patton and Philip Beitchman (New York: Sémiotext(e), 1983).

45. See my 'The Critic, the Poor Player' 285.

46. See Blau, *The Audience* 37, 142.

47. Almereyda notes that these product placements were not 'promotional throwaways...we paid for the privilege of parading certain logos and insignias across the screen.' *William Shakespeare's Hamlet* xi.

48. *William Shakespeare's Hamlet* xi.

49. See Rosemary Hennessy, *Profit and Pleasure: Sexual Identities in Late Capitalism* (London and New York: Routledge, 2000) 102–4.

50. See Fredric Jameson, *Postmodernism, or, The Cultural Logic of Late Capitalism* (Durham: Duke University Press, 1991).

51. For the idea of the 'final girl,' see Carol J. Clover, *Men, Women and Chain Saws: Gender in the Modern Horror Film* (Princeton: Princeton University Press, 1992).

52. These lines appear as an epigraph to Harold Bloom, *Shakespeare: The Invention of the Human* (New York: Riverhead, 1998). On how (and why) the film differs from Almereyda's scripted ending, see *William Shakespeare's Hamlet* 127–9; 140–3.
53. See John Berger, *Keeping a Rendezvous* (New York: Pantheon, 1991) 15–16.
54. Sigmund Freud, *Beyond the Pleasure Principle*, in *The Standard Edition of the Complete Psychological Works of Sigmund Freud*, trans. Under editorship of James Strachey in collaboration with Anna Freud, assisted by Alix Strachey and Jan Tyson, 24 volumes (London: Hogarth Press, 1953–74) Vol. 18: 39–40.

Index